A Traveler's Guide to Caribbean History

CW01019804

Don & Dene Dachner

1st Edition

Traveler's Press, Inc. Dixon, CA

A Traveler's Guide to Caribbean History

By Don & Dene Dachner

Published by:
Traveler's Press, Inc.
245 Fernwood Way
Dixon, CA 95620

Cover Design: Chuck Copeland,
   Creative Factory, Sacramento, CA.

Library of Congress Cataloging-in-Publication Data
By Don & Dene Dachner
A Traveler's Guide to Caribbean History
by Don & Dene Dachner--1st Ed.
Includes index.
ISBN 0-9657-780-0-2 (pbk.)
97-90352

About The Authors

We started to become Caribbean travelers while fulfilling an assignment to write up the Caribbean golf resorts for the publication, Golf Resorts of the World. We followed this by becoming Bridge directors on 13 Caribbean cruises. Hard work but someone had to do it.

During these adventures we developed an insatiable desire to learn more about what happened in the Caribbean, why it happened, how it happened and how the region evolved into what it is today.

Over cruise ship dinners and in resort lounges we found companionship with many folks who shared this same thirst. If you are a Caribbean traveler who would like to delve a bit into the region's history, you are one of us. During cruise ship shore excursions and island stays (when we rented cars), we explored the island, talked with locals and browsed book stores and gift shops for books on the island's history in detail.

After considerable research we determined there wasn't a comprehensive Caribbean history book written with the traveler in mind, so we wrote one to fill this niche. Our resources included books written by individual island authors we acquired during our travels, museum visits, press kits and from island departments of tourism, our notes and photos and information gleaned from the 260 book collection shelved at the University of California, Davis that relate to Caribbean history—many written in the 16th to 19th centuries.

Realizing it is difficult getting through Mitchner's Caribbean while traveling the region, we organized the book in a tightly written easy-to-read format, at a reasonable reading level and in a readable type size. While the content is as factual as can be found, we wrote to an audience of travelers, not the world of academia.

We wrote this book in two parts. Part 1 chapters describe nine eras of historical development and happenings of the region in general. You get a taste of Caribbean history in an overview of just 68 pages.

Part 2 used each of these part 1 chapter eras as they apply to 19 individual islands. You can read about the island you will visit the night before your visit—and it won't consume your entire evening.

We have included the names, addresses, phone and fax numbers of island tourist bureaus at the end of most island chapters in Part 2. We are sure you will find this book will enrich your Caribbean adventure.

Don and Dene

Table of Contents

Part 1

Part 2

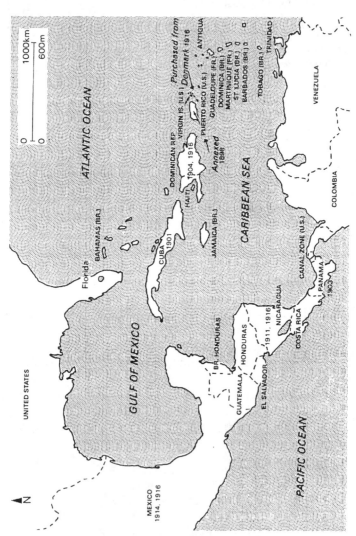

Caribbean Historical Map--1916

PART I

CHAPTER 1

CARIBBEAN GEOGRAPHY, TERRAIN AND ENVIRONMENT

GEOGRAPHY

The Caribbean Region Defined

The region discussed in this book is called the Caribbean, West Indies and, more colorfully, the Spanish Main.

In the Preface to his book "The Spanish Main--Focus of Envy" (1935) Phillip Means described the "Main" as:

> " . . .The entire Caribbean Sea and Southern half of the Gulf of Mexico, together with the islands of those waters and the mainland adjacent thereto, in a word, the whole vast area where Spanish power in America had its inception and where its vital arteries of commerce and administration lay throughout the colonial period. It is where Spain's enemies concentrated their efforts to destroy the Spanish empire in America."

No more encompassing description of this incredible region has been found that better sets the stage for a presentation of its historical past; therefore, this delineation authored by Mr. Means will be used.

If you drew a band of West Indies latitudes around the globe you would cross North Africa, the Red Sea, Arabian Peninsula, the middle section of India, Taiwan and all of Central America.

The center of the Caribbean Sea is due south of Cape Cod and Long Island.

Island Groupings

Islands are referred to as being in the Greater Antilles, Lesser Antilles, the Windwards, Leewards or Curacao Group.

Antilles means: main island group of the West Indies, including all but the Bahamas. Greater Antilles includes: Cuba, Jamaica, Haiti, Dominican Republic, Puerto Rico and the Cayman Islands. Lesser Antilles include: All the islands in the island chain from St. Thomas south to Trinidad, off the Venezuelan coast. The Curacao Group include: Aruba, Bonnaire and Curacao. The Leeward Islands. Leeward means "the direction in which the wind blows." It includes the islands from Puerto Rico to Dominica. The Windward Islands. Windward means "the direction from which the wind blows. They include the islands from Martinique south to Trinidad, but do not include Trinidad, Barbados or Tobago.

Terrain
The islands are the remains of volcanic upheavals that began 70 to 80 million years ago and rose from the seas with the Andes and other mountain ranges in Central and South America. The Dominican Republic's Pico Duarte in the Cordillera Central mountains is the highest Caribbean elevation at 10,417 feet. In contrast, the highest point in the Cayman Islands is 49 feet.

The largest inhabited island in the region is Cuba, 42,827 square miles. The smallest is Saba, 5 square miles, with its main town nestled in what is hoped to be an extinct volcano crater. The region escaped the ice age; therefore, the canyon walls in mountainous areas cut by raging rivers during periods of torrential rainfall tend to be steep and narrow. The Caribbean Sea contains trenches to the depth of over 29,000 feet. Measurements from the Sea floor to the top of some mountains reach 39,000 feet, challenging peaks in the Swiss Alps.

Environment
Over 100 inches of rainfall a year is normal in the El Yunque National Forest of Puerto Rico where it rains 10 months a year. By contrast, Aruba experiences an average of 17 inches of rainfall on its Divi-Divi tree and cactus-laden plains where precipitation is expected only three months a year.

Some islands like the Dominican Republic have seasonal rainfall from April to June and August to November. Dense, thorny woodlands and mangrove swamps can be found in certain areas in the region.

The soil erodes easily and is not naturally rich. Settlers learned early to use fertilizers.

The temperature averages from 78 F to 80 F the year around and the humidity rarely falls below 70 percent.

Most of the region has a history of devastating hurricanes. Eighty percent of them originate off the African coast and cross the Atlantic on no predictable path. Hurricane "season" is from August to October, but they have been known to strike every other month at random except May.

In October 1780, the greatest known hurricane swept through Barbados, St. Lucia, Martinique, Dominica, Sint Eustatius, St. Vincent and Puerto Rico. Its estimated 200 mile winds killed 22,000 people and destroyed large British and French fleets. Rain drops stripped trees of their bark.   Almost every island has their tale of destruction and death caused by earthquakes. On June 7, 1692 Port Royal, Jamaica was shaken into the ocean along with the infamous pirate Henry Morgan's house and his tomb. Major quakes shook Jamaica again in 1907 and 1957.

Volcanic eruptions caused extensive damage throughout the years. On May 8, 1902 Martinique's 5000 foot Mont Pelee erupted and submerged Saint-Pierre, then called the "Paris of the West", in ashes. This calamity claimed 30,000 lives. One person, a prison inmate jailed in a dungeon, survived.

The Whiteman's Graveyard

Today, the only threat to a visitor's comfort and health are sunburn, heat stroke and the pesky "no-seeum".

In the early days, one out of every three white newcomers to the region would die of disease within two years after arrival; therefore, the region became known as "Whiteman's Graveyard." The climate fostered ideal breeding conditions for a large variety of disease-carrying microbes and mosquitoes that transmit Malaria and Yellow Fever.

From 1600 to the end of the 19th century, disease had a major impact on island life and military ventures. Often entire armies were nearly completely destroyed by the mighty mosquito.

In 1655 the French landed 1500 soldiers on St. Lucia. Only 89 were alive at the end of a few months.

Malaria was endemic to islands with rain forests. When the female Anopheles mosquito lances a human, Malaria parasites enter the liver, multiply and feed on red blood cells. Before 1840, when quinine became available, about 25% of victims died on their first encounter. Malaria tended to be a rural disease. Blacks enjoy a relative immunity to Malaria.

Yellow Fever carrying Aedes Aegypti mosquitoes prefer the urban community where humans are closely packed because they cannot fly much beyond 100 yards. They like water standing in containers with hard sides like cisterns and pots. The mosquito and human carriers were transported from Africa via slave ships so outbreaks of Yellow Fever were not uncommon upon the arrival of slave ships. When the mosquito ran out of non-immune hosts, the disease would vanish. Upon recognition of an impending epidemic, the only known defense was quarantining the sick and moving from the infected area. Death from Yellow Fever is a painful and terrible one. There is no sure cure for it, even today.

Yellow Fever is endemic to West Africa and many blacks arrived with some immunity. No whites came in contact with the disease before arrival; therefore, their death toll was much greater than the blacks.

Flora

A walk through some of the islands' botanical gardens and especially through Welchman's Hall Gully on Barbados can only give today's visitor an inkling of the denseness of growth which once existed, even on today's virtually treeless Aruba and Grand Cayman.

Dr. E. Rufz, an early historian wrote of his first impression of Martinique:

"The forest, what in inextricable chaos it is! The sands of the sea are not more closely pressed together than the trees are here: some straight, some curved, some upright, some toppling, fallen, or leaning against one another . . . You do not find here the eternal monotony of the birch and fir. This is the kingdom of infinite variety." Source: Roberts: The French in the West Indies. 1942.

While some larger islands like Jamaica and more mountainous ones like Dominica, Trinidad and Tobago still have dense forests today, much of the timber has been cleared from many islands.

Sugar planters cleared lands of forests and undergrowth for planting and used the timber to stoke the fires in their boiling houses where they made sugar and rum. Boat builders and ship repairers, like those on the Cayman Islands, consumed the forests to their end in pursuit of their occupation.

Some trees fell to supply the necessary fluid to make dyes, so much in demand in Europe in the early years.

While many of the Caribbean beaches have become lined with condos and resorts, in response to the tourist trade boom, today's Caribbean governments are becoming very ecologically sensitive and are taking steps to preserve the beauty of their lands.

CHAPTER 2

THE AMERINDIANS

Caribbean (West Indies) historians generally agree that three unique tribes of peoples ventured from the East coast of South America and paddled their canoes--some about 96 feet long, holding up to 50 persons--through the Caribbean Sea to the shores of the Bahamas. These migrations took place over thousands of years, their island-hopping being the result of a basic drive--the never-ending human quest to find a better living environment.

Collectively, these early arrivals are called "Amerindians"--the Ciboneys, Arawaks and Caribs. It is thought that all tribes migrated throughout the Caribbean islands. The Arawaks tended to eventually dominate the Greater Antilles while the Caribs tended to settle mostly in the Windward, Leewards and Curacao group.

When Christopher Columbus first set foot on the island of San Salvador in 1492 authorities speculate that there were from 225,000 to 6 million Amerindians residing in the West Indies--the number being an ongoing argument among Caribbean historians. One historian places the Caribbean population at 30 million in 1989. Another places the population at 47.5 million in mid-1991. Whatever the number, there is no question that the Caribbean population today represents a mixture of the majority of the peoples and cultures of the world.

The Ciboneys (Siboneys)

These first known Caribbean inhabitants arrived in the region about 2000 B.C. They were wanderers, hunters and gatherers and had no established villages. Findings from their refuse dumps reveal no pottery, utensils, weapons (except wooden clubs and stones thrown by hand) or evidence of religious rituals or beliefs. There is also no evidence of there having been a political organization. If Columbus is to be believed, at the time of his arrival, a very small number of Ciboneys were enslaved by the Arawaks--but we find no hard evidence to support this. Their complete lack of military defense apparently led to their extinction.

The Arawaks
"A people short of everything": Columbus.

The Arawaks (meaning "meal eaters") began their migration around the birth of Christ, established villages and set up a well-defined political and religious structure. They desired a sedentary and settled life. Use of metals was unknown to them. Historians describe their pottery, glazed white with red overlays, as "elegant." Their villages were built around a square which served as a meeting place and ball-field where they played "Batey", a kick ball game like soccer. The "Great" Cacique--an inherited chieftain position--held absolute power over all decisions. This autocrat presided over feasts, dances, public festivals, law courts and assigned menial supervisory duties to "Caciques". Large islands were divided into provinces with a very complex infrastructure of ruling "Caciques" creating an inescapable class structure--upper, middle and lower--determined by birth. Mothers of new-borns applied boards to their child's head to develop a narrow skull with a slanted forehead producing beauty and perfection. The end result was a slanting forehead, protruding eyes and a flat nose with wide nostrils which made the adults look ferocious. Virginity was not considered desirable; therefore, Arawak men preferred to marry a sexually experienced woman. They liberally painted their copper-colored bodies--one reason being for protection from insect bites. They had beautiful black head hair, but no beards or body hair. Their teeth were dirty and black because of their diet.

Appeasing spirits played an important role in their life. When in trouble they called for their "Shaman", a person skilled in the use of magic, narcotics and other drugs who played the role of a doctor. When you consider a few of their many superstitions, you can understand their need for the Shamon. For example:

1. They would not eat Garfish for fear that their children would have long noses.
2. They danced all night during an eclipse to ward off the spirits who were trying to eat the moon.
3. When paddling past a place where a person had drowned, they would throw food over-board to prevent the dead person from capsizing the canoe.

They were a passive lot. Why they let themselves become enslaved by the Caribs and Spanish and eventually exterminated while offering so little resistance has yet to be explained.

The gradual and terminal disappearance of the Arawaks seems to be a combination of events. Part of their demise was no doubt due to their lack of a natural immunity to smallpox, measles or the common cold--diseases brought from Europe. Part of it came from the lack of knowledge by the Spanish that the mere removal of them from their seashore residences to inland mountainous gold fields, were death moves. Malnutrition resulted from a lack of access to the protein provided by fish.

And, of course, there were the Caribs with their obsession for conquest. Carib culture was built around success and bravery on the battlefield. The Arawaks were an accessible and ready prey.   In the order of 17th Century thinking, the survival of the Arawaks was not on anyone's list. The Arawaks were vulnerable and submissive; therefore, in the flow of human evolution they disappeared.

Arawak villages can be seen at the Indian Creek site on Antigua or Spanish Point on Barbuda.

The Caribs
"These cannibals, a people very savage . .": Columbus.

The Caribs (meaning "cannibals") arrived in Grenada about 500 years before Columbus. They followed the path of the Ciboneys and Arawaks through the Caribbean Sea to the Bahamas.

They were a male-dominated society with emphasis on military and seafaring exploits. They held major ceremonies to celebrate the birth of a boy, the admission of a boy to warrior status and the launching of a new canoe.

Each island had one or two chiefs called "Ubutu", elected according to their bravery and military prowess. This position was not hereditary. "Tuibutule Hauthe" were secondary chiefs who supervised fishing and the cultivation, storage and distribution of food. They trained most boys as warriors, the rest as priests.

The Caribs were polygamous with the wife holding very little power. The men and women lived in separate communal huts measuring about 20 feet wide and 60 feet long. Wives were considered to be servants, placed in charge of cooking, laundry and other chores such as washing and oiling their husband's hair each day. For rewards, brave warriors received captive Arawak women for wives. Husbands fasted during labor and childbirth to show their support.

Carib religion was very basic. Each person had their good god, "Icheriri" and their bad god, "Mabouya". They believed that any sickness or ill-happening was the result of a spell cast by an enemy's Mabouya. The Priest's job was to defeat the Mabouya's evil spells and deeds.

Sensationalists spread the rumor that the Caribs were cannibals. Professor Bullbrook from Trinidad summarizes the findings of historians with his statement:

. . ".That he (the Carib) was a cannibal has to be admitted, but he did not eat human flesh because he preferred it. It is even possible that he did not like it. He ate no one save a brave enemy, and he ate him entirely for the purpose of gathering to himself that enemy's bravery."

Columbus is suspected of characterizing the Caribs as cannibals to gain approval to enlist them as slaves. Columbus wrote:

. . ".These cannibals, a people very savage and suitable for the purpose are well made and of good intelligence. We believe that having abandoned their inhumanity they could be better than any other slaves."

At the time of this quote, Columbus had never seen a Carib.

While there were very separate and distinct tribes, they would come together in times of trouble.

Amulets--objects worn on the body to ward off evil spirits and provide magical power--were the men's most prized possessions, obtained from battles with the Arawaks. They were typically crescent-shaped, an alloy of Gold and Copper and framed in wood. Their size ranged from small Caracoli, worn in the ear, nose or mouth as pendants or mounts large enough to be worn hanging on the chest. The disdain for the Arawaks extended beyond death. The Caribs believed that the brave warrior souls would go to a plush mountainous heaven where they would have Arawaks as slaves. If they were cowards, their souls would be sent to a desert beyond the beautiful mountains where they would become slaves of the Arawaks. The fate of female souls is a mystery.

The Caribs were a nuisance to the Spaniards and other colonists from Europe. They would not succumb to slavery like the Arawaks. They did offer a friendly hand on some islands to help the "newcomers" with food--but when the "newcomers" raided their food supplies as a "Thank you", they retaliated.

This retaliation led to counter-retaliation which led to their extinction--the ball and musket prevailing over the bow and arrow.

Records show that the last few Grenadian Caribs jumped off a cliff in 1654 as an option to being captured by the French.

A settlement of approximately 30 Caribs, the last remaining Amerindians, exists on a reserve in Dominica today.

CHAPTER 3

DISCOVERY--THE "ENTERPRISE OF THE INDIES"

The stories related by Marco Polo that described the fabulous Orient intrigued Columbus and set him to thinking of a new way to reach the land of the Khan. The route by land had been blocked by the Turks.   The sea route around the `Cape of Storms' at the southern tip of Africa was treacherous.

His studies and association with geographers, navigators, astronomers and map-makers convinced him he could reach the Orient by sailing west.

He approached the King of Portugal who rejected the plan because of Columbus' lack of experience. He also believed, and rightly so, that Columbus' geographic conclusions were in error. Columbus then presented the plan to King Henry VII of England who declined because he had been toying with the idea of sending his own explorer on a similar expedition.

Next, he tried Spain's Queen Isabella and King Ferdinand who graciously and kindly referred the idea to a committee which promptly issued a "No." Columbus' friend and member of the Spanish court, Luis de Santangel, pleaded with the Queen to change her mind. He succeeded and she convinced the King to change his mind.   Columbus was recalled and a very liberal "Discovery Contract" gave him the go-ahead he needed for what they called the "Enterprise of the Indies."

It is unfortunate that the name Luis de Santangel is so little known, for not only did he convince the Queen to give the order to approve the world's most historic voyage, but he and an associate borrowed funds from a Court trust fund to finance the expedition. The Crown repaid the loan later.   Contrary to a popular legend, Queen Isabella did not pawn her jewels to pay for Columbus' first voyage.

The Queen's decision to approve this first voyage turned out to be an excellent investment. It is estimated to have cost around $152,000 (1991 dollars) to outfit Columbus, about the sum of a year's salary for Spain's state treasurer and tutors for a prince and princess.   During the 16th century alone the return on this investment was over 200 million percent!

The First Voyage

The three ships, Pinta, Nina and Santa Maria carried provisions for a one-year voyage.   Columbus brought a small supply of cheap beads, trinkets and hawksbells to give to the Great Khan and a few cannon, crossbows and muskets for protection.   The crew and captains of the Nina and Pinta were experienced.   Columbus' unwilling crew had been selected from various jails because no volunteers could be found to make the voyage.

A half-hour before sunrise on August 3, 1492 Columbus weighed anchor and slipped away from Palos' harbor, Spain.

On September 3 they began passage through the Canary Islands. Some men wept when they lost complete sight of land on September 9. The world was larger in circumference than Columbus calculated. His voyage covered 7500 miles rather that his estimated 2500. The King of Portugal was right.

Following is a chronicle of some significant events that took place on this first voyage:

October 6: They sighted large flocks of birds.

October 10: Men began to grumble, wanting to turn back.

October 11: At 10 p.m. Columbus thought he saw a light in the west.

October 12: At 2 a.m. a sailor on the Pinta saw land. The Pinta fired a cannon, signaling the sighting. They rejoiced but decided to wait until daylight before attempting a landing. Columbus landed at dawn on San Salvador (Watling Island) in the Bahamas.

October 13 to 22: Columbus spent these days exploring the Bahama islands.

October 23: Finding no gold in the Bahamas, Columbus set sail for Cuba or what he thought to be Japan.

October 28 to December 5: Columbus explored the north coast of Cuba. On December 5 he set sail for the north coast of Hispaniola (Haiti).

December 6 to January 15: Columbus landed and explored Haiti's north coast. On December 20 the Santa Maria became grounded on a reef and had to be abandoned.   This incident led to the establishment of the settlement he called, Villa de la Navidad in honor of Christmas.   He left about forty men to trade with the Indians and continued his voyage.

January 16 to March 15, 1493: Columbus made his return voyage to Palos, Spain.

Planning the Second Voyage

The transplant of European culture, morals and religion from Europe to the New World began with the planning of Columbus' second voyage. The first voyage was primarily a mission of discovery. The purpose of the second was to set the stage to establish an empire.

Columbus immediately became a world-renown hero upon his return to Palos on March 15, 1493. Proof that he had reached the `Indias' was in the form of an impressive assortment of foreign birds, animals, plants, trees, fruits and a enough gold to whet the appetite and imagination of adventurers to be.

The Queen lost no time in contacting Columbus. She sent a letter urging him to come to the Court ". . . so that you may be timely provided with everything you need . . . you must not delay in going back there." Outfitting for the second voyage was lavish in comparison to the meager provisions given on the first. They supplied Columbus with 17 ships, 1500 men (no women), a six months supply of food, cattle, pigs, chickens, 20 horses, seeds and plants, pets, tools and a wide range of craftsmen. The horses, never-before seen by the Indians turned out to be the most potent military weapon of all. When men mounted a horse the Indian took them as one huge monster and fled in terror.

This was to be a serious attempt at settlement.

While the goals of establishing settlements and finding the land of the Great Khan were not to be forgotten, the Queen made it very clear that every effort should be made to cultivate the friendship of the Indians and to convert them to the Catholic faith. She sent six priests along for this purpose.

The 17-ship fleet left a celebrating crowd when it departed Cadiz harbor on September 25, 1493.

The Second Voyage

The crossing was uneventful. They set a course south of the Bahamas because whenever Columbus had mentioned gold to the Indians on the first voyage they always pointed south. An air of joyous anticipation, rather than distrust, pervaded the crew and passengers.

The island of Dominica came into view on November 3. Seeing no safe anchorage, Columbus sailed north and discovered an island which he named Maria Galante after his flagship.

They proceeded along the west shores of the Lesser Antilles naming Santa Maria de Guadalupe (Guadalupe), Santa Maria de Monserrate (Monserrat), Santa Maria la Antigua (Antigua), Nevis (after Nuestra Senora de las Nieves, Our Lady of the Snows), St. Cruz (St. Croix), St. Thomas and St. John--these last three (the U. S. Virgins), he named after martyr heroines of a medieval legend.

On November 19 he entered the Greater Antillies and named a large island San Juan Bautista (Puerto Rico). From there he sailed on to the familiar land of Hispaniola.

They approached Navidad with great joy and anticipation. Joy at seeing their old companions and their settlement and anticipation over how much gold they retrieved. They entered Navidad's harbor in the evening of November 27 and sent up flares to announce their arrival. There was no response.

On the following morning they landed and instead of finding jubilant settlers, buildings and streets they found decayed corpses and ashes. Columbus learned from Guacanagari, an Arawak chief who greeted him on the first voyage, that his colony had degenerated into an undisciplined band of gold-seekers who imposed severe torture and punishment on the Arawaks. Caonabo, another Arawak chief, sent out war parties in revenge and massacred the small Spanish party.

This event greatly influenced Columbus' thinking about the Indians. Not only were they not docile and childlike, they would fight when pressed; therefore, could not be trusted. In turn, the Spaniards lost their "godlike" aura and became warlike invaders to the Arawaks. The friendly, loving co-existence between the Spanish and Indians envisioned by the Queen became dashed and the event gave her the first inkling of Columbus' shortcomings as an administrator.

They abandoned Navidad and after a month's sailing covering only 30 miles against headwinds they reached a harbor and the town site of Isabella where Columbus decided to establish their main settlement. The site, having a poor water supply and located near a malaria-carrying mosquito swamp couldn't have been worse.

Columbus began an intensive search for gold on Hispaniola. He found enough to send back to Spain to show promise of grand deposits--but actually, he shipped the best part of what Hispaniola had to offer. On February 4, 1494 he sent twelve ships back to Spain for supplies, initiating a ferry system between Spain and the New World. Columbus took the remaining ships and headed for the south coast of Cuba--what he thought to be the mainland of the land of the Great Khan. The Indians assured him there was an island to the south, so he temporarily changed course, sailed south and discovered Montego Bay, Jamaica.

After a brief stay in Jamaica and finding no gold, Columbus returned to Cuba and resumed his explorations along the Khan's mainland coast. Satisfied that he had reached Asia, Columbus returned to Isabella.

He left his younger brother, Diego in charge--another big administrative mistake. As in Navidad, too many colonists concerned themselves with nothing more than extracting as much gold as they could as fast as could so they could return to Spain as soon as possible--administrative order, be damned--and Diego would not or could not maintain control.

Another error in judgment involved putting Mosen Pedro Margarit, one of his roughest and most cruel commanders, in charge of 376 men to explore the interior of Hispaniola with instructions, `don't harm the natives'. Disregarding wishes about treatment of the Indians, Margarit went wild, pillaging, torturing and raping them.

Diego heard of Margarit's actions and demanded he change his ways. Instead of complying, Margarit seized two ships and sailed for Spain. Once there he and his followers submitted terse reports to the Crown regarding Christopher's and Diego's administrative ineptitude. These reports and the suggestion sent earlier by Columbus that the Caribs would make excellent slaves (a suggestion contrary to the Queen's dream of love and friendship) did not impress the Crown.

Isabella had unquestionably proved to be a disastrous town site so they found a new location for the New World capital and named it Santo Domingo.

Columbus sailed for Spain after a 3-year absence in March, 1496 leaving his older brother, Bartholomew, in charge of building the new city, Santo Domingo.

Upon his arrival, Columbus learned of Margarit's charges of his incompetency as an administrator and found the people swayed by Margarit's tales. The crowd did not exhibit the same jubilance upon his return as they did upon his departure.

The King and Queen requested an audience with Columbus so he could relate his findings and adventures. He enthusiastically appeared and at the same time submitted a plan for a third voyage. The Crown took his plan under advisement, but it took two years to launch voyage number three.

The Third Voyage

The time had come to reach beyond mere settlement of and communication with the known New World and to establish that evasive new route to the land of the Great Khan. It is to this task that Columbus directed his efforts during this third voyage. Outfitted with six ships Columbus set sail on May 30, 1498 on a course considerably south of the other two. The fact that gold had been found in Africa near the equator had much to do with this decision. It must follow, he concluded, that gold would be found near the equator in his New World as well.

This logic led him to the discovery of Trinidad on July 31, 1498. He sailed along the shores of Trinidad and crossed the Gulf of Paria where he found evidence of pearl fields and an interesting phenomenon—a large amount of fresh water mixed with the sea. He sent some men to investigate and when they reported on a large river emptying into the bay he correctly theorized that its source came from a mainland, not an island. He had discovered the coast of Venezuela and the South American mainland.

Finding a continent there did not square with his geographic maps. He concluded that finding an uncharted mainland, combined with strange readings from his compass and the irregular comings and goings of the ocean currents, that the river waters flowed into the sea from the Garden of Eden. He believed he had set foot on the doorstep of Paradise.

He continued along the south, then north coast of Venezuela's Paria Peninsula, making landings and meeting friendly Arawaks. The Arawaks tried to convince Columbus that he was on the shore of a vast continent, a belief he did not totally accept.

It had been over two years since Christopher left his brother, Bartholomew, in Santo Domingo and became anxious to return, so he headed north on August 15.

The Santo Domingo Disaster

During his absence from Santo Domingo, virtually all the human frailties of hate, greed, conspiracy, jealousy and cruelty reared their ugly heads.

Columbus had approved of Bartholomew's sending 300 "prisoner of war" slaves to Spain. This raised the guile of the local Spaniards who suspected the Columbus brothers skimmed some profit from the endeavor. At the same time, this upset the Crown, for "prisoners of war" or not, Columbus was supposed to be making friends with, not war with the Indians.

Bartholomew led an expedition to southwestern Haiti where he found a friendly chief, Behechio in Xaragua province. They entertained each other with food, drink and gifts for three days. Upon his departure, Bartholomew had become so elated over the established friendship that he purposely failed to collect the usual tribute of gold.

Upon his return to Santo Domingo, Bartholomew found the city on the threshold of rebellion. Mayor Francisco Roldan had incited the populace against the foreign Genoese brothers for enriching themselves at their expense. Roldan accused Bartholomew of extracting the gold tribute from Behechio and keeping it for himself.

Roldan told the local Arawak chiefs that if he were in charge he would not extract gold tribute from them. He told the settlers if he were in charge, every settler would be granted a large amount of land and Indians to work the land for gold.

Bartholomew confronted Roldan and told him of the impending return of Columbus, who had gained much favor with the Crown. Roldan, feeling threatened, retreated under the protection of Arawak chief, Guarionex. Bartholomew considered Guarionex's harboring of Roldan to be traitorous so he burned his village and massacred its inhabitants.

Columbus returned to this mess and found Roldan's 500 social diseasing-spreading men reeking havoc throughout the province of Xaragua. To make matters worse, three of Columbus' ships bound for Santo Domingo missed the port and landed in the hands of Roldan at Xaragua, who quickly to converted most of the men's thinking against the 'foreign' Columbus brothers.

Having only 70 men to face Roldan, Columbus sent his flagship to Spain with news of Roldan's rebellion, and requests for more faithful supporters, more priests and provisions. He also sent a letter telling of the new discoveries of Trinidad, findings of pearls in the Gulf of Paria and the possibility he had stood on the doorstep of Paradise.

Columbus thought, being greatly outnumbered, it would be good policy if the Arawaks thought the Spanish were united so he invited Roldan to a peace conference. The outcome was an humiliating agreement pardoning Roldan, returning him to office, granting him and his followers free passage to Spain with their gold and concubines and lastly, giving large grants of land (including the resident Indians as slaves) in the province of Xaragua to those who wanted to stay.

It is unfortunate that the land given away belonged to Chief Behichio who befriended Bartholomew such a short time before.

In October 1499 Columbus sent two ships to Spain with letters explaining his land grants and his agreement with Roldan, which he underlined as been signed under duress. These events and a letter from Roldan exhausted the last drop of patience the Crown had for Columbus and his brothers' administrative incompetency.

In desperation, Queen Isabella sent the honest and forceful Francisco de Bobadilla to go to Santo Domingo to investigate conditions. He was given full power and authority over Christopher Columbus and all other administrators to establish order and discipline by any means he saw fit.

Upon arrival, Bobadilla heard stories of cruelty invoked by the Columbus brothers and became a believer when he faced seven Spaniards hanging from a gallows. When he faced Diego, who had been left in charge of the city, he said that five more were to be hanged on the morrow. Bobadilla arrested Diego and put him in chains. The same fate met Christopher and Bartholomew.

Columbus' third voyage ended with his being sent home to Spain disgracefully bound in chains.

The Crown busied themselves for six weeks with various court matters before they gave the order to unbind Christopher.   All appeared over, but there one more voyage was to come.

The Fourth Voyage

It wasn't until 1502 until Columbus gathered himself together and presented the idea of a fourth voyage to Isabella and Ferdinand.

By this time the Crown had heard enough to know that Christopher was hopeless as an administrator; however, he had brought so much fame, honor and potential wealth to Spain, they could not deny him another chance to find the western passage to the land of the Khan.

After a routine crossing he landed on Martinique and sailed north along the Lesser Antillies until he reached Santo Domingo. The Queen forbid him to land at the site of his terrible disaster, but he disobeyed the order because he wished to exchange a vessel for another of different design. Nicholas de Ovando, the governor, aware of the Queen's wish, denied him entrance to the harbor.

He sailed west and just off the coast of Honduras he came across a large canoe transporting trade goods and manned by two dozen Indians, no doubt the first European contact with the Mayas.

On July 27, 1502 he began his southward quest for his passage along the east coast of Central America from Honduras to Panama and encountered terrible storms. He made landings at several bays, river estuaries and inlets, but none led to the strait of Cathay.

His ships had weathered to the brink of being unseaworthy and when he became sick with malaria he gave up the idea of finding his passage to India and headed to Santo Domingo for ship repair. The worms had eaten so many holes in the ships the crews constantly manned the pumps.

He couldn't make it to Hispaniola. On June 25, 1503 he ran his ships aground at St. Ann's Bay, Jamaica.

He sent for help from Governor Ovalano but he had other things pending that gave his reason for neglecting Columbus.   A year elapsed before Columbus and his 116 marooned crew members were rescued and returned to Spain.

Christopher's hopes for additional voyages vanished when Queen Isabella died on November 26, 1504.

Bath Hotel, 1778, Nevis

Maya Ruins, Cozumel

Maya Ruins, Cozumel

CHAPTER 4

SPANISH QUEST FOR POWER AND GOLD

Columbus and other early explorers in the Spanish Main could have been responsible for some of the original "good news, bad news" reports.

The good news would have been Columbus' discovery of a new passage to India and a mysterious land to explore that held great promise for findings of gold and unknown treasures.

The bad news would have contained a sizable list of unexpected, undesirable and disappointing findings such as the fact that Columbus did not discover a new passage to India.

The Spanish Main As They Found It

The gold-embellished trinkets and jewelry worn by the Amerindians came from small deposits of nuggets they found in riverbeds rather than from vast deposits. The Spaniards found gold in Cuba, Puerto Rico and Hispaniola but these deposits played out by the 1520's. It wasn't long before the Spanish lost interest in the Caribbean as a source of wealth from precious metals.

Columbus and other first-time founders certainly experienced the thrill of setting foot on newly-found land, but often found the native Arawaks or Caribs to be unfriendly. Not only were they unfriendly, but they did not display a very advanced culture and it was questioned from the beginning as to whether they could understand and be converted to Christianity--a mission most important to the Queen.

In an effort to ascertain the Arawak's aptitude for work and religious training, Queen Isabella established a special township for them in Cuba. They chose two dozen intelligent, promising Arawaks to be supervised, but not under compulsion, for a certain period of time to see if they could live in a civilized manner. The selected ones showed no interest in either work or worship. Many found the township too confining and fled to the countryside. The Spaniard's patience soon ran out and they returned the rest to slavery. The Arawaks proved to be no asset and the warlike attitude of the Caribs held no promise for anything peaceful. By 1501 (nine years after discovery) so few Indians had survived because of overwork, malnutrition and suicide that the Spaniards began to seek slaves from Africa.

Those who travel the islands today find roads and expanses of open land. The original explorers found forbidding jungles of underbrush, dense forests, entanglements of vines and few pathways. Simple land exploration was very laborious. The clear land we see today is the result of years of tree and brush-cutting to make way for sugar cane cultivation.

The Spaniards came from a semi-arid, moderately-warm climate where they could work long hours on rigorous tasks. The Spanish Main offered them a hot, humid climate that sapped their energy quickly. They found it difficult to perform even the most mundane day-to-day tasks without physical discomfort.

The tropical climate provided ideal breeding conditions for mosquitoes and microbes that transmitted fatal diseases to many non-immune Spaniards. At first they had no knowledge of the diseases' origins or any procedure for control, treatment or cure.

It is a wonder, with all these impending hardships, that the region wasn't discovered and then left alone. But there seems to be that spark in human nature that overcomes inconvenience when the promise of power and gold are at hand.

The First Settlements

Spanish laws gave minute specifications as to how a new town would be laid out. A square plaza would be the center of every town. Bordering the plaza would be a church, town hall, prison and sometimes the Governor's residence. The military barracks, facing a parade ground would be located nearby. The streets would enter the plaza at right angles, giving the pattern of growth a checkerboard shape. Even today, most Spanish-American cities conform to this design.

A need arose for a permanent settlement to serve as a harbor for commerce, refuge from storms and enemy attacks and base for westward explorations. In 1504 Santo Domingo on the island of Hispaniola (Dominican Republic) was founded and became the first American political and religious capital.

Diego Columbus, Christopher's brother, built a home and fortress there so massive that the King is said to have gone to his window in Spain and remarked, "Those walls in Santo Domingo cost me so much and must be so high that I should be able to see them from here." The town grew rapidly and soon included a college, hospital, three monasteries and a cathedral built in 1512.

Santo Domingo's prestige grew when it became the seat of the Audiencia which acted as an advisory council to Governors and a supreme court.

In 1508 Juan Ponce de Leon founded the settlement of San German in Puerto Rico and in 1511 established San Juan de Puerto Rico.

In 1511 Diego Velasquez founded Havana, Cuba and followed by establishing Santiago, Cuba in 1514.

The Westward Shift

By 1517 the three major settlements of Santo Domingo, San Juan and Havana were large enough to serve as home bases for westward expeditions.

Diego Velasquez became the governor of Cuba and patron of three explorers who made successive excursions to the Yucatan and Mexico. They were Francisco de Cordoba in 1517, Juan de Grijalva in 1518 and Fernando Cortes in 1519.

Their findings included Indians with a well-developed political organization and a military system superior to any found in the islands. The Spanish, indeed, lost several battles.

Although sometimes defeated in battle, the explorers were encouraged by the observation that they had contact with Indians who had wealth and intelligence. Plentiful trinkets made from gold and precious-looking stones, stately stone buildings and well-populated villages convinced them they had contacted an advanced civilization.

They did not always engage the Indians in battle. They sometimes managed to converse with some who told thrilling tales of a splendid empire that existed beyond the towering mountains.

Cortes' March to the Aztec Kingdom

Although Cuban Governor Velasquez considered 34 year old Cortes to be untrustworthy, he commissioned him to follow up on Cordova's report of stone buildings and gold on the Yucatan. Cortes assembled 11 ships at various Cuban ports, together with 10 canon, a plentiful supply of small firearms and gunpowder, crossbows, swords, spears and 16 invincible armored horses and knights. On the day of departure Velasquez had second thoughts and ran to the waterfront as Cortes was departing and yelled for him to return. Cortes retorted, "Time presses, and there are some things that should be done before they are even thought of."

He stopped at some Cuban ports to recruit men. At his last stop, Havana, he took a final inventory of his 550 soldiers, 110 sailors and all his supplies. Included on board was a Lieutenant Alvardo and a writer, Bernal Diez who recorded the excursion in detail. Cortes sailed for the Yucatan on February 18, 1519. Cortes' first contact with Mexico resulted in a battle with the Tabasco Indians on a small plain up the Tabasco River.   He encountered a force of 40,000 warriors armed with bows and arrows.   The sound of cannon fire terrified the Indians, but they held fast as a disciplined force--something not experienced by the Spaniards in the Caribbean.   The winning battle tactic was the charge of the 16 armored horsemen led by Cortes.   Believing the horsemen to be one-piece metal monsters, the Tabascans fled in utter disorder.

With the battle over, Cortes released two chiefs, they exchanged gifts and then proceeded to establish friendly relations.

Cortes sailed north to the San Juan de Ulua islands, the northern-most point reached by Grijalva and the gateway to the sea for the Aztecs.   Montezuma, Emperor of the Aztecs,   suspected Cortes might be Quetzalcoatl, god of the air, who had left the Empire promising to return to begin a new golden age.

The Emperor sent envoys and gifts to Cortes and negotiations which lasted for months began to arrange passage of Cortes to the Aztec capital, Tenochtitlan (Mexico City).   Interpreters were a Spanish castaway, Aguilar, who had spent 8 years with the Aztecs and Mayans and Marina, an intelligent slave girl, given to Cortes by the Tabascos.   Marina became Cortes's mistress, bore him a son and had much influence over Cortes' decisions.

Montezuma's counselors convinced him to deny Cortes access to Tenochtitlan, which he did, and at the same time suggested to Cortes that he return home.   Cortes protested, but Montezuma did not relent.   Cortes gained the favor of some coastal Tlasclan chiefs who hated the Aztecs, moved north near them, founded the city of Vera Cruz and made plans to seize Tenochtitlan.   He burned all his ships to prevent timid followers from deserting and enlisted the support of 6000 Tlasclan tribesmen.   On August 16, 1519 he began his trek to the Aztec capital.

Cortes reached the threshold of Tenochtitlan on November 8. While greatly outnumbered by figures ranging from an estimated 50,000 to 300,000, Cortes presented a fearsome threat with his 16 invincible armored knights and horses.   Montezuma greeted Cortes and ushered him into the city.

Once inside, Cortes immediately captured Montezuma, forced him to swear allegiance to King Charles of Spain and to publicly support him.

Meanwhile, Veslasquez heard that Cortes had set himself up as a missionary of King Charles instead of Veslasquez. This infuriated him and he sent Panfilo de Nariez to take Cortes prisoner and assume his command.

Cortes heard of this plot, went to the coast, defeated Nariez and sent him back to Cuba. He then confiscated Nariez's ships and stores.

Cortes left his lieutenant, Alvardo, in charge during his absence. Upon his return, Cortes found that Alvardo had taken an action to butcher over 600 Aztec noblemen during one of their ceremonies. Cortes, sensing the anger of the populace said to Alvardo, "Your conduct has been that of a madman!"

Cortes coerced Montezuma into speaking from a balcony in an effort to calm the crowd. By this time, Montezuma had lost much of his respect and credibility. The crowd showered him with arrows and stones and he was fatally wounded.

That night, July 5, 1520 known in Mexican annals as the Noche Triste, Cortes fled Tenochtitlan suffering great losses of men, equipment and treasure.

Cortes found refuge in the republic of Tlscala where he spent 10 months organizing a new army. In May, 1521 he launched a masterly campaign against Tenochitilan and conquered it by storm in three months.

With the Aztec capital under his control, Cortes rapidly took possession of the entire Aztec empire. On October 15, 1522 King Charles of Spain proclaimed Cortes Governor, Captain-General and Chief Justice of the new country of New Spain. This removed him from the shadowy shackles of Velasquez
.

Pizarro's March to the Inca Kingdom

Pizarro is described by Rogers in his book, "The Caribbean" as: "The soul of Pizarro was that of a bandit, venturesome to the point of madness, fierce and predatory. He followed a very lucky star . . ."   The tall, handsome Pizarro could not read or write but possessed the gifts of oratory and an ability to lead men. He engaged in numerous adventures, but it wasn't until he reached the age of 50 in 1522 that the opportunity for fame and fortune arose.

A minor explorer, Andagoya had returned from a voyage beyond the Gulf of San Miguel and asserted he had talked with nomadic merchants who swore that the rumored Inca capital, Cuzco, was a reality.

Pizarro made two poorly-financed voyages down the west coast of Peru. He had to abort both trips because of bad weather and low supplies.

But these first trips did not end in complete failure. His experiences produced some treasure, promise of much more and evidence that the Inca kingdom could be easily taken. King Charles, being much impressed with the potential wealth, sponsored Pizarro's third voyage with financial backing and political power afforded no other adventurer since Columbus. The only problem facing Pizarro was finding men to accompany him for he had acquired the unenviable reputation of being a reckless commander, sometimes leading his men into deathtraps.

In January, 1531 he sailed from Panama City with three ships, 180 men and 30 horses. He looted several towns on his way down the coast of Peru and sent an impressive display of jewels back to Panama City. The showing of this treasure quickly solved his labor supply.

His first goal was to capture Tumbez, a thriving city he visited on his second voyage. He found it in ruins and when he questioned some survivors he found out that there had been a civil war and that Emperor Huasca had been overthrown by his brother, Atahuapa, an action not fully supported by the Inca population.

Pizarro selected 168 daredevil adventurers to accompany him to Cajamarca where the new king, Atahuapa lived. As they traveled the trail his horses, glistening armor (the Incas had never seen metal) and bravado created awe and wonder among the spear-carrying Incas. They welcomed Pizarro's company and entertained them lavishly along the way.

When Pizarro came close to Cajamarca, Atahuapa sent an escort to usher him to the city and provided him barracks bordering the town square.

Pizarro immediately made his move for conquest. He invited Atahuapa to a reception. When he arrived, Pizarro grabbed Atahuapa, thrust him behind a locked door and slew hundreds of his courtiers and unarmed troops.

This action stunned the Incas and they didn't know what to do without their leader. Atahuapa sent for a roomful of gold and jewels in an effort to have these serve as ransom. He felt Pizarro to be in a plot with his brother to overthrow him and smuggled out orders to have Huasca murdered. Neither plan succeeded. When Atahuapa's influence began to wane and Pizarro had convinced himself that complete anarchy existed in the Inca empire, Pizarro executed the emperor.

News of Pizarro's conquest of Cajamarca and the presence of untold riches abounding in the Inca empire brought Spanish adventurers in increasing numbers. This invasion and the Inca's inability to find a leader to rally behind, stalled efforts to organize a military force to defend their empire until it was too late.

In November 1533 Pizarro entered Cuzco. Fourteen months later he founded Lima and completed the Inca conquest with the help of Atahualpa's defectors in 1535.

Montejo's Conquest of the Mayas

Cuban Governor, Velasquez had financed the explorations of Cordoba in 1517 and Grijalva in 1518 to the Yucatan where minor skirmishes took place with the Mayans and gold trinkets were found. Francisco Montejo made the first sincere effort to conquer the Yucatan and Mayas. While residing in Spain an old friend, Alonso de Avila, visited and related thrilling tales of untapped riches on a newly-found peninsula called Yucatan.

His wife, in support, sold her jewels and with a generous contract from the King he set forth in 1527 with three ships, two captains and over 400 men to conquer and settle the Yucatan. The only provision the King imposed was that no "prohibited persons" be allowed to settle--prohibited persons being the French and English.

His first settlement bordered a swamp. Soon fever overtook his men and they became mutinous. Montejo burned his ships to prevent desertion and moved his town away from the swamp. While his men were recuperating, Mayan chiefs came from miles around to view the strangers and the beasts (horses) they brought. Some Mayans were known to faint or flee at the sound of a horse's neigh.

Montejo trekked inland alternately being well-received by gift-bearing Mayans and besieged with bow and arrows with other not-so-friendly tribes. He returned to the coast with only 72 of his original 382 followers.

At this time Gonzalo Guerrero, a Spaniard converted to the Mayan tribe, deceived Montejo into thinking that his detachment under Alonso Davila had been massacred and at the same time convinced Davila that the same fate had befallen Montejo. In despair, they both withdrew to their original town, where they discovered the ruse and sailed in a ship sent for their rescue to Vera Cruz. The first invasion effort ended in failure.

Spanish invasion efforts continued and continued to fail partly because of Gurerreo's schemes, but mostly due to the ferocious fighting of the Mayas. By 1535 no Spaniard could be found on the Yucatan Peninsula.

About this time, the Mayan empires began to disintegrate. Fighting the Spanish caused them to use vast stores of food and to neglect the planting and care of their fields. Then a serious drought occurred. The Xiu of Mani decided to make offerings to their god of rain and fertility at Chichen Itza. To get there they had to pass through the land of the Cocom, their arch enemy. To their surprise the Cocums welcomed the contingent of nobles and priests and displayed friendship by giving them feasts and a large house for shelter. Once inside the house the Cocums set it on fire. All the Xius perished. This act provoked war. Villages and towns were sacked and burned. Concurrently the region suffered from a swarm of locusts. Mayan cohesion and strength began to weaken.

Francisco Montejo was aging, and while he was successfully engaged as Governor of Tabasco, he still held the dream of conquering the Yucatan. He had an illegitimate son, Francisco Montejo the Younger, whom he instructed to "pacify and populate" the Yucatan.

The senior Montejo made it very clear that the Younger was to go forth in true Christian spirit with Christian men having no public vices or sins and to treat the Indians with all possible kindness if they did not resist. Upon conquest, the lands and natives were divided among the Spaniards--the choice bits of land were reserved for special grants.

Convinced he had embarked on a mission to bring civilization and religion to a horde of ignorant savages, Montejo the Younger fought his way from town to town and found resistance every step of the way.

Two years into the expedition, beset by hunger and fatigue the force stopped at Tiho to rest and contemplate their next course. Some advance lookouts returned and advised Montejo that they were being approached by a huge military force led by a king shrouded in feathers and carried on a litter. Fearing defeat, Montejo called for his priest who erected a cross and led them in prayer.

The "feathered" one turned out to be Tutul Xiu, emperor of the realm of Yucatan. When Montejo came into view, Tutal stepped down from his litter and approached with his men. When he came close he ordered all his men to drop their bows and arrows and to clasp their hands toward the heaven as a sign of peace. To show his desire for friendship, Montejo led Tutal through the ranks of the Spaniards.

Tutal Xiu did want peace, but his main goal was to join the Spaniards to take revenge on the Cocums for their massacre.

On January 6, 1542 formal ceremonies were held to establish the town of Merida which became the Spanish capital of the province of Yucatan.

While the region was secured for purposes of explorations to plunder, Indian uprisings continued into the mid-19th century.

The Gold Road

By 1545 all the richest Indian civilizations had been conquered and attention centered on ways to transport the gold, silver, precious gems, fine cloths and artwork to Spain.   Pack mules trudged along trails from Peru, Panama City, Mexico and the Yucatan to three major ports; Nomdre de Dios, Cartegena and Porto Bello. The value of the treasure was enormous. A writer recorded the treasure in Porto Bello awaiting shipment on a particular day to be over $75 million. On that same day he counted 200 mules laden with silver bars entering the city. They stacked the bars in the town square because all the storehouses had been filled.   The galleons would assemble in May and June to begin their voyages across the Caribbean. They made stops at Santo Domingo, Havana or San Juan for supplies before venturing the sail across the Atlantic to Seville.

The treasure-laden galleons gained the attention and envy of other European nations. The monopoly enjoyed by Spain in 1525 was continually challenged for over 200 years by rival nations through piracy, contraband trade, outright warfare and diplomacy.

It is remarkable that over this period Spain lost only Jamaica, Martinique, Guadelope, western Hispaniola, Grenada, Barbados and a few other islands to other European powers.

The loss of these islands came about through disinterest and neglect. This is not hard to understand for the Aztec, Maya and Inca empires held more promise for wealth than the humid, disease-ridden island specks in the Caribbean Sea.

It is noteworthy that they never lost control of the vital Caribbean ports that served their Spain-bound treasure ships.

West Indies Map, 1622

Dunn's River Falls, Jamaica

CHAPTER 5

EUROPEAN POWER STRUGGLE AND SETTLEMENTS

"St. Dominique and Jamaica never changed hands, but lesser islands were batted about like shuttlecocks. Both sides were greedy for sugar land, and no speck of it was too small to snatch."
Roberts: French in the West Indies.

English, French, Dutch enter West Indies

The European community ridiculed Columbus' departure on his first voyage and displayed disbelief when he returned and announced the finding of a New World.

The ridicule and disbelief turned to envy with the signing of the Treaty of Tordesillas by Spain and Portugal and supported by the Pope on June 7, 1494. Spain received complete authority over all newly-discovered lands west of a "line" drawn down the center of the Atlantic--Portugal received complete authority over all newly-discovered lands east of the "line." The rationale of the treaty was the "right of conquest."

Spain enjoyed its monopoly in the Indies for 150 years. The main interference came from the English, Dutch and French who supported and sometimes financed acts of privateering and contraband dealings. They took this form of harassment in order to destroy Spain's source of wealth because they could not afford the cost of a military conflict that would certainly occur should they decide to contest the Tordesillas treaty.

The Spanish regarded these intruders "beyond the line" as nothing more than a swarm of pesky insects, so to protect themselves they built a string of fortresses along their trade routes and went about the business of transporting gold and silver to Seville, Spain. The Spanish either neglected or abandoned the colonization of islands not along these trade routes.

Over time the pirates and contraband dealers found that what the Caribbean region lacked in gold deposits it made up for with its potential for agriculture and trading enterprises. Here, trade could be developed in tobacco, cotton, supreme hard woods, dyes, sugar, spices, gums and more. With Spain's preoccupation with gold and silver, the time was ripe for settlement by others.

The Dutch were the first to trespass into the region to make use of its natural resources. Spain had placed an embargo on salt and tobacco, forcing the Dutch to seek other sources. Holland relied heavily on large supplies of salt to preserve their herring and began to share the world's interest in using tobacco. From 1599 to 1605 over 700 Dutch ships transported salt from the inexhaustible salt field of the Araya Peninsula on the coast of Venezuela to Holland. This deposit and a new source of tobacco supply found on the east coast of Central and South America caused Holland to go "beyond the line."

The Spanish Main stronghold began to break down during the 17th century. In 1604 she granted England the right to trade in the Caribbean. In 1648 she granted the Dutch ownership of all their holdings in the Indies. During this period the contest began between the English, Dutch and French for Caribbean settlements.   Below is the chronology of some major settlements during the 17th century:

1600	Dutch settle Sint Eustatius.
1624	English settle Barbados & St. Kitts. Dutch settle Berbice.
1625	English settle Nevis.
1630-1640	Dutch settle Curacao, St. Martin and Saba. English settle Antigua, Montserrat and St. Lucia. French settle Martinique and Guadeloupe.
1648	French and English divide St. Martin.
1651	English settle Suriname.
1655	English capture Jamaica. Cayman Islands ceded by Spain to England.
1667	Treaty of Breda gives the English colony of Suriname to Holland in exchange for the Dutch island of Manhattan in New York.
1684	The English takes over Bermuda.
1697	Spain cedes the western half of Hispaniola (Haiti) to France.

In 1827 Captain Thomas Southey published a 3-volume set titled: A Chronological History of the West Indies which covers the period 1492 to 1816. The first sentence in his Conclusion on Page 616 of his third volume reads: "The history of the West Indies presents little more than a melancholy series of calamities and crimes." Southey would have been more accurate had he used the word "world" instead of limiting the geographics to the "West Indies." The world was not a peaceful and prosperous planet during the 1492-1816 period. In fact, it was the poverty and cruelty that drove the average citizen to chance the hazards of settling the Indies--the "white man's graveyard." Exploring new and unknown places is not an easy task even with today's technology, so vividly displayed in T-V documentaries. But, those who settled the Indies had the problem of dealing with both nature's and human enemies.

It is interesting to peruse the writings of Southey and note some of the situations with which the early settlers had to deal. Below is a selection of some of Southey's cataloging during the 1600's:

1605
The court of Madrid sent armed ships to Punta Araya (the salt field) with orders to station themselves there, and expel the Dutch by force of arms. The Dutch continued contraband salt trade until 1622 when a fort was built.

(St. Lucia) "Upon Thursday, after dinner, Mr. Alexander Saint John, with seventeen others, went with Augramert and his father to their houses: on the road they were attacked by 300 Caribs, who lay in ambush for that purpose. . . they were all killed except John Nichols, who, with three arrows sticking in him, by running into the wood and swimming over a standing lake, got back to the others in time to put them on their guard."

1610
Sir George Somers returned again to the Bermudas, where he died of a surfeit (overindulgence) after eating pork.

1623
Thomas Warner landed on St. Christopher (St. Kitts) on January 28. They found three Frenchmen who tried to set the Indians upon them. They became friends. By September they had a crop of tobacco, which was destroyed by a hurricane. Grascocke wrote, "All this while we lived upon cassado bread, potatoes, plantanes, pines, turtles, guanes, and fish plenty: for drink we had nicknobby (a drink made from potatoes)."

1627
"The Dutch admiral Pieter Heyn attacked a fleet of Spanish galleons in Mataca Bay, in Cuba, and took or destroyed almost the

whole of them. The immense riches with which this fleet was laden are said to have enabled the United States (?) to continue the war against Spain."

1631
"Captain Henry Hawley arrived at Barbadoes, appointed by Lord Carlisle to supersede Sir William Tufton as governor. Sir William Tufton procured the signatures of some of the planters to a petition against Hawley: this petition Hawley construed into an act of mutiny, on the part of Tufton, for which he had him tried and shot by the sentence of a court-martial."

1632
"When the freebooters (pirates) took possession of the island of Tortuga, it was garrisoned by only 25 Spaniards, who considering themselves in a kind of banishment, surrendered at the first summons: it was a joy to them to quit the island . . "

1641
"The Spaniards attacked the English at New Providence, displaced the settlers, burnt their habitations, and murdered the governor, but did not occupy the island."

1642
During this year there were three hurricanes in the West Indies.

1647
"An epidemic disease raged in America and the West Indies: in Barbadoes and St. Christopher's, between five and 6000 persons died of it; at Barbadoes, the living were hardly able to bury the dead!"

1654
"While M. le Fontenay was rejoicing for the arrival of his brother at Tortuga, a vessel arrived with intelligence that he had been chased by a Spanish fleet, and escaped by running over a shoal, upon which the frigate that pursued her had been wrecked. Preparations were immediately made to defend the island."

1668
In the beginning of February, Lord Willoughby, with a great number of colonists, sailed from Barbados to reestablish the

colonies of Antigua and Montserrat, which the French and Caribs had quite desolated during the war. In passing St. Vincent's and Dominica, he made peace with the Caribs and left Thomas Warner as governor of Dominica.

Philosophies of Colonization

The Spanish colonies operated under a system of laws made by a supreme court, sitting in Spain, called the "Council of the Indies." Spain established a supreme court, the Audencia, in Santo Domingo to adjudicate regional West Indies matters.   They established townships with one township boundary touching that of another. Spain maintained total control over her colonies and were obsessed with the goal of imposing religious instruction on the Indians. While most European countries encouraged settlements by private companies, Spain and Portugal allowed settlements by the crown only.

The Dutch entered the region in earnest in the 1620's, harassed Spanish ships and forced Spain to focus attention in Brazil which the Dutch were trying to conquer. These actions left the Lesser Antilles relatively unguarded and the window opened for British and French investors and political and religious refugees to settle the region.

Private enterprise established the English, French and Dutch settlements with contracts given by the Crown that included provisions for the payment of taxes. The administration, at first, was largely left in the hands of the settlers who concerned themselves mainly with economic gain, caring little about converting the Indians' religious thoughts.

Times changed, and while the colonists retained much political power, the homelands provided governors, local councils, military support and encouragement for religious activities.

Wars, Wars and More Wars

Spain, England, Holland and France warred with each other almost continuously between the 16th and 19th centuries.   If England, Holland and France weren't warring with Spain, England and France, Spain and Holland or Spain and France, etc. were at war with each other.

This warfare spilled over into the Caribbean islands. They not only found themselves involved in the conflicts directly, but often used as pawns in treaty negotiations.   Between 1536 and 1898 the European powers signed 23 treaties addressing rights to their occupation of various Caribbean islands. By the end of World War 1 in 1917, 17 European wars had an impact on the Caribbean. The slightest provocation would rekindle the flames or warfare. The War of Jenkin's Ear is a good example.

The War of Jenkin's Ear

The 1713 Treaty of Utrecht between England, France and Spain granted England and France certain lands and rights in the Caribbean. The Spanish signed the Treaty during a period of weakness and duress and continued to harass the English. It is purported that in 1731 the Spanish boarded English Captain Robert Jenkin's ship in the Caribbean to search for contraband. During the search the Spanish captain cut off Jenkin's ear and told him to present it to the King as a sample of what happens the English captains who sail the Spanish Caribbean waters. Jenkins presented his shriveled ear to the King in 1738 when English war fever had fermented to a new high and the indignation provoked war. The war lasted until 1748 when the milk toast Treaty of Aix-la-Chappelle ended the matter, returning the lands and issues to much the same status that existed in 1738.

Some insisted that Jenkin's ear was in place during his appearance before the King, but covered by his wig.

This chapter must conclude without attempting to detail the numerous rulership changes that took place during this period in Caribbean history because of wars or treachery. Such an effort would drive the reader to tears. St. Lucia alone changed hands 14 times before England gained permanent possession in 1814.

CHAPTER 6

BUCCANEERS, PIRATES AND PRIVATEERS

"Opportunity Makes the Thief"

"Why is it that a little spice of deviltry lends not an unpleasantly titillating twang to the great mass of respectable flour that goes to make up the pudding of our modern civilization. . . would not every boy, for instance--that is every boy of any account--rather be a pirate captain than a Member of Parliament?"
Howard Pyle, Editor, The Buccaneers and Marooners of America
November, 1890

Introduction

Technically, the sea-going bandits of this era can be classified and defined into three categories:

BUCCANEER: The Buccaneer had a vengeance against the Spanish. They attacked only Spanish ships and ports.

PIRATE: Pirates held no allegiance to any nation. They would plunder and attack any ship or port--except those owned or occupied by another pirate. Pirates are also called Corsairs, Filibusters and Freebooters.

PRIVATEER: Nations hired Privateers. England would hire them to attack French, Dutch or Spanish ships and ports. The French would hire them to attack English, Dutch or Spanish ships and ports. The nation would share the bounty with the Privateer and give them protection.

In practice, these undisciplined sea-going bandits were not dedicated to one category. At one time they would be Buccaneers--at another, Privateers. In this book, these bandits will be referred to as "Pirates" when discussed as a group.

Full or part-time pirates did not make it a practice to publish their autobiographies or keep records of their escapades. A large percentage of Caribbean pirates entered the practice with the intention of retiring, with a moderate amount of wealth, in obscurity to some quiet countryside. Besides, if identified as a pirate, they would likely be tortured and publicly hanged. Therefore, much information about their activities was acquired during periods of their torture, from journalists of the time or pirates' prisoners who escaped and told their tales.

Who Were These Pirates? Where Did They Come From?

Certainly, some were rascals, scoundrels and career criminals born to the sea and dedicated to living a short but flamboyant life by taking all the risks and rewards piracy had to offer.

But, it was by circumstance, chance or force that led most men--and some women--into a life of piracy.

Reformation in the 16th century, changing the churches from Catholic to Protestant, put lots of English fishermen out of work because they supplied Catholics with fish for Friday. Being that seamanship was the only skill they possessed, they turned to piracy to survive.

During the reign of Elizabeth I, many considered themselves Crusaders against the Spanish and became Buccaneers.

Being a part of the large economic lower-class in the 15th to 17th centuries meant a life of near starvation, physical misery, political oppression and no opportunity to rise from this miserable state. The sea offered the only avenue for escape and piracy was a viable option.

There was a sharp difference in discipline between naval ships of any nation and those of a Pirate. Naval ships had strict rules that had to be obeyed. The captain had full power and could flog or otherwise punish his crew for any minor offense. The Pirate ship was totally undisciplined. In most cases the captain was elected by a group of self-appointed crew members and had little to say except in time of battle, when he took command. The crews, in a continuous state of drunkenness, would throw a sober person overboard--suspecting him of plotting mutiny. Many navy crew members tired of strict rules and beatings and opted to switch to Piracy.

When Pirates boarded a merchant ship the captured crew had two choices:
1. Join the Pirates;
2. Be unceremoniously thrown overboard--Pirates seldom took the time to make someone walk the plank. The choice was clear.

A small group of gentlemen adventurers outfitted their own ships and sailed forth for excitement. Sir Francis Drake allowed some "gentlemen" to join his crew but became unpopular when he forced them to do the same work as other crew members.

Women did venture into the world of Piracy. One of the early celebrated ones was Alvilda, daughter of a king of the Goths who chose piracy over a forced marriage to the son of a Danish king. Her all-woman crew braved the open seas in a ship propelled mostly by oars, with little help from sails. Her pirate exploits engaged the wrath of Prince Alf of Denmark and he set forth to destroy this pirate ship—not knowing who captained the ship. After a fierce battle, Prince Alf prevailed, boarded the pirate vessel and discovered the captain to be his runaway bride-to-be. He proposed marriage and she accepted.

It is known that some captains allowed women aboard and some did not. Whether they were there for social purposes or part of the fighting force is unclear. There is much written detail about Anne Bonney and Mary Reed (see this section in the Jamaica chapter) who sailed with Calico Jack Rackman, and it is assumed others actively participated in hand-to-hand combat successfully.

While being cruel to their captives, they treated their seriously wounded and those permanently unable to fight with compassion. The wounded could stay aboard as long as desired or would be given a generous monetary allotment if they chose to return to the land.

The crews of Pirate ships changed almost monthly. They held no allegiance to any captain or ship and would not hesitate to switch, with no notice, to another ship holding promise of greater booty.

The Setting

It did not take long for the Spanish to flush through the meager gold deposits on the Caribbean islands and find their way to Central and South America where they found mountains of gold and silver.

Once found, these treasures had to be transported from ports like Cartagena, Columbia and Portobelo, Panama across the expansive Caribbean Sea past the maze of islands rimming the Sea, through the Bahamas and on to Spain.

The region was a haven for seafarers up to no good. It is sprinkled with thousands of coves, islets and cays (tiny, low islands or reefs) that provide shelter from storms, hiding places suitable for ambush and places to careen (scrape their ship's bottom from barnacles, etc.) their ships. Hundreds of islands provided provisions like turtles, fruit and drinking water. The Caribbean Sea abounded with fish.   Other European countries were jealous of Spain's newly-found wealth and objected to the Pope's proclamation awarding all lands west of the Azores to Spain because of the "right of conquest." Spain's brutal and torturous treatment of captured Protestant seamen during the Inquisition, Reformation and Auto da Fe (Act of Faith) periods especially outraged the English public.

Entrepreneurs in England and other European countries observed a steady stream of relatively unprotected treasure-laden Spanish ships crossing the Atlantic and unloading in Seville. Seizing the opportunity to acquire wealth and take revenge on the Spanish, they outfitted ships armed with canons and fighting crews and sent them forth to plunder.

European countries, at first, supported these pirates. They did not consider strong efforts to settle the area because of the expense and conflict it would bring.

Therefore, with their country's support, ideal ambush conditions, supplies of provisions close at hand and the prospect of gaining great wealth, Buccaneering, Piracy and Privateering became an integral part of Caribbean history for over 200 years, beginning in the 1500's.

The First Pirate Raid

Piracy is said to be the third oldest profession behind prostitution and medicine, but it didn't arrive in the Caribbean until 1527 when King Henry VIII of England sent Captain John Rut to the Americas with two ships, the Mary Gilford and Samson.

King Henry gave Rut two missions. One was to find a northwest passage to the Grand Khan of Tartary. The other was to spy and harass the Spanish in the Americas.

On August 27, 1527, Rut sent a letter home from Newfoundland indicating he had received secondary instructions from King Henry which he was obligated to follow.

A letter exists that describes events that took place when a 3-masted English ship entered Santo Domingo, Hispaniola's harbor on the afternoon of November 25, 1527. While there is no documentation, it is assumed it was Rut, who lost one of his ships in the northern seas.

Ten men came ashore and were welcomed by the Spanish residents. The sound of canon fire from the fortress interrupted a jovial dinner and the English returned to their ship and sailed away. Who fired the canon or why is unknown.

Three days later the English ship returned and sent 30 armed men ashore to purchase meat and supplies. The Spanish outrightly refused to sell them anything.

The affronted English then proceeded to take all the hens, eggs, meat and vegetables they could find plus clothing from the settlers they met. As they left they shouted obscenities and vows to return and attack again.

Life Aboard the Pirate Ship

Pirates acquired many of their ships by capture. If a captured ship didn't meet their specifications to qualify to become an addition to their fleet, they burned it. Many of the Privateer ships were openly outfitted in English ports.

The pirates favored a ship that could reach a speed of 12 knots like the schooner which measured 80 feet long, and weighed 90 to 100 tons and could accommodate a crew of 75. Another favorite was the 700 ton East Indiaman that measured 160 feet long with a 35 foot beam. While pirate ships would carry from 100 to 200 men, this ship could accommodate a crew of 400 and 60 canon.

Living conditions were horrid. The food was putrid, water, stagnant, meat, rancid and bread infested with black-headed maggots, but this seemed to be accepted as one of the inconveniences of pirating. Typhoid, scurvy, dysentery, malaria and yellow fever were risks that took their toll. Venereal disease was rampant. Pirates often first sought the medicine chest of a captured vessel before exploring it for treasure.

While carpenters, sailmakers and surgeons were valued, the most popular craftsmen aboard were the musicians. They had to play at any time of the day or night on request, but were given a day off on Sundays.

Some captains held religious services on Sunday. Blackbeard is rumored to have shot a crew member for scoffing at a sermon.

Pirate crews didn't care much about how a crew member behaved ashore but realized there had to be a few rules aboard to maintain some degree of order and understanding about how the booty was to be shared.   Some typical rules included in these agreements are:

1. Each crew member is to have one vote in matters concerning the ship's escapades.

2. The bounty is to be divided as follows:

   A. The captain and quartermaster each receives two shares.

   B. The master gunner and boson receives 1 ½ shares.

   C. All officers receives one and one-quarter shares.

   D. Regular crew members receives one share.

3. Any crew member withholding booty to be shared after a raid will be marooned.

4. There will be no card playing, dice games or women on board, except during social events.

5. There will be no fighting on board. Quarrels will be settled on shore in a gentlemen's duel with pistol or cutlass.

6. Any crew member who deserts the ship or shows cowardice during battle will be put to death.

The pistols and rifles used during the pirate era were not too accurate. The pirates practiced marksmanship daily and gained considerable advantage over the lesser experienced merchantmen during a boarding. Their superior marksmanship and experience greatly reduced their casualties during a boarding.

Pirates did not fire canons at their prey for fear of sinking it. Usually, a shot across the bow would strike such fear among the victims that surrender was immediate and complete.

The Birth of the Buccaneer--A Strange Breed

Piracy and privateering has existed worldwide since man began to sail the open seas. True buccaneering is an historical happening that is unique to the Caribbean alone and lasted only about 30 years, from 1690 to 1720.

It seems that it was the Spaniards themselves who gave birth to the Buccaneer.   The original Buccaneers (called Cow killers) were a motley lot of mostly French escaped criminals, runaway bondsmen and political or religious refugees. They lived on the West and North coasts of Hispaniola (Haiti) and hunted wild cattle and pigs with knives and long-barreled "buccaneering pieces." They hunted in pairs, sold the meat and hides to passing ships and shared their profits equally.   They developed a special process of smoking the meat which they called "Boucan." It was their association with the name "Boucan" that led to this category of pirates to be called Buccaneers.

Although these "Cow killers" harmed nobody, the Spaniards considered them a nuisance to be rid of, so they set about and killed off their source of income--the cattle and pigs.

This action planted a seed of hatred and the Cow killers, to be renamed by historians as Buccaneers, set about and destroyed all the Spanish property they could find and killed all the Spaniards in their path.   They banded into a closely-knit group called "The Confederacy of the Brethren of the Coast" and relocated to Tortuga, just off the northwest coast of Haiti.

They developed a fleet by capturing Spanish ships, and attracted aspiring Brethren because of their successes. Their payment policy was simple and straight forward: "No prey, no pay."   Their mastery of seamanship and successes and bravery in battle attracted notice from European countries who tried to conscript   the Buccaneers to fight with them against their enemies. These efforts ended in failure because the Buccaneer's first priority was loot, not winning battles.

In 1657, by invitation from the English, they moved their headquarters to Port Royal, Jamaica.

Big Names in Caribbean Piracy

Henry Morgan, the most famous and swashbuckling of them all, William "Blackbeard" Teach, the cruelest, Jack "Calico Jack" Rackman and his two infamous female consorts, Anne Bonney and Mary Read are discussed in the Jamaica chapter under this heading because of their ties with this island.

It is estimated that nearly 6000 persons engaged in some form of piracy in the Caribbean during this era. Many books, some written as early as 1724, describe their exploits. The few pirates mentioned here can only serve to give some insight to their character and possibly whet the appetite for further reading, for their exploits are truly almost beyond fiction.

Following are three pirate personalities that must be mentioned:

Sir Francis Drake.

Drake (1532-1595), experienced many failures before successfully plundering major Spanish holdings in Central and South America. Many of his failures might be cited as investments, since they were attempts to find the best strategy for storming Spanish forts and cities. During his early escapades he made it a point to befriend the Cimarrones (runaway slaves) and the Carib Indians who gave him support in future raids.

His first major attack was Nombre De Dios, Panama which he conquered by firing canon at the city while he sent troops to attack from the rear--his newly-found tactic. Later he overwhelmed a poorly-defended mule train north of Nombre De Dios and carried off such a great treasure in gold that he had to leave behind 15 tons of silver.

After his famous voyage through the Strait of Magellan and around the world in his ship the Golden Hind 1577-1580, he was commissioned by Queen Elizabeth to "fare forth and do your worst" to the Spanish in the Indies. He left England on September 14, 1585 with 30 ships and 2300 men.

On his way he sacked and burned Santiago in the Cape Verde islands. There, a plague struck and he lost 300 men. He went on to strike Santo Domingo, Hispaniola which he quickly captured and extracted a 25,000 ducat ransom before leaving. This was a great personal blow to Spain's King Phillip's ego.

Drake's next stop was Cartagena, Columbia which he successfully conquered using his frontal and rear attack tactics. He wanted to use Cartagena as a major port for the English, but by this time his force dwindled to 800. Unable to maintain control of the city, he took a modest ransom and departed.

His last major encounter was the El Morro fort at San Juan, Puerto Rico. The Spanish soundly defeated him. John Hawkins, his mentor, died in battle. Some historians say that Drake also died at San Juan. Others say that he went on to attack Havana and died during a plague of malaria and dysentery in January 1596 off the coast of Nicaragua.

Captain William Kidd.

Captain Kidd's pirate story differs from the norm. Toward the end of the Caribbean piracy era in 1695, England's Lord Bellmont and an investment group outfitted an excellent fighting ship, the Adventure and employed Kidd and a select crew to sail the Indies with the purpose of seizing the booty of pirate ships. They did not give Kidd the usual privateering split of the loot--75% going to the captain and crew. Instead, the Crown was to get 10%, the Bellmont group 75%, leaving Kidd and crew with a paltry 15%.

Shortly after departing the Thames in England, Kidd and crew had a "man to man" talk and decided to switch to the usual 75% booty cut for the privateers.

During the Atlantic crossing they met an unprotected Spanish treasure-laden galleon. The opportunity was irresistible. They seized the vessel and its wealth and there and then decided to cut the Crown and Bellmont out completely--after all, they were pirates, so Kidd joined the ranks.

Kidd was a gentleman of sorts. He did not spill a lot of blood and had a longing to return to his family in England and the life of respectability and leisure he left. After he decided to end his pirate career he attempted to bribe officials and plead forgiveness for his wretched deeds, but it was in vain. The English hanged Captain William Kidd at Execution Dock on the Thames in 1701.

Captain (teetotaling) Bartholomew Roberts.

Captain Roberts holds the record for the most ships boarded in the West Indies and around the world--400. He accomplished this during a 3-year span, 1719 to 1722.

Born to the sea at Wales in 1682, he sailed as an ordinary crew member until 1719 when his ship was boarded by the pirate Howell Davis and chose the option to join Davis' crew. Six weeks later Davis was killed during an attack on the fort at Portugal's Princess Island. The crew elected Roberts to be their new captain.

Roberts gained the crew's support by returning to Princess Island and destroying the fort and burning two Portuguese ships in the harbor.

The man was fearless. He quietly entered Bahia harbor, Brazil where 42 Portuguese merchantmen and warships were anchored.

His boson located the most heavily laden ship and Roberts sailed up, boarded her, stripped the treasure and sailed away before the Portuguese warships could be alerted. This has been considered the most daring raid in Caribbean piracy.

Roberts didn't restrict his activities to the West Indies. After an officer stole his ship, the Rover and made off with the Bahia prizes, he sailed a sloop to Newfoundland where he successfully pirated ships, crews and stores and regained his wealth. He ravaged the coasts from Newfoundland to West Africa and returned to the Indies.

In 1721 Captain Chaenor Ogle of the British Royal Navy began a search for Roberts in his ship, the Swallow. He found Roberts and his newly-acquired vessel the Onslow and the smaller consort, the Ranger anchored in a tiny bay on the Guinea coast.

Roberts sighted the Swallow and being too busy with breakfast to bother with the boarding, sent the Ranger to seize what he thought to be just another merchantman.

The sly Ogle maneuvered the Swallow away from the Ranger just far enough to draw the attacker out of Robert's hearing range of canon shot. He then let the Ranger come close before he uncovered his canon and destroyed the Ranger. Ogle then quietly sailed into the harbor, completely surprising the breakfasting sober Roberts and his hopelessly drunken crew.

Roberts was hit in the throat with grapeshot and by his request, upon his death, was thrown overboard fully-clothed and armed with his pistols and cutlass.

The End of Caribbean Piracy

By the 1720's the European powers had discovered the value of sugar cane crops. England and France were in the process of ending their hostilities. The pirates became a nuisance, rather than an asset, so the European homelands began to unfold plans to eliminate all forms of piracy from the region. The English enlisted the services of Captain Woodes Rogers, a former privateer, to root the pirates from their sanctuaries in the Bahamas. England ordered all governors to suppress piracy and for the Royal Navy to become very active to menace pirate ships. All nations armed their merchant ships and trained their seamen to fight. The cooperative effort resulted in success.

It is estimated that between 1716 and 1726, 600 pirates hanged for their deeds. The business of piracy in the Caribbean became too risky, so those dedicated to the profession left for the South Seas.

Botanical Gardens, Barbados

CHAPTER 7

THE SUGAR ERA

The Dutch Role in the Introduction of Sugar

When the Spanish first began to establish their Caribbean settlements, they introduced a large variety of food supplies for the purposes of survival. They imported cattle, pigs, fruit trees and food plants and produced just enough sugar to meet local needs.

The serious growing of sugar cane commercial basis in the Caribbean began when the Dutch captured Pernambuco, Brazil from the Portuguese in 1630 and held it until 1654.

During the time of their occupation the Dutch learned the treasured Portuguese secrets of growing cane and how to extract the juice. In 1637 Pieter Blower, a Dutchman, brought some cane to Barbados and grew the plant to produce the popular rum, "Kill Devil". Lo!--Here was a marketable product.

The Dutch were merchants and opportunists. They had connections in Africa for securing slaves. They also had every reason to believe that sugar cane would be a very profitable crop in the Caribbean climate and knew that sugar plantations would require an enormous labor force. Putting two and two together, they arranged for some influential and monied planters from Barbados to visit Brazil to see sugar cane operations in action.

The project produced undreamed-of results. The sugar and slave trade booms soon followed.

Sir William (Colonel) Drax, one of the Dutch guests on the excursion to Brazil, brought a model of a sugar mill back to Barbados in the 1640's and with his genius for organizing the planting and processing procedures, he soon reaped gigantic profits.

The eyes of the world focused on Colonel Drax, for he had shown that the New World offered a bonanza for those willing and able to invest in the growing of sugar cane.

How They Made Sugar--From Planting to Sugar Loaf

For sugar crops to be profitable, the principles of the economies of mass production had to be applied. These principles required large investments in land, labor and capital. These requirements eliminated the many small tobacco farmers who could not convert to growing cane because of the large investment required in acreage, machinery, tools, livestock and labor.

Labor, alone, posed a problem. Sugar plantations required one worker for every two acres, compared with one worker for 10 acres of cotton and one for every 40 acres of corn. Then there was the problem of feeding and caring for the workers during the months that required little work.   The first step required the clearing the land. The Caribbean islands in those years had dense forests and undergrowth. With clearing completed, the planting could begin.

Planting originally began with a process called "holing", when they planted cane stalks upright in holes. Later, they found that laying the stalks on their side (rattooning) in a trench 6 inches deep produced more shoots which weathered the hurricanes better. At the end of a month the cane would be high enough to "hide a Hare"--as the saying went. The stalks would be 2 feet high at the end of 2 months and then the ground required weeding.

At first, they harvested the crop at the end of 12 months. Later, they found that the cane produced more juice at the end of 16 months. When they harvested, they cut the cane 5 inches from the ground, stripped the leaves (which they fed to the livestock) and transported the cane to the mill.

In order to get the best product, the cane needed to be processed through the mill within 24 hours after cutting. This meant careful planning to time the planting periods on the right sized plots to meet the capacity of the mill as the cane matured.

The Milling Process

The planters located the Grinding House of the mill (ingenio) on a small hill so they could take advantage of the law of gravity. Here they extracted the juice from the cane by running the shoots through rollers.

In the early years they powered the mill using horses or cattle. Later they employed windmills and finally, steam power. They piled the crushed cane stalks and, when dried, used them as firewood.

The juice flowed through a pipe downhill to a cistern where it was stored for 24 hours and treated with ashes (of a special type) and kept damp with water. From there the juice flowed into a series of copper pots located in the Boiling House where skimming took place. They sent the skimmed liquid to the Still House where they made "Kill Devil", alias "Rumbullion", described by a traveler as "a hot, hellish and terrible liquor."

The Emergence of Molasses

The remaining liquid flowed into a cistern and was cooled. When cool, the potting process began. Pots, 16 inches square, with a hole in a tapered end plugged with plantain leaves, held 35 to 40 pounds of liquid when filled. These pots remained in this Filling Room for 2 days and nights. Workers would knock the sides of the pots with their knuckles, and if the sound was proper they took the pots to the Curing House. There, they removed the plantain leaves and the product, "Molasses" drained from the pot. The draining process took one month.

Sugar--The Final Product--Emerges
Next, the pots went to the Knocking Room where they separated the "sugar loaf" from the pot. The loaf had three layers. The top was a frothy light brown and the bottom, a dark brown. They re-boiled these top and bottom portions and produced what we call today, "brown sugar."

They covered the middle portion, called "muscovado", with tempered clay and allowed it to cure for four months. This produced their final product--"white sugar."

Elapsed Time?
The whole process, from planting to sugar loaf, took about two years.

The Plantation Lifestyle
Rarely did the planter plan to establish permanent residence on his plantation. He wanted to amass a fortune, return home and wallow in his newly-acquired wealth. The more successful planters built mansions called Great Houses and stayed to supervise. Others stayed just long enough to get the project underway, enlisted overseers and lawyers to manage their interests, and became an absentee owner. The differences in marketing methods encouraged more English than French to stay and oversee their property.

Those who attended to their island interests enjoyed a life of opulence.

The early planters threw up anything with four walls and a roof for shelter. When these shelters disappeared in a hurricane or were found too hot and humid to inhabit, they began to give attention to their housing's location and design.

When the planter acquired sufficient wealth he would build a Great House atop a hill and designed it to take advantage of the prevailing winds. The typical house was rectangular in shape and constructed with wood and stone. Builders often used the ballast carried in ships from Europe to produce special effects.

The ground floor was tiled with stone and used as a storeroom and air space to cool the second floor. Typically, they entered the second, and main floor, from the carriage way by climbing a flight of stone steps and passing through an impressive entrance into a wood-paneled hallway lined with wall hangings and pictures. Termites were (and still are) a terrible West Indies problem and sometimes wood paneling, wall hangings and pictures gave way to these invading insects.

The dining hall, with its mahogany floors polished with coconut husks, served as the planter's social center and usually shared the second floor with the master bedroom. It was not uncommon for planters and visitors traveling about the island to spend two or three weeks as a guest; therefore, the dining hall needed to be grandiose for sumptuous entertaining where they served large quantities of food and wine. The dining hall also met the need for a place to conduct elaborate balls and marriages, plan hunting trips and discuss political matters. When not in the dining hall, they frequented spacious outdoor verandas. Guest bedrooms occupied a third story or a wing off the second. In many cases the bedroom partitions did not reach the ceilings and the windows were always kept open, except during storms, there being more concern for cooling than privacy. Massive, wood-carved four-poster bedsteads were the centerpiece of exquisitely but sparsely furnished bedrooms. Often, slaves trained by missionaries carved the integrate designs on the bedposts.

They located the kitchen in a separate building to keep away the heat and lingering odors. A smokehouse was nearby as was a"buttery" (a cool place where they kept perishables}, housing for the slaves, the carriage and maintenance buildings and a garden.

They relied on Europe to supply such amenities as glassware, china, cutlery, goose quills and chamber pots--the outhouse being located some distance from the main building. The more affluent and fastidious planters began installing tin or zinc bath tubs in the mid-eighteenth century.

It was not unusual for the planter to enlist the services of 20 to 40 servants. A typical list would include: one butler; two footmen; one coachman; one postilion (a person who rides the leading left-hand horse of a four-horse carriage); one helper; one cook; one assistant; one storekeeper; one maid; three house cleaners; three washerwomen; and, four seamstresses. Each child had its nurse and each nurse her assistant boy or girl.

About Indulgence

Eighteenth century English writer, Bryan Edwards, in describing plantation life, wrote:

"There seems universally a promptitude for pleasure. This has been ascribed, perhaps justly, to the levity of the atmosphere. . . A West Indian property is a species of lottery. As such it gives birth to a spirit of adventure and enterprise and awakens extravagant hopes and expectations--too frequently terminating in perplexity and disappointment."

Rumors that Caribbean planters overate and overindulged are not without documentation. A typical Caribbean feast is described on Page 79 of the book, Black Ivory which provides a quote from Thomas Thistlewood:

Wednesday, March 15, 1775. John Cope, Richard Vassal and William Blake dined with Thomas on Jamaica who reported the menu as follows:

"Mutton Broth, Roast mutton and broccoli, carrots and asparagus, stewed mudfish, roast goose and paw paw, apple sauce, stewed giblet, some fine lettice which M. Vassall brought me, crabs, cheese, mush melon, etc. Punch, porter, ale, cyder, Madeira wine and brandy."

The next day Thistlewood complained that he felt "very unwell, with drinking too much wine yesterday."

Sane indulgences took the form of dancing, racing, horseback riding and hunting. Insane indulgences took the form of overeating, over drinking, gambling and dueling. Dueling with pistols or swords was so common it could well be classified as having been a sport.

All this opulence had its price. Overindulgence and disease took their toll. Their policy of managing slaves through terror and cruelty meant living continuously under the specter of revolt.

When the planters made their occasional trip home they brought an entourage including slaves and displayed all the pomp and pageantry they could muster. This, they felt they had earned.

For example, Jamaica's Thomas Lynch arrived for an appearance before King Charles II in a lavishly gilded carriage, the coachman and postilion dressed in the richest costumes and the horses shod with silver horseshoes. He loaned the King #50,000. Shortly afterwards, King Charles knighted Lynch in repayment.

Flamboyancy such as this gave rise to the catchy phrase, he's as: "Rich as a West Indian planter!"

The Cycle of the Sugar Era

The 17th century witnessed the breakdown of Spanish domination in the Caribbean. The English, French and Dutch infiltrated the region, established small colonies and entered the agricultural world market with bales of tobacco and cotton.

The tobacco and cotton enterprises had a short life. By 1639 the glutting of the European tobacco market caused a dramatic drop in price. The quality of North American grown Virginia tobacco greatly surpassed that grown in the West Indies. The confines of the limited acreage on the islands made growing cotton difficult and not very profitable.

When Colonel Drax introduced sugar cane to Barbados in the 1640's it took island planters only around 10 years to enthrone "King Sugar" and switch from the small, 100 acre farm to the 300 to 1000 acre plantation.

Between 1741 and 1745 ten of the major sugar producing islands marketed 102.4 thousand tons of sugar. Between 1766 and 1770 the same islands increased their production by 62.4%, marketing 162.4 thousand tons.

Although production increased dramatically, the economic-wise West Indies planters were enjoying the benefits of a sugar monopoly and did not glut the market. They carefully rationed the land devoted to growing sugar cane and engaged their political and economic gears to control prices.

The Beginning of the Unraveling of the Sugar Era in England

It is estimated that in 1754 Jamaica had enough land to support 150 more plantations and that enough sugar could be grown there alone to supply all of Europe.

Sugar refiners and the public launched protests in the English Parliament about the outrageous increase in sugar prices. It was pointed out that sugar profits were enough to pay and clothe an army of 40,000 foot soldiers for one year.

In the middle of the 18th century French sugar sold for half the price of English sugar in Europe, so a serious move got underway to change the laws to allow French sugar to compete with English West Indies sugar.

The planters banded together and fought the opposition, using the fashionable political move of the day, by buying seats in Parliament.   In addition, the planters exerted their influence by taking such actions as opposing the annexation of St. Lucia unless settlers were directed to grow cocoa, annatto or indigo instead of sugar; voting not to allow new settlers in St. Vincent to grow sugar;

insisting that clay used for whitening not be sold by Barbadians to the Leeward Islands; and, that Tobago be settled only if Barbadians agreed to what the settlers could grow.

To strengthen their alliance to promote planter interests and to present a common front against their opposition in Parliament, the growers formed the elite Planter's Club. Absentee plantation owners/Parliament members dominated the membership.

The arrogance of the West Indies planters, the gross display of their wealth, the manipulation of Parliament and ploys to maintain high sugar prices to glean exorbitant profits, enraged all non-planter connected Englishmen and mainland Europeans.

The Sugar King Dissolves

English planter influence along with the economic importance of West Indies sugar began to break down during the War of Jenkin's Ear, 1739-1748. The planters, so occupied with profit-making, noticed but did not become concerned about events taking place in the world market that would deal a fatal blow to the West Indies sugar market.

Haitian Sugar

It became quite apparent during the War of Jenkin's Ear that French grown Saint-Dominique (Haiti) sugar was cheaper and of better quality than any grown on British islands.   In 1748 the Governor of Jamaica wrote that unless Haiti's sugar competition was destroyed, the British sugar interests would be ruined.

Java Sugar

The Dutch, seeking a better supply, introduced sugar cane to Java and shortly rivaled the English European market.

Maple Sugar

In the later part of the 18th century Thomas Jefferson introduced the production of maple sugar in the United States and this supply became a competitive product in the North American market.

Beet Sugar

But, the most important competitive blow to West Indies sugar came in the form of beet sugar, developed by a Prussian chemist, Marggraf in 1747.

Loans Called In

Edwards, (cited earlier) reminds us that not all sugar ventures resulted in success. Many planters relied on year-to-year credit and in the later years of the era when sugar prices began to fall, loans were called and property began to be repossessed.

All of the above were impending devastating economic realities that, whether acknowledged or not, along with Emancipation, must have given rise to the expression, "Out with the old—in with the new."

The bombastic, romantic, yet humanistically deplorable sugar era crashed in the middle of the 19th century.

Hamilton Sugar Mill. Nevis

CHAPTER 8

SLAVERY AND SLAVE REVOLTS

"Boccarou (the white man) make de Black Man workee, make de Horse workee, make the Ox workee, make everything workee; only de Hog, He, He de Hog, no workee; he eat, he drink; he walk about, he go to sleep when he please, he libb like a gentleman."

"Information for those Who Would Remove to America."
Benjamin Franklin.
SOURCE: McCrum, "The Story of English."

Introduction

It is difficult to conceive that just over 200 years ago, four generations back, the pig had more respect than a human being, that torture sometimes was considered a form of sport and that life on earth was considered to be a relatively unimportant transitory experience--that true life followed death.

Slavery had been an acceptable practice from the dawn of man until emancipation in the Caribbean in the middle of the 19th century. Prisoners of war always became slaves; the Moors used the Christians as slaves; slavery had always been an institution in Africa and the slavery issue needed to be dealt with by the League of Nations after World War I in 1920.

When an English lady inherited a plantation in Jamaica during the 18th century she decided to free her slaves and divide her land between them. When the matter came to the governor's attention he summoned her and asked, "Madam, have you taken leave of your senses?"

The governor's thinking was typical of the times. Humanity as we know it today was not the fashion.

The Procurement Process

The original English slaver, John Hawkins (Sir Francis Drake's mentor), transported 300 blacks from Sierra Leone on the West coast of Africa to Hispaniola in 1562. He acquired them "partly by the sworde and partly by other meanes", a practice soon found to be self-defeating because the coastal chiefs turned out to be the key source of supply of slaves from inland tribes.

In the beginning the slave trade benefitted both the Africans and the slavers--the supply emptied the jails of the unwanted and filled the slaver's holds with a profitable cargo. In short order the jails emptied and the West Indies demand for slaves increased dramatically. During the 18th century, prisoners of war became the next in line to be bartered away to slavery.

European trinkets, cloth and firearms were irresistible bargaining tools for chiefs who had access to an inexhaustible supply of African slaves-to-be. A supply network quickly became established that extended far inland. During the 18th century 70% of the Indies-bound slaves were kidnaped and trekked to the coast through this network.

While a "gentlemen's agreement" existed between neighboring African villagers that they would not attack each other, seldom did they venture beyond their villages unarmed, for good reason. When the wind carried drum beats that alerted a tribal chief with superior weaponry that slave traders were about--neighbors beware! They lost little time rounding up captives to sell--chiefs, queens and royalty included.

Olaudah Equaino, a slave who joined the English Royal Navy and became a distinctive anti-slave evangelist, recorded his capture. He wrote that when he was 11 years old, kidnapers took him and his sister and marched them to the coast. The trek took over 6 months. He passed through villages where he heard new languages and music and saw cultures completely foreign to him. He and his sister immediately became separated and while he escaped a few times, his drivers quickly recaptured him.

They chained the captives together and made them carry heavy loads to keep them tired, thus discouraging the urge to escape. While the African chiefs were busy establishing their network, the slave traders set about building forts and dungeons to receive the slaves and ready them for shipment. The outnumbered white was not in friendly territory and kept either aboard ship or near forts defended with high walls and the fearsome cannon. A few brave independent slavers received their supply at the mouths of rivers like the Niger, Senegal, Gambia and Congo; however, the majority of trading took place at fortresses financed by European governments and such monopolistic companies as the British Royal African Company which established a string of seventeen forts along Africa's West coast. The forts also served the purpose of defending themselves from other European nation's raids. The actual trading was ritualistic, carried out following a strict set of customs. Chiefs, their retinues, traders and clients all exchanged gifts, ate, drank and smoked together showing proper etiquette and courtesies. Sometimes the negotiations broke down into bloodshed, which probably came when the slaves-to-be underwent their physical examination.

The slave traders stripped the slaves and took great care not to buy any deformed or sickly, or those with poor teeth or stature. If they did not appear able to do hard labor, the slaver rejected them. Research has not disclosed the fate of the rejects, the property of a distressed native trader who had paid for him, but it is hard to believe that it could have been worse than those facing the next journey--the "Middle Passage."

The "Middle Passage"

The Middle Passage is a term used by historians to identify the voyage of slave ships from the West coast of Africa to the West Indies.   If the ship had an English captain, he was no doubt a Christian who, remarkably, felt no guilt and saw no conflict with his religion and the inhumanity of his charge: Transport as many slave cargoes as possible to the Indies in the least amount of time.

The average slave ship carried around 500 slaves, and made the crossing in about 40 days. They chained two slaves together and made them lie side by side in a space five feet long on shelves with two and a half feet of head room. They separated the men and women. Collisions, fights and curses took place as the slaves crawled over each other to reach the sparsely-spaced conical toilets. It is certain that the women were sexually abused. Most captains had rules that forbid rape, but it would be capricious to believe that they enforced them forcefully against a small crew who did not really want to be aboard.

The slaves received only slight relief from the intense heat and stench through small portholes which the crew closed during stormy periods. Twice daily the crew brought the slaves to the deck to exercise, be wiped dry and to receive a portion of lime juice to prevent scurvy. The slaves remained below during stormy periods and the heat and stench in the holds intensified.

The slave diet consisted of beans boiled to a pulp, boiled yams and rice, a small quantity of beef or pork and a sauce called "Slabber Sauce" made of palm oil, flour, water and pepper. They gave the slave only one spoon to eat with from a communal food bucket.   The slaves soon lost their spoons and resorted to hand-feeding, one method of spreading disease.

Most ships had a surgeon, a loathsome job performed by some unfortunate obsessed with drunkenness or beleaguered with financial ruin. He received his pay in the form of "head money"--the more slaves arriving alive, the more the pay. He performed the pre-voyage physical exam and went below each morning to attend to the sick, moving them if necessary. This was another practice discontinued during stormy periods.

The death rate during the crossing was appalling for both crew and slaves. It has been said that if you drained the Atlantic you would uncover a pile of human bones marking the slave ships' path that would stretch from Africa to the Indies. A 15% mortality rate was not uncommon. Flux (what they called dysentery) became a big killer because the surgeons thought it came from overheating and filth instead of the real cause--rotten food and bad water. Smallpox was the most dreaded and when any slave or crew appeared to have the disease they quickly threw him overboard. Some slaves became so sick they stopped eating, so the crew force-fed them.

Crew members always took caution against revolts but the real danger waned when the slaves lost sight of the African coast and their last chance to escape their shackles and swim home.

The Sale

The sight of land brought relief for the crew and temporary jubilance for the slaves. A ship would anchor for a week just inside a harbor while the captain and crew prepared for the sale.

The slaves received extra food rations, baths and primping, which included oiling the skin, to make them as presentable as possible for the buyers. The crew and slaves scrubbed the ship's decks and holds before they allowed any buyers aboard.   When the sale took place on board, the buyers performed a physical exam in much the same manner as that performed before the voyage. Buyers bid to purchase the strongest and most healthy. The rest remained as "refuses."

The "Scramble" sale, which terrified the slaves, took place onshore in a large corral.   The sellers herded the slaves into the corral where they waited for the beat on a drum. At the drumbeat, large doors were flung open and the mass of buyers rushed in howling and wrangling over the slaves. Some buyers would wrap ropes around groups of slaves or otherwise bind them together and pull them to a seller's station to bargain.

The slaves had no idea of what was happening to them, what the yelling meant or who these buyers were--thus the terror. They saw their family and friends being separated, but didn't know that they likely would never see them again.

Ships didn't sell all their slaves in one day. Sometimes it took a week. Often the captain would decide to sail to another island where he found buyers who would accept some of the less able. Some "refuses" always remained unsaleable at the end of the voyage. The captain freed these slaves and left them at his last stop to fend for themselves.   Consider the mixing that took place during the trek to the coast, in the dungeons awaiting shipment, during the various pickup stops made by the slave ships, the separation that took place during the sale and the merging of slaves from all over Africa on the plantations. It is no wonder that the slaves lost track of their roots.

Life on the Plantation

The slaves shuffled the last leg of their journey over the unfamiliar path to their final destination--the plantation. One can only wonder what went through their minds during those first few days of plantation work and lifestyle. After a sudden and mysterious capture they found themselves in a land they knew not where, working for a master they did not know, who spoke a language they could not understand. They were forced to work at a job they knew nothing about, using tools they had never seen, working shoulder to shoulder with blacks they did not know.   They were sick, demoralized, dislodged from family, friends and their culture.

The masters divided the slaves into three work gangs.

The First Gang performed strenuous tasks like digging, planting, cutting, burning and carrying. Members of the First Gang were both male and female, young, able and fit. During the harvest months, January and July, the First Gang ended their field work at sunset and proceeded to the mill where they performed some of the heavier duties.

The Second Gang consisted of weaker workers, mothers with suckling babies, the elderly and children ranging in age from 12 to 18 years. They cleaned up in the fields and performed light tasks in the mill.

The Third Gang consisted of the very young from about six years to the very old. Here the young served as apprentice helpers, took grass to the cattle and water to the First Gang. The young started here and worked up to the Second and eventually the First Gang.

The slaves awakened around 4:00 a.m. to the sound of a Conch Shell blast. Work, often performed in rhythm to musical chants, started in the field at 6:00 a.m. and ended at sunset, with an hour and a half lunch break. Adding the extra hours spent after dinner, the work week averaged 96 hours.

As time passed and the slaves became used to the plantation system routine they became ever watchful for ways to slack on the work, escape and revolt. In the heyday of plantation operations 95.5% of the population was Black on Dominica, 91% Black on St. Lucia, 93% Black on St. Vincent and 97% Black on Grenada.

To keep the slaves ever fearsome of the results of their disobedience the masters established and enforced a strict set of rules of conduct and harsh punishments for offenders. The rules and punishments varied from island to island and plantation to plantation, but a typical set is found in the French "Code Noir" (Black Code) decreed in March 1685.

The Code forbid work on Sundays or holy days, permitted marriage of slaves with approval of the master and forbid any congregation of slaves of different owners, even attendance at weddings. Each slave's allowance of food included 2-1/2 pounds of cassava farina and 2-1/2 pounds of salt pork or 3 pounds of fish a week. The Code required the master to provide two suits of clothes per slave per year and to take care of old and sick slaves.

The slaves could not own firearms, carry large sticks, own any property, hold public office, sell any produce without the master's permission or be a witness in court.

The Code imposed the death penalty for any slave who struck his master, wife or any free person. Theft of sheep, goats, hogs, poultry, peas, corn and the like resulted in a public flogging and branding. The punishment for running away included flogging and sometimes hanging–the government would reimburse the owner for his loss. The courts did not allow torture or mutilation. If these happened, the court confiscated the slaves.

Slaves could be sold, but the Code forbid slave families to be separated. Slaves 14 to 60 years of age could not be seized for debts, but could be sold with the plantation. The master could free any slave with 20 years service.

Male masters and their sons openly took advantage of the female slaves, much to the dismay of the white females in the Great House. The outcome produced a mixture, described by John Stewart in his book, "Account of Jamaica and Its Inhabitants." A part reads:

"Between the whites and the black in the West Indies, a numerous race has sprung up, which goes by the general name of people of colour: these are subdivided into Mulattos, the offspring of a white and a black, Sambos, the offspring of a black and a Mulatto, Quadroons, the offspring of a Mulatto and a white; and Mestees or Mestisos, the offspring of a Quadroon and a white. Below this denomination, the distinction of colour is hardly perceptible; and those who are thus removed from the original negro (nic) stock, are considered by the laws as whites, and competent, of course, to enjoy all the privileges of a white."

A 3-level plantation social structure became established. The whites enjoyed the highest social status, their prestige being based on plantation size and number of slaves owned. The free-colored found their place in the middle level status. Within this level, the mulatto considered themselves superior to the free black. The slave occupied the lowest-level status and here the domestic or skilled worker considered themselves to be superior to the field worker--one punishment for domestics being assigned to return to field work. Plantation rules limited the social activity of the slave. Sunday was a day of rest when many went to town for Market Day where they sold excess produce or craft items. The masters also allowed days of rest on Christmas, New Years and Easter. At the end of the workday, groups would congregate outside huts and sing and tell stories.

On some plantations Saturday night dances were allowed but frowned upon. Black organizers planned the event and charged admission to cover the cost of the musicians and free-flowing liquor. The master would punish the organizers if those in attendance became too unruly.

Revolts and Rebellion

The slaves considered, planned, attempted and carried out revolts and escape attempts from the day of their capture until emancipation in the 1830's. Some did resign themselves to their fate but most wanted their freedom.

Some islands like Jamaica and Haiti have mountainous regions, ideal for hiding after an escape, but the planters left few hide-outs on most islands after clearing the land to grow their cane.

Rebellion took many forms. Whenever possible the slaves would work slowly, "drag their feet", burn fields, poison animals and sabotage machinery. They would steal food or items that would inconvenience their masters. Even though the punishment involved a savage flogging, slaves would runaway to visit lovers, kin or to protest. Given the opportunity they would poison or otherwise kill a brutal master.

The successful plantation master found ways to deal with individual rebellions. The possibility of group uprisings is what worried him the most. Table 17 in Jan Rogozinski's book, "A Brief History of the Caribbean" shows that 81 conspiracies or uprisings took place between 1649 and 1843, 194 years, which involved from a few dozen to over a thousand slaves.

The largest rebellion in the United States involved less than 500 slaves and at no time did the rebellions threaten the white society as they did in the Caribbean. The first major revolt took place in St. Dominique (Haiti) in 1791 after several years of colonial unrest. The number of slaves which had increased from 255,000 to 480,000 during the 12 year period, 1779 to 1791, willingly joined the revolt. The revolt's success became an economic disaster for Haiti which boasted of 780 sugar and 2000 coffee plantation in 1788. The new government divided the sugar plantations into small plots, giving them to the former slaves. Twenty-three years after the revolt, Haiti disappeared from the sugar market and the number of coffee plantations dropped to 1000.

Plantation owners all over the Caribbean desperately tried to keep the Haiti revolt news from reaching their islands. They allowed no sanctuary for refugees of any color fleeing from Haiti, but this kind of news quickly found a way to slave's ears. It sparked increased vigilance and fear in the hearts of the planters and kindled hope in the hearts of the slaves.

Historians estimate that during the slaving years, between 9 and 11 million blacks made the "Middle Passage", 4 ½ million coming to the Caribbean, 355,000 to the U.S. and the rest to South America, mainly Brazil.

The 19th century saw the end of the slave trade and emancipation.

CHAPTER 9

POST-SLAVERY ERA

The Emancipation Fallout

With emancipation, the Caribbean entered a new era. The region was left with a residue of cultures recruited over hundreds of years to supply menial labor for the sugar, tobacco and related plantations. These transported, used, then abandoned persons had come from virtually every corner of the world including Africa, Europe, India and China. Most of them had no experience with leadership or even self-survival--political, social or economic.

Those formerly possessing absolute power to make decisions in their best economic interests found themselves in the almost untenable position of having to negotiate rather than mandate.

The major economic rug--sugar--had been pulled out from under the entire region.

So, you had millions of people of different cultures, with few survival skills, no concerned leadership or functional political system, a dying economic base, a legacy of social strata and racial bias all living together on the most densely populated island specks in the world.

But, what they did have was freedom--and therein lay their hope for the future.

The Economic Evolution

When the nearly free source of labor vanished and the sugar beet appeared, the sugar plantation era as it was known from the 16th century came to an end.

Most absentee owners felt no allegiance to those persons dependent on their operations and simply took whatever they could glean from a quick sale, or simply abandoned their holdings and disappeared to conduct some other endeavor from their homeland.

Some resident planters, who apparently had fallen in love with the exotic isles, remained to fight an uphill battle to retain their economic way of life. Indeed, Liz Armstrong, today's owner of the Buccaneer Resort on St. Croix is a prime example. Her grandfather, a descendent of St. Croix's first governor, opened the resort and golf course in 1947. Sounds from the floor of today's sugar mill tower are now those of laughter and celebration during cocktail parties and course in 1947. Sounds from the floor of today's sugar mill tower are now those of laughter and celebration during cocktail parties and have replaced the sounds of yesteryear's grinding of cane stalks and the chanting of impoverished slaves.

The middle and late 1800's saw agriculture and business take a turn toward the small enterprise. Large land holdings were broken up into a small acreage, from 10 to 50 acres, and the Sunday market provided an outlet for those to sell items of their handicraft.

In order for the plantation to survive, the masters had to train some slaves in the crafts of carpentry, masonry, care of livestock and iron work. Over the years, skills in agriculture outside the growing of sugar had been handed down as a result of the masters allowing their slaves a small plot to grow subsistence crops. Some leaders emerged who formed partnerships to raise capital to invest in projects or to participate in group work activities such as net fishing which still exists on Tobago today.

The freedom to apply the skills they had learned, the support from a number of denominations of churches which included financial donations and educational services, and some grants from the homelands, gave many hopes in the beginning years for upcoming prosperity.

While the newly freed men accomplished self-survival, the development of a better standard of living beyond the survival level still depended on international economic conditions. These worsened toward the end of the 19th century and "hard times" fell upon the Caribbeans.

The economic condition began to improve, or at least change, on some islands when United States of America (U.S.A.) entrepreneurs began to appear on the scene around 1904. They made investments in sugar, banana and coffee plantations covering millions of acres and utilized the most modern production techniques.

The thirst for any form of income, the lack of any kind of "watch dog" organization on the islands to administrate how income would be derived, and the willingness of local authorities to spread their arms to receive offers that would be self-enriching, thus opening the doors to a new breed of plantation masters–the American Capitalist. Once again the Caribbean agricultural treasures faced exploitation, with those engaged in the production of goods reaping few financial rewards. Library shelves are filled with historians' and political analysts' reflections and predictions relating to the U.S. involvement and its impact on the Caribbean economic scene. The U.S. involvement in economic matters (and political matters as well) has been called intervention and exploitation by many of the emerging islands' leaders. Fear did exist that the U.S. had designs on invading and gathering all the Caribbean islands into their collection of states, mainly for economic gain. But, the U.S. was not the only international presence during these formative years. Formerly English-owned islands tended to depend on English markets for their goods, the formerly French-owned islands became dependent on France for a favorable balance of trade and so it went throughout the region. This continued economic dependency on U.S. and European ties gave rise to indignation among leaders of the times like Sir Grantly Adams of Barbados, Eric Williams of Trinidad and Norman Manley and Alexander Bustamante of Jamaica.

Strongly supported by the British government, an effort was made, beginning in 1958, to establish a "West Indies Federation." Island leaders held numerous meetings and conferences. Tentative agreements were drafted and oratory took place. Over the years from 1958 to 1962, while wrangling was taking place to establish the Federation, some dramatic economic events took place on two islands with the most influential leaders--Jamaica and Trinidad. Oil had boosted Trinidad's economy which was enabling Eric Williams to implement his Socialist economic programs and Jamaica, under Manley, another avowed Socialist, was enjoying the prosperity of foreign investment in bauxite mining projects.

Fear arose in Williams and Manley that, while profits would be gained from such a Federation, they would only be drained back to support the smaller and less fortunate Caribbean islands. They felt Jamaica and Trinidad had nothing to gain from such a Federation.

Jamaica and Trinidad withdrew from the Federation formation in 1962 and the effort was aborted. Efforts have been made in subsequent years to establish some coalition of Caribbean states, but nothing significant has resulted going into the mid-1990's.

While the hopes and dreams of a long line of Caribbean descendants for economic stability are yet to be realized, the feeling of most in the mid-1990's is of a positive nature. The construction of airfields to protect the Panama Canal during World War II and the forthcoming jet airplane age has added a "new kid" on the economic block--tourism. This, bananas, coffee, oil, bauxite mining and light manufacturing have replaced hogsheads of sugar, puncheons of rum (except in Puerto Rico), bars of silver and woods used for dyes in economic importance.

The Political Evolution

The United States began their fight for independence with their "shot that was heard around the world" on July 4, 1776. Their Declaration of Independence was clear and Constitution thoroughly written to establish rules for a radically new form of government. This war for independence involved a collection of 13 individual states that had joined together in a common cause.

Shortly after this revolution, the seeds of independence began to germinate in the Caribbean. After emancipation and the collapse of the sugar industry, the more than 30 Caribbean island and island groups became an economic drain rather than asset for their European homelands. As a result, neglect in political as well as economic support became homeland policy and the locals began to strive for more political power to deal with their problems.

But, the Caribbeans did not enjoy the luxury of being able to communicate with each other by foot, horseback or horse and buggy as did their North American counterparts. Only the wealthy had the means to travel by boat over any significant distance on any regular basis and   most of those who could have been strong political leaders soon left the region, for in those formative years political dedication did not provide the motivation for most to endure the rigors of Caribbean living.

Therefore, the yet-to-be Caribbean nations had to negotiate for local political control from positions of weakness, pretty much on an individual basis, rather than from the power through a collective effort. As unique as it was, the wholesale slaughter of whites by blacks in Haiti in 1804 introduced the first Caribbean step toward independence.

Again, library shelves are filled with documents, doctoral dissertations and historians' analyses relating to the circumstances, leaders and accounting of events that led to the varying degrees of independence these island nations now have.

Below is a chronological table that shows the year and island that have achieved independence by choice and acceptance from their homeland:

YEAR	ISLAND
1804	Haiti
1844	Dominican Republic
1902	Cuba
1962	Jamaica
1962	Trinidad & Tobago (T & T)
1966	Barbados
1974	Grenada

1977	St. Lucia
1978	Dominica
1979	St. Vincent & the Grenadines
1981	Antigua & Barbuda
1983	St. Kitts & Nevis

Aruba, French Guiana, Guadeloupe, Martinique, the Netherlands Antilles and Puerto Rico have selected the status of Associated States which means that they enjoy local self-government. The U.S. Virgin Islands are now a territory of the United States and have local self-government, but are considered U.S. dependencies.

Anguilla, Bermuda, British Virgins, Caymans, Montserrat, Turks & Caicos settled in as British dependencies.

Capitalism, Socialism, Papa Doc-ism, Marxism--Or What?

During the 18th and 19th centuries--and well into the 20th, embryos of new political ideological models were fermenting and germinating all over the world.

The Soviet Union was aggressively promoting their political and economic concept that the world must adopt Karl Marx's Communistic philosophy of,"Each to produce according to his ability and each to receive according to his need."

The United States of America was committed to the concept of Democracy, Capitalism (Free Enterprise), human rights and individual freedoms.

England, while still recognizing their King or Queen, turned with many other countries of the times to Socialism which nationalized some major types of business, while allowing small business to subsist. This political concept fell between Democracy and Communism.

Opportunity opened the door for "Papa Doc" and "Baby Doc" in Haiti and their dictatorial philosophies also found their way into the Dominican Republic and Cuba.

So, the United States, Soviet Union, England and Haiti became role models for the emerging Caribbean leaders and only current history can record the results of their influence on the emerging political decision-makers.

Free Enterprise, Communism, Socialism, the Dictatorship, and/or a melding of some forms of all these political concepts have or are now being experimented with in these tropical isles who are venturing forth to find their place in today's "real world."

The Sociological Evolution

Not only did the Caribbeans have to deal with emancipation, economic and political problems, they had to deal with multi-racial and cultural mixes and an incredible assortment of religious missionaries and movements that had permeated the region since its discovery.

The Religious Influences

One of the major edicts given to Columbus and subsequent explorers by the Spanish Crown was to see to it that all aborigines found be given instruction in the Catholic faith.

The Quakers made serious attempts to settle in the British West Indies and were a predominant influence in the Emancipation movement.

The Church of England (Anglican), Baptists, Morovians (they have a highway named after them leading from the St. Thomas airport to Charlotte Amalie), Wesleyans, Presbyterians and Jesuits have been mainly responsible for the introduction and establishment of elementary, secondary and institutions of higher learning in the region.

The region has produced some religions of its own. Obeah, Voudun (Voodoo), the Shouter-pocomania groups and the Jamaican Rastafarians are religious movements that have faithful followers.

Racial and Cultural Complexities

The white population seems to be predominant on the economic scene due to inheritance and/or overseas connections, but not so in the political arena because of the sheer number of non-whites who have been able to support aspirants to positions of leadership.

These non-whites are not easily classified as to race or culture. Knight, in his book, The Caribbean , cites two censuses taken in Jamaica where attempts were made for Jamaicans to categorize themselves.

In 1960, their choices were: African, Afro-European, East Indian, Chinese, European, Afro-Chinese, Syrian, and Other.

In 1970, their choices were: Negro-Black, Amerindian, East Indian, Portuguese, Chinese, White, Mixed, Syrian/Lebanese, Other and Not Stated.

One might expect such a mix in the United States, known to be the "melting pot of the world" with a population in excess of 200 million. Jamaica's population was 1.6 million in 1960 and 1.8 million in 1970 and, of course, most of these had not become residents by choice.

The Language of the Caribbean

The present-day traveler can get by quite well with a command of the English language, but will be befuddled by some of the rapid-fire, confounding, indescribable dialects spoken by the locals, once one gets off the beaten tourist track.

These enduring language "hand me downs" are cherished Caribbean heritages and hopefully will become a permanent part of the region's culture. Two books written by Litos Valls, <u>Ole Time Sayin's</u> and <u>What a Pistarckle!</u> provide the reader with a collection of words and "famous quotations" interpreted in English.

When one considers that in the beginning years communication was discouraged and even forbidden as a matter of policy by those in power, the Caribbeans must be commended for overcoming this enormous barrier to political and economic survival successfully.

The Social Scene in the Caribbean in the `90's

Education has become a major item of emphasis on many--but not all-Caribbean islands. Literacy rates are reported to be 70% or more in Jamaica and St. Lucia and up to 90% in Trinidad, Barbados and the Bahamas. Barbados is considered to be one of the most literate countries in the world.

When one sets foot on a Caribbean island these days, one will not face the threat of the bow and arrow as did Columbus.

One could likely be descended upon by a herd of taxi drivers on Jamaica who might swarm about you like killer bees, or one could suffer the indifference of Martinique shop owners who post signs reading, "Buy, but don't touch" and might turn away in disdain if you do not speak impeccable French.

These are the kinds of problems that come with the emergence of a new industry and those that local authorities and tourist boards are addressing these days. There are even classes in high school on some islands that deal with how to treat tourists and travelers. This beats having a master pondering the problem of how many lashes a person should receive for stealing a dozen bananas.

In the `90's, the steel band, snorkeling, diving, sailing, cruise ships and elaborate resorts are being advertised on worldwide television to attract people of the world away from their role of total absorption in their professions, occupations or jobs to total absorption in relaxation in luxurious surroundings.

This is a true role reversal for the Spanish Main.

Nelson's Dockyard, Antigua

Nelson's Dockyard Officer's Quarters, Antiqua

CHAPTER 10

ANTIGUA, BARBUDA AND REDONDA

SIZE
Antigua: 108 square miles
Barbuda: 62 square miles

GEOGRAPHY
Both Antigua and Barbuda are of volcanic in origin. Before the sea level fell, around 9,600 B.C., the islands were one. They are somewhat mountainous, the highest point being 1358 feet on Antigua.

CLIMATE
Semi-arid with an average temperature of 72 degrees. The reported rainfall has diminished over the past 300 years.

CAPITAL
Antigua: St. John's   Redonda: Uninhabited
Barbuda: Codrington

AMERINDIANS
Archaeologists carbon dated charcoal remains of campfires at Jolly Point and have determined that these were left by the C(S)iboneys around 1775 B.C. The Ciboneys (Stone People) lived off the land and sea, eating seaside grape, cherry, locust (stinking toe) and seafood. There is evidence that the Arawaks used the stone implements made by the Ciboneys after they moved on.

The Arawaks arrived around the birth of Christ. Archaeologists have found over 40 Arawak village sites on Antigua, the main ones being at Indian Creek, Mamora Bay and Mill Creek. When they carbon dated pottery pieces they found them to be from 300 A.D. to 1200 A.D. The Arawaks brought pineapples, peanuts, papaya, cotton and tobacco with them from South America. Around 1200 A.D. some Arawaks continued their Caribbean migration and found their way to Hispaniola and Puerto Rico where they developed into a more advanced society called the Tainos.

The Arawaks also established a village site at Spanish Point on Barbuda.

The Caribs began arriving in the region around 1200 A.D. They settled mainly on Dominica, Guadalupe, St. Vincent and St. Kitts. Historians believe that the Caribs only visited Antigua to raid the Arawaks and gather food and other items not found on their home islands.

DISCOVERY

There is no record that Columbus landed on Antigua, which he named Santa Maria de Antigua after a shrine representing a miracle-working virgin in the Seville Cathedral. It is there where he prayed before his second voyage.

It is assumed he sighted Antigua (named Waladi by the Caribs) on November 11, 1493 after leaving Redonda and continued his northern journey.

SPANISH QUEST FOR POWER AND GOLD

Antigua gained but short attention by the Spanish. In 1520 a cadre of settlers led by Captain Don Antonio Serrano landed with the intention of establishing a settlement. After a number of encounters with raiding Caribs, they aborted the attempt.

EUROPEAN POWER STRUGGLE AND SETTLEMENTS

The   potential of profits from agricultural efforts by growing tobacco and sugar began in the 1600's. The English began their claims in the West Indies in 1625 by granting the Earl of Carlise settlement rights on a number of islands, including Antigua and Barbuda

The famous French privateer, d'Escambuc, and a friend of the Earl, a Mr. Williams, occupied the island for a short period in 1629.

The effort that resulted in the permanent settlement of Antigua came in 1632 when Sir Thomas Warner, Governor of St. Kitts, sent his 22 year old son to Antigua.

The English settlement grew and made the transition from growing tobacco to sugar cane. The population increased from 750 in 1636 to 1200 in 1640.

The year 1666 found England at war with Holland and France. The French landed on Antigua, conquered it, and devastated the towns and plantations. At the same time Caribs from Dominica raided the island and carried off the settler's wives. Three months after the French conquest, the English, Dutch and French signed the 1667 Treaty of Breda which returned Antigua to England. The French left the island so impoverished and in disrepair that other European nations left it to remain under English control from then forward. Returning after the French occupation, the English built Fort James to guard St. John's Harbor in 1703 and started Fort Berkeley in 1704 to guard English Harbor.

The English began to recognize the potential of English Harbor as a haven from hurricanes, naval base and site for ship repair in 1671 when the ship, Dover Castle, rode out a hurricane there.

The English erected the first buildings which were to become Nelson's Dockyard in 1725 and by 1743 the site became the major English naval base in the Caribbean.

Admiral Lord Nelson, a Senior Captain at age 27, commanded the Dockyard from 1784 to 1787 and for a short time became the Commander-in-Chief in the English Leewards. His anti-United States policy, which suppressed trade, made him very unpopular. When he left the island he was so sick he had a cask of rum placed aboard to preserve his body in case of death.

He went on to defeat Napoleon's fleet in the famous Battle of Trafalgar on the Southwest coast of Spain between Cadiz and the Straight of Gibraltar in 1805.

Interestingly, English records show that 100,000 English died in the West Indies during the Napoleonic Wars. Of these deaths, 50% were due to disease, 30% due to accidents (usually when drunk), 13% by peril of the sea and only 7% by enemy action.

BARBUDA

The Crown gave the Earl of Carlise proprietary rights over Barbuda along with many other West Indies islands in 1627. The Caribs ran off English settlers in 1628 and 1632. In 1668 Governor Willoughby of Antigua granted James Winthorpe a lease on Barbuda for a yearly payment of "one ear of corn." Winthorpe used Barbuda to grow crops to feed those on Antigua, but gave up in 1685.

King Charles II then issued a lease to Christopher and John Codrington and the island remained under lease by the Codrington family for nearly 200 years. During this time they introduced sheep, cattle, mules, horses and deer to the island. They became major suppliers of these items along with green turtles, fish, vegetables, lime, lumber, leather goods and hammocks to the Royal Navy.

The Codrington family moved to Somerset, England and became absentee owners. Administration by the Codringtons eventually came under the management of a minor and the business began to operate at a loss. The Crown foreclosed on the Codrington lease and ended their reign in July 1870.

The Antigua governor then issued a succession of 5 leases over the next 18 years. All failed because of either the lack of government support or unsuccessful attempts to establish large plantations—which the island could not support.   Barbuda reverted to Crown rule in 1901. By 1906 the introduction of the cotton gin made cotton growing profitable along with horse and cattle grazing.

BUCCANEERS, PIRATES AND PRIVATEERS

As mentioned, one reason the English established Nelson's Dockyard was to serve as a naval base to attack pirates and privateers; therefore, the island did not pose as an attractive place for pilferage.   Dutch buccaneers did use Barbuda's coves as a refuge after pillaging Spanish ships in the early 1600's.

THE SUGAR ERA

Christopher Codrington went to Barbados and returned with a knowledge of "modern" sugar production techniques. He established a plantation on Antigua around 1674 which he named Betty's Hope. This model became an inspiration to English investors.

In 1706 there were 27 mills in operation on Antigua. This number increased to 78 by 1710 and by 1748, 175 windmills and 64 cattle mills dotted the island. Antigua remained a major sugar producer for the next 200 years. Between 1766 and 1770 Antigua ranked third in sugar production in the Caribbean, behind St. Dominique and Jamaica with an annual average of 10.7 thousand tons. Today 109 mill site ruins can be found on the island.

The English built forty-three forts about the island to protect the plantations from Carib raids. After 1689 the 43 gun Fort George served as a refuge for the 500 white inhabitants. Added protection came with the construction of the Shirley Heights fort after the American Revolution and it also served as a base for Nelson's Dockyard.

BARBUDA DURING THE SUGAR ERA
The clever Codringtons had a "Right to Wreck" clause written into their lease. Under this clause they could claim the right to cargo salvaged from ships which ran aground off the coast of their island. Barbuda lies low on the horizon and on days when the visibility was poor it was often not sighted until too late to avoid the reefs. The Antigua and Barbuda Museum has recorded 145 known shipwrecks that occurred since 1695. When times were hard in their agricultural endeavors, mainly due to periods of drought, the Codringtons made up the difference from the bounty recovered from shipwrecks. It was not uncommon for over-zealous wrecking crews to begin salvage before getting permission from the captain.
The last large ship to be impaled on the reefs was the 7800 ton Dutch vessel, the Amersfoort in 1927.

SLAVERY AND SLAVE REVOLTS
The sugar boom brought slavery and a disproportional number of blacks to whites to Antigua. In 1787 a census reported 2,600 whites and 37,000 slaves.
The slaves continually protested their predicament by being surly, careless in their work, faking illness or by simply running away. There were single plantation uprisings such as the one where the slaves of Colonel Martin murdered him in his bed because he refused them time off during the Christmas holidays.
A major uprising plot was foiled in 1736 when the planters were to congregate in St. John's at a ball to celebrate the coronation of King George II. Plans had been laid by 350 slaves to enter the ball, seize Fort James and Fort George at the same time and kill all the whites. Some last minute event caused the postponement of the ball and the plot was uncovered and quelled.
Another attempted uprising took place in just 3 years before emancipation when the government suppressed the Sunday Market, the only free time allotted the slaves. This plot was also uncovered before it materialized and was suppressed by the militia.
Emancipation came to Antigua on Friday August 1, 1834 and 29,000 slaves became free. Antigua was the first Caribbean island to free the slaves and the only island to bypass the Apprenticeship Program. Emancipation Day passed quietly and most slaves appeared for work for wages on Monday morning.

SLAVERY ON BARBUDA
Slaves on Barbuda enjoyed unheard-of freedoms. Codrington's business on Barbuda was one of a supplier of goods. His workers

needed to be tradesmen with skills as hunters, tanners, saddle and shoe makers, masons, coopers, sail makers and carpenters.

Codrington's success depended on the quality of production of his skilled workers and to keep them happy he allowed them freedom to move about, establish their own villages and generally live a self-sufficient life. The threat of being sent to Antigua to work on the sugar plantation was enough to keep the slaves living an orderly life.

Major confusion surrounded emancipation in 1834. The island of Barbuda was claimed to be private property by Codrington because of the lease, but was it? The lease still came up for renewal from time to time.

Codrington granted the slaves their freedom and gave them land anyhow. The lease came up for renewal in February 1854 and so many legal issues arose, the Crown in desperation, reissued the lease for 50 years with an annual payment of "one fat sheep, if demanded."

POST SLAVERY ERA

Antigua joined the other sugar-producing Caribbean islands in a post emancipation depression. Revival came in 1905 when the Antigua Central Sugar Factory opened and processed 1,634 tons of sugar. The new factory's process of producing gray crystals replaced the muscovado sugar and accounted for 86% of Antigua's exports in 1915.

A labor riot came to Antigua in 1918 when laborers received no action on their demands for a fair day's wages for a fair day's work. A confrontation with the police ended with two demonstrators killed, and they gained nothing.

Extreme conditions of poverty existed in 1939. Houses still had dirt floors, clothing was supplemented with burlap bags and flour sacks and working hours were from 6 a.m. to 6 p.m. for pitifully low wages.

Then came the labor movement in 1939. Very limited changes took place until 1951 when Union field officers went to the estates to negotiate rates of pay. The owners would not deal, so a three months strike was called.

The workers met at the now historic sites of the Tamarind tree north-east of Bethseda and Betty's Hope to consider their resolve. The decision was made to "live off the land" and this they did for nearly a year until on January 1, 1952 the Antigua Sugar Syndicate conceded and gave a 25% wage increase.

A constitutional conference and elections held in 1966 resulted in Antigua, Barbuda and Redonda becoming an Associate State of Britain as of February 27, 1967.

POST SLAVERY BARBUDA
Barbuda came under the governing power of Antigua in 1901. Barbudians wanted their independence from Antigua and fought hard to gain it. Their efforts ended at the 1980 Independence Conference where it was decided to grant Barbuda a seat in the Antigua Parliament and to grant a liberal amount of powers to a Barbudian Council. Today, Barbuda is a semi-autonomous dependency of Antigua.

REDONDA
This is a rocky, precipitous and forbidding volcanic island about a mile long and 1/3 of a mile wide with King John's Peak rising to 1000 feet.

A polished stone axe and other items indicate that the Caribs probably used the island as a way station.

Columbus sighted the island on November 11, 1493 and described it as an inaccessible rock. He named it Santa Maria la Redonda, meaning St. Mary the Round.

Entrepreneurs found Redonda's natural resource, bird droppings (guano) satisfied a worldwide demand for calcium phosphate. When they mined the guano to bedrock they found deposits of aluminum phosphate and in 1895 they had completed an overhead cable way and shipped over 5000 tons of ore.

A skeleton crew was kept after World War I to maintain the equipment, but when a hurricane blew away the buildings in 1929 the owners abandoned the property. Some machinery can be seen today.

Matthew Dowdy Shiell, a famous science fiction writer who vied for a column in a Sunday paper with Jules Verne, sailed by Redonda in 1865, laid claim to the island and proclaimed his son to be King Phillipe I of Redonda. The son made a game of this by touring Europe with a retinue of courtiers and granted some of his friends titles.

The Antiguan government went along with this, tongue in cheek, and a succession of "Kings" followed. As of 1991, Jon Wynne-Tyson of Sussex, England has laid claim to be Juan II, the "ecological" King of Redonda.

In 1978 the government attempted to reactivate the phosphate mine. They opened a post office to try to produce some revenue from philatelists and stationed a postmaster/caretaker there.

Hurricane David washed away the post office in 1979 and the birds once again are enjoying the island's solitude.

Your island contact

Ms. Yvonne Magilney, Director General
Antigua & Barbuda Department of Tourism
P. O. Box 363
St. John's, Antigua, W.I.
Phone: (809) 462-0480
Fax: (809) 462-2836

The Farley House, Barbados

CHAPTER 11

BARBADOS

Name Derivation: Barbados means "The Bearded Ones." This is believed to refer to the bearded fig trees.

SIZE
166 sq. miles

GEOGRAPHY
Mostly a gentle-rolling limestone plateau dipping into occasional gullies. Mt. Hillaby, 1116 ft. is the highest point. Rocky cliffs and rough surf typify the Atlantic side while sandy beaches and quiet surf characterize the Caribbean side.

CLIMATE
One of the more healthy in the Caribbean. North-east trade winds and its tropical setting bring 14-18 inches of rain during most months. Temperatures are only moderately warm.

CAPITAL
Bridgetown

AMERINDIANS
There is evidence that the first wave of Amerindians, the Ciboneys, arrived around 350 A.D. Archaeologists believe the Arawaks, who arrived around 800 A.D., killed off the Ciboneys and became the first permanent residents. Archaeological digs have located 56 Arawaks settlement sites, mostly located in the northwest cliff sides facing the Atlantic Ocean. The third wave, the Caribs, finding the island more suitable for agriculture than hunting, just passed through in the mid-13th century.

Few, if any, Arawaks occupied the island when the English landed in 1627. Theories set forth by historians for the Arawak's absence include: raids by the Spanish who took them by force or trickery (they convinced some that they had come to take them to visit the land of their ancestors); raids by the Caribs who took the women for wives; they fled to avoid capture by the Spanish; and, a prolonged drought destroyed their crops, forcing them to migrate to another island.

The lack of interference by Amerindians enabled the English to concentrate on the business of agriculture instead of warfare--a luxury not afforded them on other islands. The settlement experienced rapid growth.

DISCOVERY
Columbus never set foot on Barbados. There are claims by both Spanish and Portuguese explorers of having landed here early in the 16th century, but neither country laid claim to Barbados.

On May 14, 1625 James Powell, captain of a merchant ship owned by Sir William Courteen, landed on Barbados and claimed the island for England's King James I. He did this by carving the notice, "James K of E and this island" on a tree. From that time until its independence in 1966, Barbados remained under English control. Powell felt the island to be ideal for agricultural development. After two years of political negotiations between Powell, Courteen and royalty, settlement began with the first colonists, financed by the Courteen group, landing and establishing a village near Holetown on February 14, 1627.

When the English arrived, they found the island well-stocked with pigs. How they got there is another Barbadian mystery. Some historians believe the Arawaks brought them and others feel that the Portuguese dropped them off to breed for supply meat or that they swam ashore from shipwrecks.

SPANISH QUEST FOR GOLD
The geographic location of Barbados is such that it did not serve as a suitable supply depot or harbor for Spanish treasure ships. They found no show of gold or silver. The only asset of interest to the Spanish was the Arawak slave supply. When they exhausted the supply of Arawaks, the Spaniards left the island alone.

EUROPEAN POWER STRUGGLE
European powers never seriously threatened English control of the island. Its out-of-the-way location, unfavorable trade winds and use limited only for agriculture did not make the island an attractive place to fight over in the early days.

The "European Power Struggle" took place between the Crown, which by precedent of discovery possessed sole ownership, and several private entrepreneurs. Matters got complicated when the Crown issued a grant to the Earl of Carlisle to administrate the Caribbean islands, including Barbados. The Crown, whose attention to these kinds of matters was slipshod at best, forgot that a grant had been issued to the Courteen group. Soon after, the Crown issued a third grant to the Earl of Pembroke.

The island administration remained in complete confusion until Carlisle, after much intrigue and bald faced robbery, was named "Proprietor", and received an all-inclusive administrative second grant. He issued his financial and political supporters large parcels of land. Carlisle appointed a succession of Governors and some of them began their reign by executing their deposed rivals as a matter of good politics.

By the early 1630's Carlisle had helped a small group of wealthy, well-connected elite secure large land holdings and political power in the Assembly. This "planter elite" became a major political force in Barbados and England clear through the Sugar Era.

The Carlisle grant stipulated that all laws were to be approved by the freeholders; however, there was the usual loophole. The grant also allowed the Proprietor (Carlisle) to rule in times of emergency--the emergency to be identified by the Proprietor. Barbados remained in a state of emergency while Carlisle ruled.   He appointed Governors and established an Assembly to represent the freeholders--but Assembly members had to be unswerving "yes men."

By 1640 the population of Barbados had grown to over 10,000 and the second generation of Carlisles became the Proprietors. They established a Council and Assembly and wrote a constitution that gave the planter elite some control over island matters. The execution of King Charles I by Parliament in 1649 gave Barbados a political jolt. Subsequent negotiations ended with the Carlisle grant being voided and Barbados becoming a Commonwealth. The planters negotiated a concession to transport their sugar only on English ships in return for a guaranteed market.

BUCCANEERS, PIRATES AND PRIVATEERS

Barbados was not on the Spanish flotilla trade routes; therefore, had little plunder to interest buccaneers. Only a few French pirates engaged in minor skirmishes along the west coast. One serious outside interference came during the American War for Independence in the late 1770's when the French set up a blockade. As a result of this blockade, needed supplies could not be landed and thousands of slaves died of hunger and disease.

News of the successful exploits by such buccaneers as Henry Morgan reached Barbados around 1665. This enticed large numbers of landless freemen to emigrate to Jamaica to seek fame and fortune.

THE SUGAR ERA

The first agricultural efforts in Barbados did not succeed too well. Tobacco, the first major crop, was introduced during a time of rapidly falling prices and when the Carlisle and Courteen feud took the form of each taking turns burning each others crops. The Dutch are given credit for bringing sugar-growing technology, refining machinery, financing for large-scale plantations and a marketing outlet for sugar to Barbados and the West Indies. Their interest in enticing growers in the West Indies to grow sugar wasn't entirely to sell machinery and technology or to be neighborly. They saw a vast potential market for African slaves, partly because of English law that forbid those of the Jewish faith to contract white indentured servants. A good number of Caribbean planters were Jewish.

The Dutch West Indies company developed their sugar technology in Brazil from 1630 to 1654. Around 1640 some Barbados growers went to Brazil, came back and tried the crop.

Sugar plantations became an immediate success. By 1647 the majority of planters owning 200 acres or more had converted to sugar. With reference to sugar cultivation, Governor Atkins said in 1676, "As for the lands in Barbados I am confident that there is not one foot that is not employed down to the seaside". Most of the large planters arrived early in Barbados and forced the smaller ones to sell when sugar came on the scene. In 1654 there were 11,200 landowners with the average farm being 10 acres. Thirteen years later the number had dwindled to 745 with the average farm being between 300 and 500 acres.

Many small farmers emigrated to Jamaica or the U.S. States of Virginia and Massachusetts to raise crops like tobacco that brought adequate returns on a small acreage with little capital investment.

Sugar plantations required that the planter make a considerable investment. A 500 acre plantation fetched 400 Pounds in 1640. In 1648 the same plantation sold for 7000 Pounds for a half-interest. A 300 acre plantation that would produce 180 tons of sugar and 34 puncheons (a cask containing from 72 to 120 gallons) of rum required 230 slaves, 7 servants 220 head of cattle and 12 horses.

By 1680 175 planter elites controlled 60% of the land and 60% of the slaves. Barbados was "King Sugar" of the West Indies from the mid-1600's to the turn of the century, exporting most of the sugar grown in the region.

Planters in Jamaica and the Leewards soon noticed Barbados' success with sugar. They entered the market and surpassed Barbados' production by 1715. This should be no surprise when you consider that the area of Barbados is 166 square miles compared to Jamaica's 4244 square miles.

Barbados history is rampant with tales of modest investments growing into vast fortunes in short periods.

Thomas Modyford arrived on Barbados in 1647, bought 500 acres, earned a fortune and became Governor by 1660. He extended his interests to Jamaica and the Crown made him Governor of that island in 1664. At his death in 1679 he owned one of the largest plantations in the West Indies.

James Drax, who married the daughter of the Earl of Carlisle, arrived in Barbados in the 1620's and acquired 700 acres. It is said he planted cane first and by 1654 became the richest planter on Barbados--if not in the entire West Indies. The planter elite accumulated great wealth and became extremely influential in the politics of England and Barbados. Sugar production grew as planters became more skilled at preparing sugar for sale--a process that took two years from planting to shipment. In 1712 Barbados planters sold 6300 tons of sugar. This figure tripled by 1800.

THE DECLINE OF KING SUGAR

Several social and economic events took place around the middle of the 19th century that had a dramatic negative impact on King Sugar. The major source of cheap labor--the slaves--disappeared in 1838 with emancipation. The security of having prices protected by tariffs disappeared with the enactment of the Sugar Duties Act in 1846, designed to gradually remove tariff protection for West Indies sugar. In the same year the West Indies Bank, with headquarters in Bridgetown, went bankrupt. This bank provided most of the credit for the planters.

The sugar industry entered a short-lived depression period. The planters quickly stepped up to the task of survival by first moving to cut wages. Next, they bolstered yield by using chemical fertilizers and introducing modern technology such as steam power. Finally, they increased the acreage planted, which gave a greater total cash yield on a small profit margin.

Planters survived on this marginal basis until 1884 when sugar cane prices started to drop dramatically with the introduction of subsidized sugar beets. During this period many of the merchants assumed plantation ownership by foreclosing on the planters' indebtedness. This shift of ownership also began the acceptance of the merchants into the planter's elite social realm.

The merchant/planters did not abandon their estates like those in Jamaica. They enjoyed a short period of prosperity during World War I while Europeans ravaged their English homeland. A central mill proved to be successful in Cuba and Puerto Rico. Slowly, between 1911 and 1921, the small, inefficient Barbados plantation mills gave way to the more efficient central mill. While plantation life as it was known in the 1750's had disappeared, this change enabled sugar to remain as the major economic base until tourism took its place in the 1970's.

SLAVERY AND SLAVE REVOLTS

Indentured servants, a mixture of voluntary servants, political refugees and convicts and rogues who came from England, Scotland and Ireland made up most of the labor force in the beginning. They signed 5-7 year contracts to work for a Master in return for the Master's payment for their passage to the colony. While the contract did include certain provisions to protect the servant, these provisions were subject to review by the Barbados judicial system. If a servant brought a complaint about a Master not complying with a contract provision, there was but one outcome--they flogged the servant.

Richard Lignon, a much-cited Barbados historian, published his work, A True & Exact History of the Island of Barbadoes in 1647. On Page 44 of the 1970 reprint he wrote:

"As for the usage of the Servants, it is much as the Master is, merciful or cruel; Those that are merciful, treat their Servants well, both in their meat, drink, and lodging, and give them such work, as is not unfit for Christians to do. But if the Masters be cruel, the Servants have very wearisome and miserable lives."

It is generally agreed that they treated the slaves better than the indentured servants during this period. Lignon writes:

"The slaves and their posterity, being subject to their Masters forever, are kept and preserved with greater care than the servants, who are theirs but for five years, according to the law of the Island. So, for that time, the servants have the worser lives . . ."

Lignon didn't mention that during this time a slave cost 200% more than an indentured servant; therefore, the slave was a much-more valued commodity.

The supply of indentured servants changed around the 1680's. New English laws were enacted to reduce the number of emigrants from Ireland and Scotland to the West Indies because the motherland was suffering a labor shortage. Barbados' servant contracts did not provide the glitter of those written for Jamaica, which provided for an allotment of 20 acres of land upon completion of servitude.

The floodgates of the African west coast slave supply began to open in the 1660's with the increase in supply numbers provided by the African chieftains and the improvement of transportation efficiency by the Dutch. Slave labor gained a clear cost advantage over the indentured servant and became the new sought-after labor resource. Between 1651 and 1700 an estimated 118,200 Africans were imported to Barbados.

Slaves arrived at Bridgetown, after suffering a 15% mortality rate during the "middle passage", in deplorable physical condition. Upon arrival captains would anchor for a week while they prepared the slaves for sale by bathing and fattening and scrubbed the ship to remove the stench. When ready, the planters/buyers boarded the ship to bid for the slaves, who were paraded naked before them to disclose any deformities. Upon purchase by their new Master, the last leg of their journey was a footpath trek to their new Island home.

The ports from which the slaves left Africa for Barbados and the owners of the carrying ships can be identified. No records were kept as to who came from where. Slave ships often recruited slaves from more than nine different tribes, each with their own language and settled in different locations lining the entire length of the African west coast. After arrival, they intermixed and by 1817 only 7% of the blacks were African born, the rest being Creoles with no knowledge of their ethnic background.

The slaves lived under a very strict set of rules. They brought some of the rules from Africa. Lignon relates in his 1647 book on Barbados history that the slaves were very jealous of their wives. He never saw one glance at another's parts which should have been covered, when naked. Nor did he ever see them kiss, embrace or even cast a "wanton" glance in public.

Lignon tells of a woman who bore twins. This proved to the slave husband that his wife had committed adultery and the penalty for this act was death by hanging--the husband to provide the rope. The Master heard of this and tried in vain to explain that the birth of twins is an act of nature, not infidelity. The husband refused to change his mind so the Master said that if he hanged his wife, he would be hanged with her on the same limb at the same time. The husband relented but never, to Lignon's knowledge, spoke to her again.

In 1661 the Council enacted the slave code, "Act for the Better Ordering and Governing of Negroes" and amended it three times to give a legal structure for handling the slaves. African slaves were described by authors of the code as "heathenish, brutish and a dangerous kind of people whose wicked instincts should at all times be suppressed."

The Act provided that the Master should feed and clothe the slave. Clothing meant providing drawers and caps for men and petticoats and caps for women--once a year.

The Act classified crimes as private or public.

The punishment for a private crime such as running away, stealing, burning cane or striking a Christian, included being branded, whipped, having their noses slit or having a limb removed. A popular punishment not written into law, but widely accepted as normal, was castration.

The punishment for a public crime such as rebellion, the threatening of a white person or theft of a pig was death. The Island Treasurer compensated the slave owner for this loss of capital because a slave was legally defined as "real estate." A Master could be liable for a fine of 15 Pounds for willfully killing a slave.

The slaves also lived under social restrictions. The Anglican church considered the slaves to be intellectually unable to understand the concepts of Christianity; therefore, they did not expose them to religious teachings in the early years.   They could not beat drums, honk horns or use other loud instruments. Their houses were searched once a week for stolen goods or weapons. Slaves could not leave their plantation without a ticket provided by their overseer or appear in court to testify against their Master.

The slaves and servants lived by the bell during their six-day work week. A bell would sound at 6 a.m. to start the day's work, at 11 a.m. for dinner, at 1 p.m. to resume work and at 6 p.m to end the day. Lignon wrote: "Sunday was a day of pleasure."

BUSSA'S REBELLION
The topography of Barbados, being relatively flat and easily traversed on horseback, did not provide safe refuges for runaway slaves like the mountains of Jamaica. The planters, well-aware of the slave's distaste for them, lived in fear of uprisings; therefore, always held a well-trained militia in readiness.

Events took place around the beginning of the 19th century that stirred the hope for freedom among the slaves. Haiti gained independence from France in 1804; the 1807 Slave Trade Abolition Act abolished the slave trade; and, the abolitionists began to gain strong support in England.   The planter elite on Barbados did not materially change their 1661 slave code. The 1807 Slave Trade Act did not bother them because they had engaged in a program to encourage and foster natural slave population growth.

The slaves on Barbados became more restless, aggressive, uncooperative and arrogant after 1807. The planters recognized these feelings, but had no idea that a rebellion was being planned. An African-born slave named Bussa led Barbados' only rebellion. His position as chief driver on the Bayley plantation in the parish of St. Phillip gave him enough freedom to move about and organize others who held positions of trust and responsibility on their respective plantations.

The rebellion was carefully planned by decentralized groups that met throughout the island and reported to Bussa. The rebellion started at 8:30 p.m. on Easter Sunday, April 14, 1816--three days earlier than scheduled.

While the goal was to take over the island, the slaves seemed content to burn crops and generally destroy their master's assets rather than to concentrate on killing whites. They did not harm the many poor whites left unprotected by the Militia.

The revolt lasted only 4 days. On Tuesday morning Bussa's armed force met the Imperial troops. Bussa died leading his men to battle. The following day the Militia, Imperial troops and the West India Regiment (an all-black fighting force) quelled the rebellion.

It has been estimated that 1000 slaves died on the battlefield or were executed and one Militiaman and two West India Regiment soldiers lost their lives in action.

The rebellion gave the slaves no immediate gains. Instead, it served to strengthen the planters' resolve that further slave repression was necessary. To quote John Beckles, Attorney General, speaking to the "spirit" of the slave:

" (their spirit) will not be subdued, nor will it ever
be subdued . . (it) behooves us to be on guard, to keep
a watch that we may not again be caught so shamefully
unprepared. The comfort and happiness of our families
require it--the safety and tranquillity of the island
call for it."

Freedom for slaves came 22 years after the ill-fated Bussa's rebellion.

POST SLAVERY ERA

The 1820's saw intense slave-related struggles between the planter-dominated Barbados Assembly and the abolitionists' powers in England's Parliament.

The Consolidated Slave Law, passed in 1825, contained the first significant concessions by the planters. This law gave slaves the right to own property, right to give evidence in court in all cases and reduced the fee they had to pay to get their freedom. The planters retained the right to flog and imprison their slaves.

The next step in emancipation came with the 1833 Emancipation Act. This Act freed the slaves, but instituted an apprenticeship program. Those under 6 years old were completely freed. Those over six were required to serve their Master for a period of 12 years. The reasoning behind the 12 year "apprenticeship" plan was to give the emancipated slave time to adjust to freedom and the planter time to adjust their economies and social changes brought about by workers who were free.

The 83,150 emancipated slaves received no pay, except for work in addition to the "slavery-day tasks", but did receive allowances of food and clothing and up to ½ acre of land.

The planters argued that since the policy of the use of slaves, which the Crown once cherished, is now considered to be criminal because of a newly-found humanitarianism, they should be paid for their losses. Parliament agreed and each slave owner received #20 compensation for each slave.

The Crown and colony Assembly negotiated modifications to the 1833 Act up to August 1, 1838 when the Crown mandated full emancipation, including abolition of the Apprenticeship System.

The planters did not accept this change with a spirit of wanting to better the former slaves' education, health care, housing or relief for the poor. They held tight to strengthening social control over the freed blacks to ensure an adequate labor force.

Planters argued that education for blacks would do more harm than good. First, an education would raise false hopes that they could better themselves. Second, an education would make them unhappy with their subordinate social status. It took 40 years after emancipation for the government to initiate the beginnings of basic education for the ex-slaves.

A cholera epidemic struck Barbados in 1854 and claimed over 20,000 lives. Bridgetown, with its polluted water supply, open cesspools, canals being used to remove waste from households and the gutters filled with filth, became known as the most unsanitary town in the West Indies. It took this epidemic--which killed both whites and blacks on the same scale--to spark interest in health care reform. The Governor appointed a new health board and health classes were taught in schools.

Emancipation laws called for a program of social welfare. To the Assembly this meant establishing a strong police force and a court system being given extensive powers to prosecute and punish the ex-slaves for the slightest infraction.

The ex-slaves did not fare too well in the labor market. Strict laws were enforced, such as the one that held that if a worker worked for an employer five consecutive days, he would be under contract for one year.

In the years immediately following full emancipation the ex-slave had the choice of starving, working under unbearable conditions or emigrating.   The Dutch and English experienced a labor shortage and saw Barbados as a prime source of seasoned workers. They launched a strong campaign to attract freed blacks. The Barbados planters countered with a propaganda campaign about yellow fever, malaria and cholera being rampant in the other colonies and passing a law making it illegal to encourage workers to emigrate. The lure of better wages and working conditions was overwhelming and by 1870 over 16,000 freed blacks emigrated to other colonies.

In 1875 the Crown decided that it would be to the best interest of Barbados if they would join in a confederacy with the Windward islands and become a Crown Colony. The planters fiercely opposed the idea while the freed blacks and poor whites felt that any change would better their lot. A riot, reminiscent of Bussa's Rebellion, ensued and the planters won as they did in 1816.

The 1875 riot resulted in serious negotiations for a new constitution and governmental system. An executive committee was formed which included members of the Crown Council and Barbados Assembly being appointed by the Governor. This marriage between the Crown and planter lasted until the late 1950's.

While social conditions improved for the blacks, low wages and poor working conditions continued.

A new opportunity came for black workers in 1904. The United States had undertaken the task of building the Panama Canal and needed workers. The U.S. set up a recruiting office in Bridgetown and by 1914 contracted at least 20,000 blacks to work on the canal. The higher wages given in Panama led to increase in wages demands on Barbados. During labor demonstrations workers would chant:

> We want more wages, we want it now,
> And if we don't get it, we going to Panama.
> Yankees say they want we down there,
> We want more wages, we want it now.

Many blacks working the canal had families in Barbados and planned to return. They sent money home and their families, for the first time, were able to make some investments. They formed societies with similar goals of today's credit unions. The planters saw this as a threat and in 1905 passed the Friendly Societies Act which made it illegal for any society to own more than one acre of land. The societies then assumed the role of a savings bank. A member could make weekly deposits and receive a lump-sum withdrawal in December for Christmas. The freed blacks were not without leaders willing and able to further their cause for better working conditions, wages, education and social reforms. Clement Payne, a dynamic and intellectual leader arrived in Barbados in March 1937. His dedication to the organization of workers into trade unions quickly gained him a large following. The government considered him to be a threat that had to be removed. They charged him with falsely claiming to immigration officials that he was born in Barbados when he was in fact born in Trinidad. His trial and conviction outraged his followers who made plans to rescue him from the police on the morning of July 27. They found that he had secretly been deported during the evening of July 26.

The act of deporting Payne enraged his followers and a riot occurred in Bridgetown. Armed with stones, bottles and sticks, they broke windows, overturned cars, fought the police and racked havoc on establishment property. The riot was not subdued until late that evening. New leaders appeared. Clennel Wickham's newspaper articles inspired Charles O'Neal to form the Democratic League which led Errol Barrow to form the Democratic Labour Party. The 1937 rioting spurred Grantly Adams to form the Barbados Labour Party (BLP) in 1938.

In 1940 Adams was elected to the Assembly and became president of the Barbados Worker's Union (BWU). In 1954 he resigned from the BWU and became premier. Errol Barrow, a World War II hero, appeared on the scene, won a seat in the Assembly and took leadership of a small group of left-wing members of the BLP. He became disenchanted with the BLP and formed his own party, the Democratic Labor Party (DLP) which he led for the next 32 years.

Grantly Adams was victorious in the 1956 election and became the first and only premier of the West Indies Federation, a plan proposed by England to consolidate government in the West Indies. The Federation, which was dissolved in 1962, demanded much of Adams' time and he neglected problems of 20% unemployment, high cost of living and low wages. Barrow stayed at home, campaigned on the issues close to the heart of the voters and won the 1961 election. The DLP retained power until 1971. Barbados gained independence on November 30, 1966 and Errol Barrow became its first premier.

Your island contact:
Mr. Hugh Foster, Public Relations Manager
Barbados Tourism Authority
P. O. Box 242
Bridgetown, Barbados, W.I.
Phone: (809) 427-2623
Fax: (809) 426-4080

Bomba's Shack, Tortola

The Virgin Islands Mining Company, Virgin Gorda

CHAPTER 12

BRITISH VIRGIN ISLANDS

SIZE
Anegada: 13 sq. mi.
Tortola: 21 sq. mi.
Virgin Gorda: 8-1/2 sq. mi.

GEOGRAPHY
Mostly hilly, with the highest point being 1728 feet on Tortola.

CLIMATE
Generally agreeable with temperatures ranging between 77 and 86 degrees. Temperatures do not fall beyond 68 degrees during the nighttime. Hurricane season is between June and October.

CAPITAL/MAIN TOWN
Administrative Center for all British Virgin Islands--there are 50 in all covering 59 sq. mi.: Road Town, Tortola.

AMERINDIANS
Carbon dating indicates human habitation of the islands around 400 B.C. Archaeological finds substantiate the presence of the Arawaks around 1080 A.D. and that the Caribs occupied the islands between 1393 and 1443.

Little is known about pre-Colombian Amerindians, but it is suspected that the Caribs drove off the Arawaks during their migration through the Indies, but made no permanent settlements.

The Caribs apparently did not present a significant problem to early settlers because no mention is made of conflicts by historians.

DISCOVERY
Columbus sighted the British Virgins on November 17, 1493 after leaving St. Croix on his second voyage.

He sent a ship to explore the islands and islets and after finding so many he named them `Las Once Mil Virgines' in honor of the legendary St. Ursula and her 11,000 martyr virgins.

It is suspected that he gave the islands this name to impress Isabella and Ferdinand with the number of islands he had discovered.

While it is assumed he named Virgin Gorda (Fat Virgin) he likely had no part in the naming of other islands in the group such as Dog, Cockroach and Mosquito. For over a century after discovery the British Virgins remained historically dormant and only modestly settled.

SPANISH QUEST FOR POWER AND GOLD
Unfriendly topography, unpredictable currents, numerous dangerous rocks and shoals, their small size and lack of mineral wealth provided no attraction for the Spanish.

The Caribbean was filled with more desirable settlement sites that offered some promise for gold deposits, pasture land and better-located harbors; therefore, the Spanish just ignored this island group.

EUROPEAN POWER STRUGGLE AND SETTLEMENTS
The Treaty of Westphalia (1648) granted the occupation of certain islands in the Caribbean to the Dutch. Shortly afterwards some Dutch buccaneers and a few settlers made the first serious attempt to inhabit Tortola. They built a fort at Soper's Hole and introduced sugar cane.

The Dutch carried on their activities without incident until 1665 when English naval commander John Wentworth, hearing that England was at war with Holland, attacked Tortola. He captured a Dutch ship and took possession of 67 slaves which he sent to Bermuda.

Some Dutch remained, but English buccaneers drove most of them away in 1666 and raised the English flag.

The Third Dutch War (1672-74) broke out and Colonel William Stapleton officially took possession of Tortola. England felt the British Virgin group to be strategically located. Besides, in the 1700's it was fashionable to occupy any Caribbean island if for no other reason than to keep some other country from occupying it.

Disputes arose between England, Holland and Denmark over the rightful ownership of not only the British Virgins, but also the future U. S. Virgin Island group. Spain made repeated attacks on Tortola for the purpose of plunder and torture in 1685 and 1686, but the English managed to retain possession of the islands most of the time during this unsettled period.

While the English wanted control of the Virgins, they discouraged settlements because they didn't want to go to the expense necessary to defend them. In spite of discouragement, a census taken in 1717 counted 317 whites on Virgin Gorda and 159 on Tortola, `The Land of the Turtle Dove'. A report to the Crown on February 20, 1756 tallied 267 small arms and 66 cannon available for the Virgin Island defense. It requested 300 more small arms and 58 more cannon.

The strategic location of Tortola came into play during the American Revolution when the need arose to protect English interests from American attacks and to support the English privateers who were harassing American shipping. Fort Burt and Fort Shirley were built during this period.

The English retained possession and control over the British Virgins from this time forward.

BUCCANEERS, PIRATES AND PRIVATEERS

The treacherous coastlines of the British Virgins that discouraged settlers and merchant shipping provided harbor haunts for the adventurous "Brethren of the Sea."

It is said that Sir Francis Drake viewed the "Virgin's Gangway", later to be known as the Sir Francis Drake Channel, from "Drake's Seat" atop Crown Mountain on the island of St. Thomas. He was one of the first to sail it in 1586.

Another popular legend surrounds Dead Man's Chest Island where the pirate Blackbeard is supposed to have abandoned a mutinous crew and to be the setting for Stevenson's Treasure Island.

Still other legends surround the island of Anegada. Pirates frequented the harbors of Freebooters Point, Bone's Bight and Treasure Point. Islanders believe that the many buried treasure sites on this island are guarded by a person buried with the treasure. The treasure can only be found if this "tired spirit" decides to reveal the location of the treasure to someone so he will no longer be obligated to guard it.

Norman Island is named after Norman, a buccaneer who salvaged a Spanish galleon and is said to have buried its treasure on the island. The cache has been reported to have been found several times, but from time to time adventurers still search for it.

In the early days the settlers stuck to agricultural pursuits and merely co-existed with the pirates, with no desire to participate in the profession. The outbreak of the American Revolution in 1776 brought change and the `golden age' of privateering began.

In 1776 six English vessels left Tortola with 1421 hogsheads of sugar, 225 bales of cotton and 186 tons of fustic (a tropical tree from which yellow dye can be extracted). American privateers captured the vessels and confiscated their cargo.

In retaliation, some wealthy Tortola planters outfitted 7 ships and they intercepted 29 American ships and the privateering war was on.

The Crown allowed the planters to keep only one-half of the booty, but after a petition, the Crown allowed all privateers to keep all their booty. As a result, even members of the English Council and Assembly began to finance privateers and ships were openly outfitted in English harbors.

The profit incentive moved privateers to extend their activities to include ships of neutral nations, including those dealing with Danish controlled St. Thomas and St. Croix. This resulted in some embarrassing political situations between England, Denmark and the neutral nations, so the Crown issued orders for privateering to be restricted to American ships only.

The Virgin Islander's ignored the privateering orders until the arrival of a new governor, Thomas Shirley in 1781. He managed to cut off all support to those who attacked any but American ships. Privateering of American shipping continued until the end of the American War for Independence.

Of course, smuggling went hand in hand with privateering. There were legal channels to dispose of booty, but it was more profitable to either smuggle goods by not reporting them to authorities or to bribe cooperative authorities for false clearances.

The Crown became increasingly concerned over the loss of income by illegal privateering. Of the 82 reported captures between 1803 and 1815, none were reported by privateers. Letters of protest continued to be received from friendly nations demanding that England do something about their marauding privateers, who now could be redefined as pirates.

The Crown took action by establishing a Vice-Admiralty Court in Tortola, increasing the number of naval vessels which did their own privateering and monitored English piracy and establishing Road Town in Tortola as a free port.

The free port concept allowed goods to pass through Tortola without customs, which dramatically increased the flow of trade. The only requirement was that certain goods that left Tortola had to be re-packaged, which had a significant negative impact on pirated goods. Between 1782 and 1785, 385 ships arrived and departed British Virgin ports. Tortola became a major rendezvous port. In May 1799, 260 vessels assembled at Tortola to form a fleet to cross the Atlantic.

All this activity, plus the cooperative support of all European nations to eliminate all forms of pirating led to the gradual decline in the pirating business in the Virgins and elsewhere in the Caribbean.

THE SUGAR ERA

While privateering was a major economic base, the British Virgins were not to be left out of the sugar era. Rapid expansion in sugar and cotton production began in 1735. By 1751, when Virgin Gorda and Jost Van Dyke joined Tortola, one million pounds of cotton and 1000 casks of sugar were reported to be exported from the Virgins.

One of the larger planters on Jost Van Dyke was Quaker William Thornton. Upon hearing that there was a competition for the design of a capitol building in Washington D.C., he drew some plans and presented them to General George Washington and they were accepted. Later, upon the request of Thomas Jefferson, he designed some buildings for the University of Virginia. For this he received a prize of $500.

The prosperity of the sugar era was short-lived in the British Virgins. The entrance of the 19th century found deteriorating soil conditions, falling sugar and cotton prices, a general depression in Great Britain and increasing competition from Cuba and Brazil. In 1831 the cost of marketing sugar exceeded the price received. Another shattering economic blow came from a hurricane on September 21 and 22, 1819, virtually leveling everything standing and leaving many plantations on the doorstep of bankruptcy.

Virgin islanders made a plea to the Crown for financial assistance. This was refused with a statement, "(financial assistance) might be construed into a precedent for claiming Gifts from the Crown." Under the British colonial system, colonies were valued only to the extent that they contributed to England's prosperity.

Almost continual drought, the ending of slavery and a number of hurricanes eventually eliminated sugar and cotton exports from the economic picture. In 1839 the Virgins exported 3429 barrels of sugar. This dropped to 144 in 1852.

Left with this indifference by the homeland and after having lived through so many economic setbacks, the British Virgin Islanders returned to what they did best--being a base for smugglers, which they turned into a fine art.

SLAVERY AND SLAVE REVOLTS

Slavery appeared in the Virgins around 1672. The source came from pirated Spanish ships, the St. Thomas slave market and some immigrants who brought their slaves from other islands. It wasn't until the middle 1730's, with the coming of the sugar plantation, that

Virgin Islands imported slaves directly from Africa at a reduced cost. This practice ended abruptly in 1808 with the passage of the Imperial Act, which ended the slave trade.

Slave labor was the most effective capital investment in agricultural techniques in the Virgins. Of the 39,000 total acres in the islands, only 700 are flat. This meant that much land had to be terraced and slaves were the more effective tool than the plough.

The planters gave their slaves certain privileges, grants of land for subsistence farming and adequate food in the early years when the numbers were small. As sugar production increased, slave plots were taken away or reduced in size, rules became more strict and good food scarce. As on other islands, they had a low social status and poor housing.

In spite of the suppression, the slaves were not a meek and submissive lot. They, like slaves on other islands, took a variety of roads to resistance. Some stole boats and rowed to Puerto Rico where they could be free if they entered the Catholic faith. Others worked slowly, faked illness or committed suicide. Arson and pillage became such a problem in Tortola that 24-hour watches had to be established.

There were some revolts. In May 1790 slaves revolted on the Pickering estate because they believed that emancipation had taken place and their masters were not complying. Two of the ringleaders were tried and sentenced to death.

Slave conditions improved in the 1820's with the stoppage of the importation of new slaves. Now that the supply had stopped, the need arose to take better care of the slaves they did have. The use of the cartwhip for punishment was abolished. Allowances for food and clothing became more generous and subsistence plot sizes were increased.

An unprecedented event took place in 1811 when Arthur Hodge, known for his cruelty, was brought to trial for killing his slave, Prosper. The fact that he was brought to trial at all and executed to boot showed an attitude change beginning to take place among the planters.

The planters encouraged marriage between slaves and tolerated religious instruction by the Quakers and Wesleyan Methodist missionaries as long as it did not interfere with the slave's performance.

Quakerism made a short appearance in the 1740's, but their beliefs came to odds with slavery, even though they did own slaves. Fearing Quaker influence might help the movement toward emancipation, one of their leaders, Lieutenant Governor John

Pickering was replaced by Captain John Hunt who did not favor Quakerism.

While the Quaker movement didn't remain, their model of humane treatment of the slaves, with corresponding reciprocal cooperation showed the value of religion among the slaves. Emancipation of the slaves took place in the Virgins in 1834.

POST SLAVERY ERA

Emancipation did not bring immediate total freedom to the slaves. Not only did the planters fear financial disaster with the disappearance of their work force, they also feared reprisals and disorder from the freed slaves. To reduce tensions, the Crown introduced the Apprenticeship Program to ease the slaves into freedom and provide a period of adjustment for the planters.

Rules came with the Program. It limited the workweek to 45 hours of compulsory work. If the worker wanted, he could work additional hours for agreed upon wages. He could not change his residence or leave the estate without a pass. Punishments were enforced for insolence, rioting, resistance or escape. In some ways the master had more control over the apprentices than they did over their slaves.

The apprentices did receive some rights. Masters could be punished for assaults on apprentices and apprentices could sue their masters in court. The number of Virgin islands falling under the administration from Tortola made supervision of the Program difficult. After much apprehension in the beginning, masters and slaves seemed to resign themselves to the Program's rules. Although things seemed to be jogging along peacefully, many felt that the apprentices were not receiving the training necessary to cope on their own in a world of freedom. The Program was not working in the Virgins or elsewhere; consequently, in April 1838 the Crown abolished the Program and the apprentices gained their freedom.

The collapse of the sugar industry, accelerated by the Sugar Duties Act of 1846 which equalized duties of foreign and British sugar prices and the departure of the Reid, Irving and Company, the Virgin's last contact with England placed the Virgins in dire financial straits.

The freed apprentices faced the options of emigration or subsistence farming which was difficult because planters owned the land.

Gradually the freed men gained control of land, owned but abandoned by planters, through a series of land acts or by one way or another. In 1897 there were 3 owners of 500 acre parcels, 45 between 100 and 500 acres and 408 below 100 acres. Only 291 properties were less than 20 acres.

Peasant farming took the place of the sugar plantation. The major emphasis turned to rearing livestock, pigs, goats and sheep and growing yams and potatoes.

The Virgins entered the 20th century in economic shambles, a result of poor planning, neglect by England and incompetent administration of social services. A legislative council was established in 1937, but it met irregularly and mainly for ceremonial purposes to take care of administrate matters, not making any attempt to address economic problems.

The British Virgins did improve somewhat economically as a result of its participation in World War II and began to receive some attention from England.

England provided some aid to improve pasture lands and establish agricultural stations. Between 1946 and 1962 significant increases in rearing cattle, sheep, pigs and goats took place and the economic picture brightened.

The government showed some interest in tourism in 1953 when it passed the Hotels Aid Ordinance to encourage the building of hotels. Interest in the tourist industry really grew in the 1960's when they saw the tourist boom beginning to take place in the nearby U. S. Virgins and the government took a firm stand to support this industry's development.

The twelve miles of paved road built on Tortola in 1958 was greatly extended over the next 12 years. The telephone and radio broadcasting systems found their way to the islands in the 1960's and the self-government achieved in the 1950's resulted in more governmental interest in the Islands' development.

The dark age of slavery has turned into the British Virgins being a vacationer's playground.

Your island contact:
Mr. Russell Harrigan, Director of Tourism
B.V.I. Tourist Board
P. O. Box 134, Road Town, Tortola, BVI
Phone: (809) 494-3134 Fax: (809) 494-3666

CHAPTER 13

CAYMAN ISLANDS

SIZE
Grand Cayman: 76 square miles
Little Cayman: 11 square miles
Cayman Brac: 14 square miles

GEOGRAPHY
No point on Grand Cayman is more than 60 feet above sea level. The island is nearly completely surrounded by reefs. North Sound divides the island, with the western part being of dry forests and the eastern half having freshwater swamps and mangrove trees.

CLIMATE
Tropical climate with highs in the 90 degree range in the summer and lows of 75 degrees in the winter months.

CAPITAL
Georgetown, Grand Cayman

AMERINDIANS
The finding of some art objects and tools indicates that the Arawaks did at least pass through the Caymans. The number of items found leads archaeologists to believe that they did not make any long-term settlements here. One possible explanation for the Arawak's lack of interest in the Caymans is the absence of clay deposits which they used to make pottery.

DISCOVERY
Columbus departed Porto Bello, Panama in April, 1503 to return to Spain after his fourth voyage to the "New World." He planned to stop at Dominica on his way to Hispaniola to take on water. Winds blew him off course and on Wednesday, May 10 he sighted the Caymans. His son, Ferdinand wrote, "We were in sight of two very small and low islands, full of tortoises (turtles), as was all the sea about, insomuch as they looked like little rocks, for which reason these islands were called the Tortugas."

About 20 years elapsed before Las Tortugas appeared on a recognized map. By this time the island's name had changed to Cayman—the Carib name for the crocodile family. One legend has it that someone mistook the iguanas on Grand Cayman for crocodiles and named the island Cayman. A more plausible explanation seems to be that they were renamed after the discovery of an abundance of creatures of the crocodile family found on the shores of Little Cayman.

Grand Cayman remained unsettled and unexplored for 150 years after it was chartered.

SPANISH QUEST FOR POWER AND GOLD

The Spanish did not prize the islands because they did not lie on a trade route and offered no gold or silver. Spain showed little concern when they ceded the Caymans to England, along with Jamaica, in the Treaty of Madrid in 1670.

EUROPEAN POWER STRUGGLE AND SETTLEMENTS

Sailors did find the Caymans to be a desirable stop to stock up on water, wild geese, doves and turtles. In 1592 Captain William King wrote in the publication, The Principal Navigations, "Two turtles, with their eggs, can feed ten men for a day." In 1643 Captain Jackson wrote, "The island is much frequented by English, French and Dutch ships." While the islands provided needed water and food, there are no accounts that describe wreckage caused by unchartered reefs, hurricanes and the wrath the Spanish put upon invaders who crossed "The Line" drawn by the Pope.   Buccaneers, pirates and privateers found the Caymans a haven for supplies and harbors to career (repair) their ships. Their presence, the islands' out-of-the-way location and the limited agricultural opportunities delayed the consideration of the Caymans as a place to establish a settlement.

It is sometime difficult to identify what is Cayman legend and myth and what is historical fact. Some mystery even surrounds the identity of the original settlers. Bodden (which could have been spelled "Bowden") and Watler which could have been spelled "Walter") are two family names involved in the founding of Bodden Town in 1658, Grand Cayman's original capital.   It is said they deserted Cromwell's army. No Bodden, Bowden or Watler appears on Cromwell's regimental list; however, a Thomas Walter does.

How the Early Settlers Survived

Bodden Town provided a good location to sight ships and an excellent harbor for the turtle trade, a major industry in the early days.

During May, June and July each year female turtles, accompanied by males, arrived from Cuba, Mexico, Honduras and Nicaragua. They waddled up the gently-slopping beaches three times, fifteen days apart, and laid 80 to 90 eggs each time—legend places the figure at 300.

Cayman "turtlers" would wait until a female had laid her third batch. They would attach a long rope to one of her back legs and when she returned to the sea her lover would come to greet her--a fatal mistake. The turtlers would slowly drag in the rope, the male tagging along, and when back on the beach they captured two instead of one.

Another occupation said to be practiced by a few of the early settlers was "wrecking." This involved the decoying of ships onto reefs and then plundering the cargo when the crew abandoned the ship.

The English Crown began issuing land grants in the 1700's for the purpose of settling and lumbering. The island had great stands of mahogany trees, some with trunks measuring 4 to 5 feet in diameter. Lumbering, along with shipbuilding entered the economic scene.

It was not uncommon for ships to arrive at Boddon Town in need of crew members. Many Cayman Islanders took to the sea and would return with tales of the outside world.

Trade increased with Jamaica in the early 1800's. The seas surrounding the Caymans produced an abundant supply of seafood to add to Cayman's exports to Jamaica.

The Wreck of the Ten Sail

The reefs surrounding the Caymans, which today provide countless exciting dive sites, snared over a hundred hapless ships in days gone by.

In February 1794 the most famous shipwreck calamity, cited as "The Wreck of the Ten Sail", occurred. Myths and legends surround the incident, but recent studies performed by the Cayman National Museum have pieced together what and how it actually happened and are in the process of recovering and displaying artifacts from the shipwrecks.

A convoy of 58 merchant ships carrying West Indies sugar and rum left Jamaica headed westward toward the Yucatan Channel where it would encounter the Gulf Stream, circle through the Florida

Straits and head across the Atlantic Ocean to Great Britain. English Navy Captain John Lawford, sailing the newly commissioned frigate Convert, was in command of the convoy.

A leaky ship delayed the cast off and caused the convoy to arrive at the Caymans after sunset on the second day. At midnight, in rough seas and high winds, the sailing master recommended to Captain Lawford that their course be changed more to the North. Lawford gave the order to the fleet.

A few hours later the Captain heard a cannon shot, North of his position, which he interpreted as a warning signal. Some merchant ships had disregarded his orders and passed the Convert. Shortly afterwards he sighted breakers and some shipwrecks, and the sailing master's earlier misjudgment of their position became apparent.

Lawford immediately gave orders for the convoy to disperse and changed his course to avoid the reefs. Misfortune befell Lawford when another ship, in its attempt to avoid the reefs, collided with the Convert. By the time they broke loose from each other they had drifted too close to the reefs to escape running aground.

Sunrise revealed that nine ships and the Convert had wrecked on the reefs. The weather prevented other ships in the convoy to provide help. Some Cayman Islanders sighted the disaster and helped bring the crews ashore. Estimates are that at least eight people perished in the disaster.

Grand Cayman had experienced a hurricane a few months earlier and the food supply would not support the shipwrecked crews in addition to the one thousand residents. Lawford arranged for some ships to pick up the stranded crews. They did and the convoy continued on their voyage to Great Britain, stopping at Havana for supplies.

A few months after the Wreck of the Ten Sail, Captain Lawford and his crew faced a court martial in Jamaica. The court acquitted all of them and blamed the incident on a strong current that carried them off their charted course.

Among the many legends that surround the Wreck of the Ten Sail is that Prince Henry fell victim to the reefs and was rescued from the jaws of death by the bravery of some Cayman Islanders. As a reward for their bravery, King George mandated that no Cayman Islander would thereafter be conscripted into the military and that they would be free from taxation forever. No evidence has ever been produced to support these romantic happenings.

BUCCANEERS, PIRATES AND PRIVATEERS

In the early days the Caymans lacked any organized settlements, serious fortifications or military presence. Neither the Spanish or English governments showed any real concern about happened there. As a result, the islands became a comfortable oasis for pirates of all descriptions.

Henry Morgan, Blackbeard, Neal Walker and Calico Jack are among the names handed down who are said to have frequented the islands. There they would pause to engage in merriment, gather supplies, make repairs and plan future raids.

Legends say that the caves on the islands house treasure chests stored for safe keeping by the pirates. Only one chest has been rumored to have been found by a man who is said to have flown away before disclosing its contents. Archaeologists believe that if any chests exist they have been buried by overburden laid down over the years by a series of hurricanes.

It would seem unlikely that the caves hold any sizable caches since the pirates divided the loot after each raid. They tended to find ports to squander their share or return home when their share reached any appreciable amount.

THE SUGAR ERA

The Caymans remained lazy islands during the hey day of the sugar era. Sir George Nugent became Governor of Jamaica in 1801 and in 1802 he sent staff member Edward Corbet to make a personal report on what Nugent's wife had described Grand Cayman as ". . . a very low and miserable island."

Corbet counted an armed force of 80. He noted plantations that grew cotton, yams, plantains and a little coffee. Almost every settler grew some sugar cane, which they made into syrup. This was the only reference he made to sugar production.

Corbet made many comments and observations on social issues. For example, he reported that because of the great number of Boddens, Coes, Ebanks, Watlers, Fosters and Edens who were connected by marriage, it was impossible to gather an impartial jury. Judges moved trials for serious civil or criminal cases to Jamaica. Many of these names are common in the Caymans today.   Corbet took the first census in 1802. He counted 933 residents, 551 of them being slaves. He found that most of the inhabitants had been born on the island. Little Cayman and Cayman Brac were uninhabited.

SLAVERY AND SLAVE REVOLTS

A few slaves arrived between 1734 and 1743 during the time when England issued land grants to encourage settlement. In 1781 an African slave ship ran aground on the Cayman reefs and the slaves were sold to pay expenses. A few other slaves trickled in with settlers who immigrated from Jamaica.

The treatment of slaves, in general, seemed to be more compassionate than on other Caribbean islands and in the U.S.

Nathanial Glover, a former Cayman Islander slave owner, wrote in 1841, "Slavery only existed here by name. The owners generally were overindulgent and the children of the slaves were usually brought up in the houses of their masters and were often playmates to their children. They were much better provided for than now."

One explanation for the more humane way the Cayman Islanders treated their slaves could be that no master owned a great number of them. In 1835 116 masters owned 954 slaves. The largest owner was Mary Bodden who placed a claim to the government to be reimbursed for her loss of 45 slaves. Next in line was John Webster who claimed 39.

The male slaves worked mostly in the fields, but the work was less rigorous or demanding than that of the sugar plantation. Very few worked in the trades. The women worked as domestics.

When the slaves were liberated, they initially settled in the northern section of Grand Cayman.

THE POST-SLAVERY ERA

The Caymans continued as quiet island settlements and stepchildren to Jamaica well into the 20th century. Sailing ships used the Caymans as a stop for turtles, fresh water and trading when leaving Jamaica and sailing the Windward Passage. The arrival of the steamship in the mid-nineteenth century allowed ships to take a more direct route east and the islands became isolated.

The Cayman Islander's took advantage of the opportunity to showcase their wares and way of life at the Jamaica Exposition in 1891. Their exhibits of rope, dyewoods, baskets, hats, sponges and seashells sparked a renewal of trade.

By 1905 the Cayman Islanders had paid off their debt to Jamaica and laborers were making twice the wages of those in Jamaica or Trinidad. The turtle industry flourished and shipbuilding, which eventually consumed the islands' lumber resources, continued until 1939. Their low taxes and high standard of living became the envy of English economic observers.

The Caymans Emerge

Cayman's entrance into modern technology was slow, but began to emerge after World War II.

The first automobile arrived in 1914, and the number increased to 47 autos and 5 motorcycles by 1940. Today everyone owns a car, for the island sports more than 60 miles of roads. In the 1940's, only Georgetown had electricity, which was switched on one hour before sunset until midnight. By 1970 most of the island had electrical service. There was one restaurant, with six tables, in 1949. Galleon Beach, Georgetown's first hotel opened in the 1950's, but it proved too small and new accommodations opened on Seven Mile Beach in 1956. In 1969 Grand Cayman hosted 19,000 tourists. The first wireless arrived in 1930. An airfield opened near Georgetown in 1954 and overseas telephone service came in 1967.

Jamaica became an independent state within the British Commonwealth in August 1962. The Caymans followed the trend for independent status and the British ratified a new constitution which freed them from Jamaican administration and made the Caymans a direct dependency of the British Crown in 1962.

The Caymans Today

Tourism and offshore banking have replaced turtling and shipbuilding, but the Cayman social graces and culture remain.

The once-vacant Seven Mile Beach is now lined with resorts and condos. The islands have become world-renown for their dive sites.

Cayman financial laws offer tax advantages and investment incentives to the banking industry. Cayman island and offshore banking sites are now home to 550 banks and trust companies with over US$400 billion of assets.

The Cayman Islanders now enjoy one of the highest per capita incomes in the Caribbean.

Your island contact:
Miss Angela Martins
Director of Tourism
Cayman Islands Dept. of Tourism
P. O. Box 67
Grand Cayman, Cayman Islands, B.W.I.
Phone: (809) 949-0623
Fax: (809) 949-4053

Cuban Embassy, Grenada

Lava Fields, Grand Cayman Island, Cayman Islands

CHAPTER 14

CUBA

SIZE
44,218 Square Miles

GEOGRAPHY
Largest and most populated (10,300,000) island
in the Caribbean. Only 20 miles off the east
coast is the Cayman trench, where the depth of
the Caribbean reaches 23,600 feet. The island
is relatively flat with hills on the east and
west ends. Highest peak is Pico de Turquino,
on the south-east corner. Many islets ring
the coasts.

CLIMATE
Temperatures range from 45 to 100 degrees with the
average temperature in Havana being 77 degrees with
75% humidity. USA summer months are Cuba's rainy
season. Average rainfall is between 35 and 60
inches.

CAPITAL
Havana (La Habana)

AMERINDIANS

The Ciboneys migrated down the coast of Florida, crossed the
Straits of Florida and at first occupied the shores of western Cuba.
Over time they ventured southward in significant numbers and
eventually established settlements throughout the island.

Arawaks, leaving in flight from the Caribs in Puerto Rico, arrived
and met the Ciboneys. They drove the Ciboneys to the hills and
enslaved those they captured. By the time of the arrival of
Columbus the island was extensively inhabited by the Arawaks, with
only a small group of Ciboneys remaining on the western shores.

The demise of the Amerindians on Cuba began in 1510 when King Ferdinand ordered an expedition to follow up the rumor of large gold deposits to be found there. Diego Columbus received the order and dispatched Diego Velasquez, the richest planter on Hispaniola, and 300 men to conquer Cuba.

Velasquez had been informed that the Arawaks were peaceful and docile and would pose no problem. But, the Arawaks had been in touch with the Arawaks on Hispaniola who had told them that they would have to stand and fight for their very existence and that any hospitality they showed the Spaniards would only be rewarded with slavery and death.

Among those issuing warnings about Spanish treachery was an Arawak chieftain, Hatuey, who had been driven from his small island off the coast of Hispaniola. When he arrived in canoes with around 400 of his tribesmen, the resident Cuban Arawaks thought he was another attacking Carib and fled to the hills. Soon he convinced them he was a friendly brother and became a leader in the struggle against the Spaniards.

In an impassioned speech to the Arawaks he was reported to have said, while holding a basket of gold above his head:

"Here is the God which the Spaniards worship. For these they fight and kill; for this they persecute us and that is why we have to throw these into the sea, so that when they get here they won't find any stones like these and they will believe there are none."

Hatuey continued his speech which implored the Arawaks to also take up arms against the invaders. The Arawak chiefs were suspicious of Hatuey, who they viewed as being a foreigner, from the start and did not believe the tales of inhumanity and brutality he related.

When Hatuey's lookouts spotted Velasquez's ships, Hatuey threw everything made of gold into the sea and sent the women and children to the mountains.

Hatuey ordered his warriors to station themselves in the forest lining the beach. When Velasquez's men entered the forested area they got their first taste of guerrilla warfare in the form of a cloud of arrows. This began the first Cuban war. Instead of flushing through the island in a matter of days, the Spanish found themselves in defense in a makeshift fort for over 3 months--a situation never before experienced by a Spanish Caribbean fighting force.

Velasquez faced mutiny and it was only because he was able to convince his men that the entire Arawak effort would collapse upon the capture and death of Hatuey that he kept control of his command. His patience was rewarded by the revelation of a Hatuey traitor of the location of Hatuey's encampment.   Hatuey was captured and burned at the stake on February 2, 1512 after refusing to reveal the location of gold deposits.

Velasquez sent Panifila de Narvaez and 150 men inland to search for gold.   Father Bartolome de las Casas accompanied Narvaez and documented his horror at seeing the slaughter of the Arawaks by Narvaez. He wrote, "No tongue is capable of describing to the life of all the horrid villainies perpetrated by these bloody-minded men.   They seem to be the declared enemy of mankind."

He described a day when Narvaez arrived at the village of Caonao. There, 2500 Arawaks greeted them and gave them water, bread and fish. With no provocation, the Spaniards turned on the villagers and left no one alive upon their departure.

Casas recorded seeing over 7000 children killed during a four month period and their parents driven to work in the mines, where they soon died of overwork and malnutrition.

Casa's numerous writings describing the Spaniards' brutality are almost beyond belief, especially when the Crown had issued orders that the Indians in the New World were to be treated humanely and converted to Christianity. In short order all significant Arawak resistance ended and the survivors found themselves enslaved.

On December 12, 1512 the King sent a message to Velasquez thanking him for conquering Cuba and commending him for his "humane treatment of the natives."

It seemed only proper to the Crown that those responsible for conquering Cuba be given a reward. This reward came in the form of the encomienda which gave those who qualified the right to the labor of a specific number of Indians, up to a maximum of 300.

Under the encomienda program the Arawaks were to be temporary workers, fed, clothed and instructed in the Christian faith so they could "be civilized on earth and saved in heaven." The altruistic purpose of the enomiendia was quickly forgotten and the program disintegrated into nothing more than slavery.

King Charles heard of the misuse of encomiendia and was about to abolish the program when the Spaniards in Cuba advised him that if he did this all the Arawaks would arise and kill all the Christians. He appointed Bishop Ramirez to investigate the allegations against encomiendia, but the Bishop had Arawaks of his own under the program, so his investigation effected no recommendation for change.

The Crown issued an order that encomiendia workers were not to be used in mining; however, no one ever read the order, so it was ignored. Encomiendia finally ended in 1550, but by then the Arawaks were well on their road to extermination.

The last major Arawak uprising came under the leadership of Chief Guama in 1529. In 1532 the Spanish dispatched a large force into the mountains and overwhelmed Guama. Those who were not killed were enslaved.

It is estimated by historians that by 1557 the Cuban Arawak population had been reduced to less than 2000.

DISCOVERY

Columbus learned of a large island to the west during a visit with some Arawaks on his first voyage. Thinking this must be off the coast of the land of the Khan, he sailed forth and discovered Cuba, which he named Juana after King Ferdinand's son, on October 28, 1492.

Columbus sailed along the coast expecting at any time to come across the great cities of the Khan, but only found small villages of Indians who fled on sight.

A force landed and spent three days exploring the interior in an effort to find the Great Khan's capital. They didn't find Khan's capital, but they became the first Europeans to witness the use of tobacco. Father de las Casas described the finding, based on Columbus's diary, in his book, History of the Indies. It reads in part:

". . . and they light it at one end and at the other they suck or chew or draw in with their breath that smoke with which their flesh is benumbed and, so to speak, it intoxicates them, and in this way they say they do not feel fatigue." Columbus described the island as "the fairest land human eyes have yet seen." He was awe-struck by the perfumed November air, variety of beautiful birds and tropical beauty of the forests.

But, the Crown wasn't interested in tropical beauty. They had a thirst for the gold, jewels and spices to be found in the land of the great Khan. As a result, the Spanish bypassed the island at first, but soon found it to be a valuable location for a military depot and way station for ships returning to Seville with treasures from Mexico.

SPANISH QUEST FOR POWER AND GOLD

The discovery of gold in the early 1500's attracted gold miners, those with skills in crafts and farmers. Growth continued until around 1535 when the mines began to play out and wild tales of riches to be found in Mexico and Peru began to circulate throughout the island. Then, the settlers had but one thought: Dios me lleve al Peru! (Take me to Peru).

The numbers of emigrants to South America from Cuba were so substantial that the Crown ordered the death penalty for anyone leaving the island without permission.

By 1602, 13,000 of the 20,000 remaining Cubans had settled in Havana working to service the ships' crews on their way to Seville and marketing Spain's newly found rage--tobacco. Havana merchants also supplied the Conquistadors headed for South America with dried meat and casava bread.

Gradually, as the 18th century began, settlers began to profit from the richness of the island's soil. Stock raising, tobacco, sugar, coffee, cotton, indigo and beeswax became important exports.

The Crown and the Church were not about to stand by and see the profits roll in without extracting their due. The Crown levied a number of duties and taxes on exports and the Church, under the title laws, extracted a 10% tithe on agricultural products. This left the planters with a very small margin of profit.

Alarm grew among producers over the Church policy to pressure planters to bequeath their land to the Church upon their death in order to assure themselves eternal life in the hereafter. The Marque of Barinas wrote King Charles II, "Within 50 years all property (in Cuba) will be in the hands of the clergy and the laity will have only an insufferable burden to suffer."

The Crown's policy of monopoly of trade and the clergy's tithe policies continued until the beginning of the 19th century. The realm engaged in continual wars to protect their possessions and by 1596, after the defeat of the Spanish Armada by the British in 1587, Spain was bankrupt. Their only hope to replenish their exhausted coffers came from their West Indies islands. Tobacco became a major income producer and in 1717 the Crown issued an edict that all tobacco be sold through Seville. Disobedience was punishable by death.

Not only did the planters ignore the edict, but they began protesting by smuggling through Dutch, French and English outlets. Don Valdes notified Madrid that even the clergy openly engaged in smuggling activities, and through this, fortunes were made.

Protests also took the form of armed uprisings by the tobacco growers. The government suppressed these and it wasn't until the British captured Cuba in 1762 that change took place. The following year Cuba was traded back to Spain for Spain's interests in Florida.

The freedoms of trade and religion allowed during the British occupation had a lasting effect on Spain's monopolistic control of the island. Cuba's step toward independence from Spain began in 1764 when the Crown, realizing the impossibility of controlling smuggling or reaping any benefits from a revolutionary population, began making trade concessions.

The 19th century saw sincere efforts to gain relief from Spanish rule. One group, the reformists, wanted to remain associated with Spain, but to be given more autonomy in government. Another group sought to gain statehood with the United States. A third group wanted complete independence.

By 1808 the reformists, made up primarily of wealthy planters, began to emerge as the leaders in Cuba's move to effect political change. News of the French conquest of Spain reached Cuba on July 14 of that year. The Cubans pulled together for Spain and declared war on France.

About this time military revolutionaries (juntas) began efforts to free themselves from Spain. By 1824 Spain had lost control of all the American mainland, northern, central and southern.

While some forces within Cuba wanted to establish a junta, a variety of circumstances aborted the efforts. One fear of the wealthy planters was that independence from Spain could lead to the freedom of slaves. Significant numbers of Spanish sympathizing emigrants from mainland revolutions, those fleeing New Orleans (after the Louisiana Purchase) and from Haiti were not about to support independence from Spain. Consequently, Cuba remained a Spanish supporter during this revolutionary period.

But, Cuba was not without those who would periodically appear to plot for Cuban independence. The combination of tight Spanish control, the non-support of the wealthy slave-owning planters and spies who infiltrated the organizations and exposed them before they could become a significant menace, crushed all these efforts.

Meanwhile, the newly established United States of America had become an important economic and political factor to Cuba. In 1826, Mexico and Columbia, fearing Cuba could become a military base for a Spanish effort to re-conquer the Americas, wanted to invade Cuba and free the island from Spanish control. USA led the opposition to this move, which raised the rancor of Cuban workers for independence. Many Cubans were convinced that the USA was planning to annex Cuba and put it under the control of American business interests. They also felt the USA had designs on conquering the entire West Indies.

Cuban rebellions against Spain continued. A major revolution started in 1895 and the USA turned its sympathies toward the rebels. When the American battleship Maine, sent to Havana to protect American citizens in February 1898, mysteriously blew up in the harbor, the USA declared war on Spain.

The famous battle of San Juan Hill took place in July, 1898 and on December 10, 1898 Spain signed the Treaty of Paris which relinquished all Spanish claims in Cuba.

The United States retained a temporary military government until 1909 when the forces left, giving Cuba its independence.

EUROPEAN POWER STRUGGLE

Spain lost control of Cuba to England for a year in 1762 and to the USA in 1898, which precluded Cuba's independence.

While Cuba was desirable, Spain's military entrenchments and the loyalty of the Cubans warded off serious European nation's attempts to occupy the island. The importance of Cuba to Spain was of such a magnitude that it never became a pawn in treaty agreements until the Treaty of Paris in 1898.

BUCCANEERS, PIRATES AND PRIVATEERS

In the early years an immediate need arose to protect Spanish trade routes and to build forts to ward off the harassing buccaneers and pirates. Sir Francis Drake had ravaged the Cuban coast in 1586. Spain's King Phillip realized that the era of Spanish naval superiority had ended and fortifications were needed at strategic locations to supply shelter and support for their fleets' journeys through the Caribbean seas. Construction on forts began at major ports like San Juan and Cartagena.

Havana became a well-fortified city, the last stop for treasure ships heading back to Seville, but Cuban coastal settlements still suffered from frequent visits by the "Brethren of the Sea."

Spain's defensive activities turned to aggression after the War of 1812. Spain's Latin American possessions were in the process of fighting for independence. Their need for naval support to suppress the revolutions and the Latin American trade with the U.S. exceeded their capacity to perform effectively. In desperation, Spain commissioned large numbers of privateers to prey on Latin American and U.S. merchant ships.

This resulted in a withdrawal of support of the Latin American revolutions in the 1820's by the U.S. because American business was heavily invested in Cuba and couldn't risk trade restrictions with Cuba by Spain. Thus, privateering made a significant impact on Cuban-American economic policy.

THE SUGAR ERA

Several efforts to build sugar mills and import slaves began in 1523, but because of the lack of financial backing and bickering between planters and government officials over contracts, sugar plantations didn't begin to function until 1590.

Taxes, export duties, trade restrictions, tithes and lack of financial support made sugar production a headache in Cuba until after 1790. A combination of the revolution in Haiti which totally destroyed its sugar and coffee production and the European wars between 1792 and 1808   opened the door to profitable Cuban agricultural ventures.

In 1790 Cuba produced 14,000 tons of sugar for a price of 2 to 4 reales. Ten years later, Cuba was producing 34,000 tons of sugar for a price of 28 to 30 reales. A powerful class of planters emerged and more capital and land became devoted to sugar.

Coffee and tobacco also developed into significant export commodities. Nearly 250,000 tons of coffee were exported annually between 1825 and 1830 and 245,097 million cigars left the island during those years.   Coffee plantations suffered a series of hurricanes between 1844 and 1846 and at the same time Brazil entered the coffee market. The combination of these two events either bankrupted coffee growers or turned them to producing sugar.

The vast land area, which includes almost as many square miles as all the rest of the Caribbean islands combined, and the rolling hills with its virgin soil continued to attract sugar investors, many of whom were experienced growers who had fled Haiti.

Cuban planters were among the first to recognize the coming of the end of slavery and to begin to upgrade their cane processing methods by using machinery. They introduced steam power in 1817 and by 1860 92% of the mills were partially mechanized. They opened their first railroad in 1838 and by 1860 many plantation-owned feeder lines led to main lines which led to the ports, cutting transportation costs by 70%.

Statistics can sometimes be boring, but those on Cuban sugar are astonishing. Production rose from 40,000 tons in 1815 to a little over a million tons in 1894. The average annual net profit was 18% on the capital investment. The largest customer in 1877 was the United States which imported 82% of Cuba's sugar. Spain was second with 6%.

Plantations were not large--they were monstrous. In 1857 the Santa Susana encompassed 11,000 acres, with 1,700 in cane and using 866 slaves; the Avala, encompassed 5,000 acres with 2000 in cane and using 600 slaves; and, the Purisima Concepcion and San Martin group that grew cane on 3,500 acres with a labor force of 989.

While the sugar industry was prospering, production per mill had increased from 30 tons per mill in 1790 to 500 tons in 1870. The political scene was festering. Spain's continued taxation and the unlimited powers given to military officials finally brought many plantations to the brink of bankruptcy. Slavery ended legally in 1880 and illegal slave use became costly. Many planters started to build large central mills to cut costs. The investment was so large that investors from the United States had to be solicited to construct the mills. In 1895, one huge mill, the Central Constancia, produced as much sugar as the entire island of Jamaica. By this time, U.S. interests dominated sugar production in Cuba, with only around 20% of the original planter class remaining.

The American interests increased to such a proportion that, when the political instability approached the crisis peak, U.S. President James Polk offered Spain $100 million for Cuba in 1848. Spain refused. Six years later President Franklin Pierce upped the offer to $130 million. Spain rejected the offer again.

The sugar industry in Cuba, stimulated by U.S. capital, continued to expand, while most of the other Caribbean islands were experiencing a rapid collapse of sugar being of economic significance. Of the 2000 sugar mills in operation in 1860, only 158 existed in the 1930's. While 447,000 tons of sugar was produced in 1860, over 5 million tons were produced in 1925. Over one-third of the sugar mills were owned outright by U.S. investors. Between 1902 and 1939 sugar accounted for 80% of Cuban exports.

In 1958, when Fidel Castro came to power, sugar accounted for 90% of Cuban exports and 33% of its national income.

SLAVERY AND SLAVE REVOLTS

Importation of slaves to Cuba began in 1524 when the Crown issued special charters for merchants to bring them to work in the gold mines. The traffic was welcomed by all. The Crown enriched its treasury by levying a tax on each slave upon arrival and even the clergy welcomed them for domestic and business uses.

The slaves wasted no time in organizing revolts. The first to be quelled took place in 1533 at the Jobabo gold mines. Following a French buccaneer raid on Havana in 1538, they rose in revolt and sacked the city. Many incidents of flight to the hills and group suicide were recorded.

An uprising of 300 slaves occurred at a sugar mill west of Havana in 1727 and another major uprising took place at a copper mine in 1731. Revolts never ended until the abolition of slavery in 1886.

Slave revolts became so frequent and rampant that King Charles III issued a slave code on May 31, 1789. The code required the masters to feed and clothe their slaves, instruct them in the Catholic religion, compel them to hear Mass and to provide a priest for this purpose. Masters who abused slaves became subject to fines and criminal prosecution and were not to work slaves more than 270 days a year.

The code required slaves to obey and respect their masters. Those under 17 or over 60 were exempted from a full days work. A full days work was defined from sunrise to sunset, except during harvest time when the work day was extended. Punishment for non-compliance included being put in stocks or irons or being flogged--not to exceed 25 lashes. It should be noted that a slave caught running a tavern or selling tobacco or wine in 1557 was subject to a punishment of 50 lashes.

While the Crown's intentions seemed honorable, giving the slaves some rights and protection from their masters, in actual practice the Code was strictly applied to the slave's, but officials were easily bribed to ignore the provisions as they applied to the masters.

To counter and restrain uprisings and runaways, the slave owners moved their slaves from huts to barracks--large rooms with one door and high, barred windows where men, women and children all slept together. Some plantations built watchtowers and blockhouses in the fields and mill yards. These were manned 24 hours a day and equipped with bloodhounds to track down slaves who ran to the hills.

In 1708 the Crown decreed that a slave could buy his freedom. A slave could earn money when he was "rented" to another plantation. A small down payment would be made, followed by installments. It took a virtual lifetime to reach the final payment and by this time the slave was old and not too productive. The slave rejoiced at gaining his freedom and the master was delighted to take the money and buy another younger, more productive slave.

About the time that the slave trade got under way in Cuba in the 1790's, abolitionists were gaining ground in England. England and Spain entered into an anti-slave traffic agreement along with France and Portugal in 1817. Spain entered the agreement because of their feeling obligated to return a favor to England after their help in the war with Napoleon Bonaparte. Only England had an intention of living up to this agreement. The amount of profits for merchants, planters and bribes to government officials coming from sugar production, which was dependent on slave labor, overshadowed moral obligations.

The largest importation of slaves (26,000) took place in the year Spain signed the agreement. By 1820, when slavery was to be abolished, there were over 236,000 slaves in Cuba and there was no sign of compliance by Spanish or Cuban officials.

England's charges of Spain's indifference to the fate of the "children of Senegal" were countered with Spain`s accusation that England's only interest in the slave trade was to destroy Cuban sugar production so England could achieve a monopoly on sugar through its production in India.

The 1817 agreement granted England the right to search ships for slaves, with the understanding that those slaves found aboard would be freed. This article, which relinquished sovereignty of Spain's shipping to England even received the disapproval of the United States Secretary of State John Quincy Adams who stated in 1822, "The right of search is even more evil than slavery itself."

The Conspiracy of La Escalera

Spanish control over Cuba began to seriously unravel in 1843. Major slave revolts occurred in March and November and whites and freed colored were becoming increasingly and openly disenchanted over Spain's imperialistic tactics.   Moreover, those favoring annexation to the United States and those falling in behind the English abolitionists were seen as rising threats to the Crown and to the end of slavery.

Near Christmas time in 1843, a planter in the Matanzas province "claimed" to have uncovered a slave uprising conspiracy. This led the over-zealous new Captain-General O'Donnell to move in. He tortured and killed suspects and concluded that the conspiracy was not confined to the Matanzas province, so in 1844 he spread his search for conspirators throughout Cuba.

During 1844 thousands of Cuban blacks and mulattos were executed, banished, imprisoned or just disappeared. The conspiracy acquired the name, "La Escalera" (The Ladder) in memory of the truss used to tie suspects while being lashed. The year 1844 became known in Cuban history as "The Year of the Lash."

The fact that a conspiracy ever existed is in doubt and is still an issue among historians. Some say it was a substantial revolutionary plan. Others say it was a minor revolution, but exaggerated by Spanish officials so they could use their powers. Still others maintain that Spain manufactured the entire incident so they could justify their policy of imperialistic repression.

The End of Slavery
Cuba and Puerto Rico formed a Reform Commission to discuss economic, political and social reforms. They agreed on economic and political issues most of the time, but were worlds apart on social issues. Puerto Rico commissioners dropped a bombshell on November 27, 1866 when they announced they were ready for the emancipation of slaves. Cubans were horrified, but international pressures forced a discussion on the issue. Cubans felt they wanted control of their island before considering the slave issue, but Puerto Ricans felt differently.

After five and a half months of discussion, the Reform Commission adjourned with an agreement on a plan for emancipation.

The commissioners returned to a hostile island administration. Captain General Lersundi would have no part of the Commission's recommendations and, instead, levied additional taxes.

Finally, after years of pressure from abolitionists, Cuba conceded to a program in 1879 called "Patronato". a plan to gradually free slaves over an 8-year period. The 8-year provision was a form of payment to slave owners, which guaranteed them free labor for this period. The abolitionists did not like the law and it was not popular with the slave owners because it required them to feed, clothe and pay them wages. Gradually, they freed the slaves rather than to have to support them during the slack seasons.

By September 1886 only 26,000 of the 200,000 slaves in 1873 were still enslaved. On October 7, 1886, two years before the end of the Patronato, a royal decree ended slavery in Cuba.

POST-SLAVERY ERA
The period from 1902 to 1959 was racked with political and economic corruption including graft, malfeasance, lack of competent leadership and blatant neglect for the needs of the rural areas and Afro-Cubans. This extended down to the local areas where 20% of those running for office in 1922 had criminal records.

Havana became a recreational brothel for foreigners, offering open prostitution, gambling and accommodations in lavish hotels. Havana, and a few other major cities, had the most of everything. Only 6% of the homes in the rural areas had electricity in 1958, compared to 87% in the cities. Over one-half of the dentists, nurses and chemists lived in Havana, with 17% of the population. Havana boasted of one doctor for every 220 persons, but in rural areas the ratio was one doctor for every 2,243 persons. Havana suggested a picture of an affluent Cuba-- but this affluence was spread among a very few. Most of the populace were destitute. By 1959, 75% of the agricultural land was owned by large local or foreign corporations. For example, Julio Logo, the world's largest sugar vendor owned or controlled over 1,000,000 acres; the Cuban-American Sugar Company, 500,000 acres; and the Vertienties-Camaguey Company owned 800,000 acres.

There was glimmer of hope for reform in 1933, but Fulgencio Batista came to power in 1952 and became the most openly corrupt of all.

Then a little-known revolutionary named Fidel Castro, exiled to Mexico, returned to Cuba aboard the yacht, Granma with 80 sympathizers in 1956. A new era in Cuban history began.

He had written the following passage in his book, History Will Absolve Me in 1953:

"Cuba could easily provide for a population three times as great as it now has, so there is no excuse for the abject poverty of a single one of its present inhabitants. The markets should be overflowing with produce, pantries should be full, all hands should be working. This is not an inconceivable thought. What is inconceivable is that anyone should go to bed hungry, that children should die for lack of medical attention . . . What is inconceivable is that the majority of our rural people are now living in worse circumstances than were the Indians Columbus discovered in the fairest land that Human eyes had ever seen."

Source: Knight, The Caribbean. 2nd Edition, 1990, Pg. 227

Castro had made a revolutionary move in 1953 that was a bit premature, but a second effort succeeded in 1959, when Batista's government had degenerated into a state of total disarray. Castro gained control with an army of 803 men (he claimed an army of 500) and Batista fled Cuba to Florida with most of the country's treasury on January 1, 1959.

Cuba Under Castro

Castro, vehemently anti-American, immediately began to dismantle everything smacking of Capitalism. He started with agricultural reform by reducing land ownership to 995 acres by either company or individuals. Over the first 3 years he issued over 1500 decrees, completely restructuring Cuba's economic, political and social society.

Castro appropriated lands and plantations of foreign countries and issued 4-1/2% 20 year bonds payable in Cuban currency in payment, the amount paid being based on considerably low land value reassessments. The U.S., Cuba's major buyer of sugar, countered with import quotas and the impasse between the two countries began.

Castro began to woo the Soviet Union with agreements on supplying them sugar. This was followed by Cuba's move to refine the Soviet Union's oil at Cuba-based refineries. When Standard Oil, Texaco and Shell companies refused to refine the oil, Castro nationalized them. The U.S. countered with the ending of all imports of Cuban sugar. Furthermore, the U.S. was not sure whether Castro's wooing of the Soviets were just political maneuvering or some part of a blueprint culminating in a Communist takeover--something the U.S. would not allow in the Western Hemisphere.

The United States broke diplomatic relations with Cuba on January 1, 1961. The fiasco at the Bay of Pigs on April 17, 1961 caused Castro to announce he was a Markist-Leninist and that Cuba was to be a socialist state with no elections. He arrested and imprisoned over 100,000 persons suspected of being anti-state sympathizers. Many anti-Castroites fled to the United States, thus leaving Cuba without any opposition to Castro's rule.

The next Cuban-American crisis came in October 1962 when a U.S. U-2 aircraft spotted Soviet ballistic missiles being installed in Cuba, 90 miles from the Florida coast. Negotiations between the U.S. and the Soviet Union ended with the removal of the missiles.

Castro was outraged at the missile removal and began to woo China to replace the Soviet's economic help. The Soviets desired the location of a friend close to the U.S. and mended their rift with Castro, but the relations continued to be strained.

Cuba's trade partners changed dramatically between 1959 and 1978. In 1959 they carried on 98% of their trade with countries with "market economies", the U.S. being the largest with 67%. In 1978, trade dependency shifted to the Soviet bloc which accounted for 82% of Cuba's trade, 69% being with the Soviet Union. Between 1961 and 1979 the Soviets supplied $22 billion of military and economic aid to Cuba. In addition, the Soviets provided subsidies for Cuba's sugar and oil industries.

Meanwhile, several other Caribbean nations feeling their way through the uncertainties of gaining recent independence were leaning towards Socialism, but didn't find Castro's road, which required so much dependence on the Soviet Union, to be an acceptable one to follow.

As the years went by, significant improvements in education, employment, housing and income took place in Cuba, but the question remains as to whether this was the result of political or economic organization changes implemented by Castro, the continual financial support of the Soviets, or some combination of the two. By any standard and for whatever reason, conditions had certainly improved since the days of Batista and his forerunners.

Evidence does suggest that the good that did happen resulted from Soviet support and a momentary time of prosperity during the 1970's and that conditions began to worsen in the 1980's.

Jacobo Timerman, a noted Argentine journalist and radio and T-V news commentator and supporter of Castro's revolution made trip through Cuba in 1987. The jacket of his book <u>Cuba: A Journey</u> which describes his experiences reads in part:

"And everywhere he confronts unavoidable evidence of the abuse of human rights, the suffocation of civil society, the bankruptcy and hypocrisy of the Cuban political system, the inability of the government to organize an economy that can provide the people with basic necessities."

In 1987 Castro was quoted in <u>Cuba Socialista</u> in a speech to the Fifty-third Plenary National Congress of the Confederation of Cuban workers as saying, "We must correct the errors we made in correcting our errors."

Great House, Trinidad

Harvested Sugar Cane Field, St. Lucia

How The Islands Used To Look

CHAPTER 15

DOMINICA

SIZE
290 Square Miles

GEOGRAPHY
Mountains rising from the sea to nearly 5000'.
Forested, rugged terrain.

CLIMATE
Typical East-Caribbean climate with heavy rainfall at
higher altitudes.

CAPITAL
Roseau

AMERINDIANS

Historians assume that the Arawaks inhabited Dominica around
the birth of Christ because of the findings made on the nearby
islands of Guadeloupe and Martinque. Dominica has not
experienced many archaeological digs.

There is no mystery about the presence of Caribs. After
discovering and passing along Dominica's rugged windward coast
during his second voyage, Columbus landed on Marie Galante. He
sent a ship to the leeward side of Dominica to find a harbor. Upon
his return, the captain reported finding a suitable harbor, did not
land, but sighted people and huts on the beaches.

Columbus did land on Dominica on his fourth voyage but made
a hasty retreat when he found the Caribs to be hostile.

The Europeans made few attempts to settle Dominica until the
1700's. The Caribs heard of the literal extermination of the Arawaks
on Jamaica and the brutal treatment all Amerindians were receiving
at the hands of the Spanish throughout the Caribbean. The
Dominican Caribs vowed that they would not suffer the same fate.
Their commitment to freedom from oppression and the mountainous
nature of the island that gave them protection, enabled the Caribs to
survive the thrusts of persistent European invasions.

The Dominican Caribs remained a thorn in the British and French
sides long after the Amerindians on other Caribbean islands were no
longer considered to be a threat to European settlement plans.
Dominican Carib raids on Guadeloupe and Martinique became

common occurrences. When the English and French were at war, the Caribs would take sides, first with the English, then with the French--whoever wooed them most successfully.

In 1642, Father Breton took it upon himself to befriend the Dominican Caribs, learn their language and convert them to Catholicism. He did succeed in learning and recording the Carib language, but utterly failed to convert any to his faith.

A son, to be known as "Indian Warner", was born in 1630 to General Warner, the English Governor of St. Kitts. The mother, Warner's wife, was a full-blooded Carib. When General Warner died, Indian Warner's stepmother persecuted him and even though his stepbrother Phillip supported him, he was forced to flee to Dominica. There, he took refuge among his mother's people and learned to live in traditional Carib ways and became their chief.

Indian Warner remained in contact with the English and in 1664 led 600 Caribs in 17 canoes to assist the English in an attack on St. Lucia. This began a period of intrigue between Indian Warner, Phillip, the English and French during which the Europeans began to question the value of the Caribs as allies.

The Carib epoch of Dominica's control ended when Phillip threw a party for the Caribs and plied them with brandy. A drunken brawl ensued and Indian Warner was killed. The Caribs sought revenge, but the English attacked and burned their camp (now called the town of Massacre), destroyed their canoes and significantly reduced the Carib's fighting force.

The English punished Phillip for the traitorous act against his stepbrother by jailing him for 18 months in the Tower of London. They then returned him to Barbados for trial. The court acquitted him and in 1676 he became the Speaker of the Antiqua House of Assembly.

The Caribs continued to raid, with small parties, English and French properties and the Europeans caught the Caribs in battles between themselves. A 1686 treaty between England and France declared Dominica a "no man's land", but the Carib killing continued.

In 1647 the Dominica Carib population was estimated to be 5000. This number fell to 2000 by 1700, 500 in 1713 and 400 in 1730. A small settlement of Caribs, the last surviving Caribbean Amerindians, exists on a reserve on Dominica today.

DISCOVERY

The discovery of Dominica did not arouse much interest in Columbus. During his presentation of events and findings made on his second voyage to Queen Isabella he passed over Dominica quickly by using a crumpled sheet of paper (a method also used by other explorers to describe the topography of Caribbean islands) to describe Dominica's terrain.

The rugged terrain and the hostile Caribs caused the Europeans to avoid any serious settlement of Dominica for around 200 years after its discovery.

SPANISH QUEST FOR POWER AND GOLD

Dominica became a way station for Spanish treasure ships to stop and replenish their supply of wood and water on their return voyage to Seville, Spain.   The crew took great care to arm themselves against the Caribs while ashore.

The island was no haven for those who became shipwrecked. The Caribs would strip the ships of sails, nails, iron and wood. Seldom did any crew survive.

BUCCANEERS, PIRATES AND PRIVATEERS

Aside from Dominica being the site of an occasional pirate raid, Dominica did not play an important role in this era of Caribbean history.

EUROPEAN POWER STRUGGLE AND SETTLEMENTS

Spain never showed an interest in settling Dominica. In the early years, other European countries had more promising locations for settlements to scramble over than to fight a well-entrenched tribe of Indians in an almost impenetrable mountainous jungle.

Accounts of early English and French attempts to settle Dominica and the ensuing battles with the Caribs are found in the "Amerindians" section of this Chapter. When the threat of Carib attacks vanished, small groups of French lumbermen moved in and by 1727, 50 to 60 families occupied the island.

By 1745 Dominica had joined the sugar era, a few plantations were producing and the population had grown to over 3000.

Dominica got caught up in the Seven Years War (1756-1763). In 1761 English Prime Minister William Pitt ordered Lord Andrew Rollo and 2000 troops to capture Dominica. Rollo landed at 4:00 p.m. on June 6. A few moments later the surprised French garrison surrendered.

The 1763 Treaty of Paris granted Dominica, along with Tobago, St. Vincent, Grenada and the Grenadines to England.

British occupation after the Treaty of Paris was short-lived. France gave help to the Americans in their 1776 Revolution and this conflict provided France with the excuse to re-capture Dominica, which they did in 1778.

In 1782 the French assembled an invasion force in Martinique to attack Jamaica. Spies informed English Admiral Sir George Rodney when the French fleet left Martinique and Rodney, seizing a favorable wind advantage for his ships, engaged the French in battle. This defeat led to Dominica, now more of a strategic location between French-held Martinique and Guadeloupe, to be returned to England in the Treaty of Versailles in 1783.

Dominicans lived under fear of French invasions and Maroon attacks. The last French attack came during Napolean's rise to power in 1805 and the renewed French interest in gaining power in the West Indies. At dawn on February 20 the English sighted French warships flying the English Union Jack flag entering Roseau's harbor. An all-day battle ensued and a strong stand at Fort Shirley dashed all hopes of French success. This was to be the last French invasion attempt.

Dominica became an English Crown Colony in 1898. On November 3, 1967 Dominica became an independent English commonwealth state.

THE SUGAR ERA

Dominica entered the sugar era around the 1780's, considerably after most West Indies islands. Often, planters alternated sugar crops with coffee.

Dominica's climate and size did not offer the plantation owner desirable living conditions, so absentee ownership became the norm. Successful planters had sugar plantations on several islands and would employ attorneys to manage their interests onsite. Landowners never considered Dominica as a possible permanent residence so, as a result, Dominica cannot boast of elaborate "Great Houses." Those assigned to Dominica begged for re-assignment. One attorney included this passage in a report he sent to his superior: "When we look around and see the many drunken, ignorant, illiterate, dissolute, unprincipled Characters, to whom the charge of Property is confided--it is no wonder the Estate goes to ruin and destruction."

Toward the end of the 19th century only one sugar estate remained and its production did not provide enough product to even satisfy local needs.

The major reason for the decline of sugar was the introduction of Limes. Lime production started in the 1860's and by 1916 Dominica had become the largest Lime producer in the world. In later years,

Dominica's agricultural marketing problems have been partially solved by the Geest "banana boats" that provide regular shipping services to Britain. This has enabled the island to enter several commercial markets such as vanilla, citrus fruits, cocoa, coffee, coconuts and bay leaf.

SLAVERY AND SLAVE REVOLTS
By 1778 the population of Dominica included 1600 whites and 14,000 slaves. The whites invoked the same strict slave laws as those on other islands to reduce the threat of slave uprisings. While unrest and resentment existed among the Dominican slaves, they chose slowdowns and minor sabotage as ways to protest, instead of armed rebellion.

Dominica, like Jamaica, provided runaways with built-in hideaways in the form of densely forested mountains. This terrain attracted runaways from Martinique and Guadeloupe as well as Dominica. Each time the islands changed hands between England and France, starting in the 1760's, Dominica's "Maroon" colony's population grew in the period of confusion during the changeover.

By 1785 a number of organized Maroon camps, each with their own chief, were strung out in Dominica's mountains. Not only did these Maroon chiefs raid the estates, they sent recruiting agents to encourage estate slaves to join them.

The planters countered the Maroon's force by establishing a militia, financed by a special tax.

The militia located and attacked a major Maroon camp. Most of the men escaped to the cover of the forest. The militia took the women captive and questioned them about camp locations and numbers of Maroons in them. The women revealed enough information to enable the militia to successfully rout the Maroons from their camps and disrupt them as an effective fighting force.

The major Maroon threat ended and the planters relaxed some of the slave laws to reduce their temptation to escape.

New invasion threats came to Dominica during the French Revolution and Dominica found itself poorly manned for defense, so they formed the West Indian Regiment. This regiment consisted of all blacks, whether freed or not. They fought some battles quite heroically.   Unfortunately, the Dominican Governor, Cochrane Johnstone, treated them badly and after an incident involving the killing of some Regiment members, the Regiment disbanded themselves and became Maroons.

Maroon activity resumed around 1802 and an outright war broke out in 1812. The planters' fighting force now included some former

Maroons who were as familiar with the mountain area as the remaining Maroons. Their knowledge helped the militia to locate camps and kill the Maroon leaders. The last real Maroon battles took place around 1815. By this time England had banned further slave trading and, like it or not, the planters knew that the end of slavery was in sight.

At midnight on July 31, 1834 the 14,175 Dominican slaves became free.

POST-SLAVERY ERA

The usual English system of apprenticeship (advertised as a training program, but in reality just extended the slavery concept) lasted only a short time before it was scrapped in 1838.

The estate owners faced a severe labor shortage and tried in vain to attract indentured servants from India, Portugal and China. The locals preferred to work a small plot of their own and have the independence that went with it.

The last years of the 19th century found Dominica struggling with issues relating to political, religious and social bickering, lawsuits over land ownership and the imposing of a land tax which incited a riot in 1893.

A writer, Anthony Trollepe wrote, describing Dominica in those years, "It is impossible to conceive a more depressing sight. . . . Everything seems to speak of desolation, apathy and ruin."

The beginning of the 20th century found Dominica under the able leadership of Hasketh Bell. During his six-year term he built roads, telephone lines, acquired an Andrew Carnegie grant to build and stock a library, initiated electricity service, built a sawmill and produced a surplus in Dominica's treasury. Thoughts and plans for Dominican independence from Britain as a Crown Colony began in 1932 when Dominica invited 17 West Indian delegates to a conference to discuss a confederation. Lacking a suitable agreement, Dominica separated itself from this group in 1940.

Dominica actively supported the West Indian Federation in the 1950's. When Jamaica and Trinidad pulled out of this scheme, Dominica set about to work with some other islands in the Leeward and Windward group, the "Little Eight", to form a federation. This idea also failed because of the inability of leaders to reconcile their differences.

Unable to establish a federation, Dominica's leaders drew up a plan to become a self-governing state in association with Britain. Britain granted statehood to Dominica on November 6, 1967.

Lennox Honychurch, author of the book, "The Dominica Story" (from which most of the information for this Chapter was gathered) ends his book with the following lines: "This story of the politics and personalities which has brought us to the present day has created what we are. We now will have to create what we will be."

Your island contact:

Ms. Marie Jose Edwards, Director of Tourism
Dominica Division of Tourism
NDC, P. O. Box 73
Roseau, Commonwealth of Dominica
West Indies
Phone: (809) 448-2351
Fax: (809) 448-5840

Fort George, Grenada

Grenada Harbor, Grenada

CHAPTER 16

GRENADA

SIZE
133 square miles

GEOGRAPHY
Varied volcanic landscape with two lake craters,
gradually sloping hills, excellent bays and harbors
and numerous streams, waterfalls and fertile valleys.

CLIMATE
Danger from hurricanes from June to October. Tropical
humidity and temperatures with rainfall ranging between
60" to 200".

CAPITAL
St. George's

AMERINDIANS
The first English colonists found Arawak women serving as slaves for the island-dominating Caribs.   This evidence and discoveries of numerous Arawak pottery remains and artwork chiseled in rocks indicates that a large settlement of Arawaks once inhabited Grenada.

These findings also indicate that Grenada typified the Caribbean Amerindian migrations. The peaceful Arawaks settled the island first. The warlike Caribs arrived next and followed their policy of running off or killing Arawak men and enslaving their women.   The first English settlers who arrived in 1605 found the island well-inhabited by the Caribs. · Nevertheless, three shiploads of settlers from England headed for Trinidad dropped 200 would-be settlers off on Grenada. The Caribs resented these intruders and by open attacks and guerrilla warfare reduced the English settlement to shambles.   The few survivors fled to England when their ships returned from Trinidad.

The French governor of St. Kitts made an attempt to settle Grenada in 1638, but met the same fate as the English.

The first successful attempt to settle Grenada occurred in 1650 when the French governor of Martinique, posing as a visitor to the Caribs, arrived with cannon, militia, built a fort and started a tobacco plantation. Soon the Caribs, who welcomed these Frenchmen as "visitors", realized they had been duped--the French had really come to settle. The Caribs began to retaliate by ambushing Frenchmen at every opportunity.

The French tired of being cooped up in their fort, the only safe place on the island, so they asked for and received over 300 soldiers and prepared to attack the Caribs.

Meanwhile, the Caribs received reinforcements from St. Vincent and Dominica and made plans to attack the French fort, head on. The French learned of the Carib attack and carefully planned a counter-attack.

The Caribs started their assault and the French waited patiently until the Caribs came within a few yards of the fort. The French opened up with a volley of cannon and gunfire that caught the Caribs totally by surprise and they fled in total disarray.

The French then went on the offensive and chased the Caribs to the sea. Many died in their retreat, but some managed to escape in canoes and on logs.

The most tragic tale of this incident involved the fate of around 40 Caribs who fled to the northern part of the island. They found themselves trapped between the pursuing French and a 1000' cliff. The Caribs made their choice between capture and death. They covered their eyes and leaped.

The site became known as Leaper's Hill. Later, the Dominican Order of the Catholic church laid the foundation of a church there.

The Carib survivors of the ill-fated attack on the French and those on St. Vincent vowed that every white man in their islands must be killed. To this end, they re-established small villages on Grenada and began a series of raids.

The French responded in 1664 by conducting a comprehensive military sweep throughout the island, killing all Caribs in sight, burning their villages and destroying their canoes and boats to prevent their escape.

This military effort was so thorough that it exterminated all but a few Caribs who escaped to outlying areas. The Caribs no longer posed a threat to the settlers.

DISCOVERY

Columbus sighted Grenada in 1498 during his third voyage. There is no record of his setting foot on the island. Apparently, the island's location and other factors did not spark interest for further exploration, for while they claimed it as theirs, the Spanish never made an attempt to settle it.

SPANISH QUEST FOR POWER AND GOLD
It is possible the Spanish made some landings to secure Amerindians to work as slaves elsewhere and made some feeble attempts to find gold on Grenada. Beyond this, the island played no role in the Spanish quests for gold in Central and South America or fight for power in the region.

EUROPEAN POWER STRUGGLE AND SETTLEMENTS
After the aborted attempt by the English to settle Grenada in 1605, the French got their turn occupying the island for 113 years, 1650 to 1763. In 1763 the Treaty of Paris deeded Grenada to the English.

During their 113 year occupation the French Crown bought out the holdings of the French West India Company, who had been granted ownership of the island, and brought Grenada's administration under total management of the Crown. French colonial policy did not allow input or any control over island affairs by the colonists. This policy applied to all their colonies.

Tobacco and sugar contributed most to the island's economic welfare, and the Crown prospered, much to the distaste of the colonists, by invoking high taxes and employing a detachment of tax collectors to collect them.

By 1753 coffee and cocoa plantations became established, along with the procurement of slaves. By 1763 Grenada boasted 81 sugar and 205 coffee plantations.

The 1763 Treaty of Paris, which ceded Grenada to the English, brought dramatic changes to the island's administration.

The Treaty placed Grenada in a Federation that included the Grenadines, St. Vincent, Dominica and Tobago. All lands were declared Crown property and the Crown sent Commissioners to sell property in a public sale to British subjects only. This left the French the options of swearing allegiance to England and operating their estates on a 40-year lease or selling their property to British subjects.

Grenada prospered under British rule until 1779. During this period the island became England's fourth largest producer of sugar, behind Jamaica, Antigua and St. Kitts. Grenada also supplied 82% of English imports of coffee.

1779 found England at war with France over France's assistance to the colonists in North America in their fight for independence.

England had a fleet of warships based in St. Lucia and France had a fleet in port at Martinique. When the English fleet sailed off to St. Kitts to convoy some merchant ships, the French saw their opening and attacked St. Vincent and Grenada.

The outnumbered English militia offered little resistance to the French and capitulated on July 5, 1779. The French immediately set about to construct forts to make the island invincible.

The eighth article of the Treaty of Versailles signed in 1783 returned Grenada to English rule. A number of social unrest took place between the French and English colonists. The English voided all marriages performed in a Catholic church and required couples to remarry in the Anglican church. Election law reform virtually eliminated all French from holding office and denied Roman Catholics the right to vote. In general the English did all they could to harass the French through the Roman Catholic church.

Persecution and oppression eventually lead to rebellion. After 12 years of British rule the French and free blacks were ready for it. The last threat to English rule on Grenada came on March 2, 1795 when French Catholic, Julien Fedon, and 100 slaves razed the town of Grenville. Before long Fedon gathered support and on March 4 he issued a proclamation demanding the British to surrender to him. They refused, made a counter-demand for Fedon to surrender, and the rebellion developed into outright warfare lasting for 15 months. Thousands died, sugar estates and towns were burned and 3 years of crops destroyed. Finally the British received reinforcements and they crushed the insurgents.

British soldiers chased Fedon to the edge of a precipice. He jumped off into the sea, never to be seen or heard from again.

The English completed the forts started by the French and from that time forward Grenada has remained under British control. Grenada became an independent state in the English Commonwealth in 1974.

BUCCANEER, PIRATES AND PRIVATEERS
This is one era that Grenada apparently escaped. No reference to piracy acts were found in historical writings on Grenada.

THE SUGAR ERA
The English inherited the sugar and coffee plantation system from the French and invoked few changes.

The police system continued to maintain control of the status quo of plantation life to provide protection to the owners from slave revolts. The strict laws limiting every move of the slaves was continued and the very rigid social status structure, tied to racism, continued. The estate owners maintained total control over the judicial and political systems.

By 1824 Grenada counted 123 sugar, 22 coffee and cocoa and 163 lumber and pasture plantations. The Grenada sugar industry suffered their decline in the same manner as other West Indies islands. Starting with the abolition of slavery and ending with some 70 financial institutions supplying credit to the planters filing bankruptcy, the industry slowly decayed.

In an effort to salvage some sugar estates and prevent economic decline Britain enacted the Encumbered Estates Court Act in 1854. This forced the sale of highly indebted estates by near-bankrupt planters to well-financed merchants. This brought forth so many legal problems, the act was abolished in 1855.

Meanwhile, while sugar production declined, planters began to switch to cocoa. By 1878 there were 73 sugar estates and 103 cocoa estates. Cocoa replaced sugar as the main export in the later years of the 19th century and has continued as a major export to the present day.

Nutmeg and Other Spices

In the 1840's some Grenadian sugar planters went to the East Indies to help introduce sugar growing and manufacturing techniques. They brought back a plant called nutmeg.

Planters didn't take nutmeg production seriously until around 1860. Today, Grenada produces 1/3 of the world's supply and nutmeg is Grenada's number one export. One tree, producing 3000 to 4000 nuts a year can keep a Grenadian from starvation. Grenada, the "spice island" also produces cloves, black pepper, allspice, ginger roots, turmeric and bark from the cinnamon tree.

Bananas

The first serious commercial effort to grow bananas in Grenada came in 1934 when the Canadian Banana Company signed a contract to buy all Grenada's bananas.

The industry really became an economic boom in the 1950's. The government established the Grenada Co-operative Banana Society in 1954. All bananas headed for export had to be passed through the Society. The Society signed a contract with the Geest shipping lines to export bananas to England. In 1953 Grenada exported 49,863 stems. In 1958 they exported 948,000 stems--an increase of 2000%.   Today, the big three, cocoa, nutmeg and bananas have replaced sugar as the important agricultural exports.

SLAVERY AND SLAVE REVOLTS

Records of when and the number of slaves were imported to Grenada are sketchy, but no doubt the largest number of slaves arrived between 1735 and 1779 during the height of the sugar boom.

They exhibited the usual resistance practices such as slow-downs, burning buildings, killing animals and sabotaging machinery. The island topography provided some choice locations that could be used as hiding places; therefore, many slaves chose to escape the plantation shackles and become Maroons (the name given runaway slaves).   The Maroons carried out organized raids on the estates, seizing food and supplies and throwing fear of a major uprising into the hearts of the planters. In frustration, the British offered volunteers three times a militia man's pay to seek out Maroons, plus a bounty for each Maroon captured. The volunteers had some success, but most of the Maroons merely retreated farther into the remote regions of the island.   A good number of Maroons joined in the Fedon Rebellion. This is the only open Grenadian rebellion in which Maroons or slaves participated that was worthy of mention by historians.

The slavery era ended in the 1830's in Grenada as it did in other English colonies. Over 18,000 freed Grenadian slaves participated in the so-called Apprenticeship Program.

POST-SLAVERY ERA

Grenada made the transition from Apprenticeship to complete freedom peacefully but the legislature provided little help in the form of medical care, job training or education for the newly-emancipated. Some privately-owned "Alms Houses" opened, but many paupers wandered the streets of St. George and the countryside.

Aside from the paupers, four types of workers emerged:

1.   "Tenants-at-Will" continued to occupy the dwellings on the estates rent-free and in return agreed to provide continuous labor at a specific wage rate.

2. A "Peasant" society emerged. These persons bought, rented or leased small plots to farm on their own. They would work   part-time on the estates for extra money.

3. "Metayage", a system of share-cropping came into being around

1850 when planters found it difficult to pay wages. The planter supplied land, machinery, etc. and the share-cropper supplied the labor on a specific plot on the estate. After the harvest, the planter paid the share-cropper and agreed-upon price.

4. "Tradesmen" practiced such trades as carpentry, masonry, fishermen and blacksmiths. Women became domestics, washerwomen and seamstresses.

Child labor continued. The 1871 Census showed that 11,265 children were not in school. Between 1838 and 1890 over 6000 East Indians and Africans immigrated to Grenada as indentured servants. Most of the indentured stayed in Grenada or immigrated to other Caribbean islands at the end of their indenture.

The British Colonial Office faced a governmental problem in 1838. If they left the political organization as is, the planters and whites would become a white dictatorship. If they allowed the 500,000 emancipated a voice in government, there would be a black dictatorship.

Britain solved the problem by leaving it in the hands of a dictatorial English governor to solve. He solved the problem by allowing free elections for members of an Assembly. In order to vote, a person must be an adult male who owned a plantation or estate of a specified size and have a minimal yearly income. These qualifications, and a few others, limited the number of voters to 1% of the population which just happened to be a combination of white and black planter elite.

This governmental format didn't last long and in 1876 Grenada became an English Crown Colony. There was continual dissatisfaction with this form of government and in 1932 a movement began to demand self-government. Grenada achieved Associated Statehood with Great Britain on March 3, 1967. Grenada operated under this system until February 1974 when it became an independent country within the Commonwealth.

Enter Eric M. Gairy and GULP
"From the time I have come to Grenada and started the Trade Union movement and the political organization, people have tried to get rid of me, and I don't think they can make it. LOTS OF THEM WHO HAVE TRIED ARE LYING IN THE CEMETERY."
Prime Minister Eric Gairy at a press conference held on February 9, 1974 in Grenada. Source: DaBreo, D. Sinclair, The Prostitution of Democracy.

E. M. Gairy entered the political scene in 1951 as a strong advocate of worker's rights and social reform. The general population rejoiced over the emergence of a leader with charisma and ideals aimed at bettering their lot. But Gairy's real impact and true nature as a political leader began to unfold in 1967 when he won the election as Premier representing the Grenada United Labour Party (GULP).

Beginning in 1967, Gairy's sympathy for worker's rights drifted to sympathy for Gairy's rights. In his effort to make himself politically and financially prosperous, he implemented programs that made the populace dependent on government and crushed dissent by Parliament members–by 1979 Parliament had become his personal property.   He created a highly centralized bureaucracy that depended on his Cabinet (over which he had total control) to make all important decisions. He disregarded the Constitution when it came in conflict with his own interests, called in all the public's firearms to prevent armed rebellion, took governmental control of private estates (being careful not to pay his opponents for their land), and assumed control of all producer cooperatives.

Gairy carefully screened Public Service employees and when he found those in opposition to GULP and Gairy he had them transferred, demoted or discharged. Gairy gave concessions and monopolies to his supporters with the understanding that these would be withdrawn if their loyalties changed.

Enter the NJM

Gairy began his political suicide when his militia beat up six members of the New JEWEL (Joint Endeavors for Welfare, Education and Liberation) Movement, known as the NJM in 1973. The NJM had replaced the original JEWELL movement by merging several political organizations.

This act of brutality was the "straw that broke the camel's back" for the 15-30 year old set who did not know the Gairy of old who had won the hearts of their fathers by initiating efforts to benefit the working class. They only knew the brutality and corruption they saw in the '70's.

Gairy continued to harass, beat and even kill NJM members individually and in meetings. On November 4, 1973 over 8000 Grenadians gathered and the NJM presented a document, known as the "People's Indictment" stating 27 reasons why Gairy must go. Gairy responded with 54 reasons why the NJM must go and intensified his beatings of NJM members.

Gairy's most expensive error occurred on November 18, 1973, known as "Bloody Sunday." His militia brutalized several NJM members during one of their meetings and this action resulted in a general strike. Grenada experienced continual conflict between Gairy and the NJM until November, 1979, while Gairy was addressing the UN about UFO's (Unidentified Flying Objects) from outer space. The NJM took the government over by force in his absence.

Enter Maurice Bishop and the PRG

In 1976 the leadership of the NJM came under Maurice Bishop, a tall, radiant and mesmerizing orator and his sidekick, Bernard Coard, a student of economics and financial affairs. Both Bishop and Coard embraced the concepts of Marxist Communism and worshiped Lenin. The first thing Bishop and Coard did after the NJM took control in 1979 was to abolish Gairy's 1973 constitution and establish a new government order, the People's Revolutionary Government (PRG). The PRG immediately abolished all laws and replaced them with "People's Laws" signed by Bishop. Bishop's goal was to fashion a government to operate in the Soviet-style of Communism. He began by nationalizing the electric and telephone companies, banks, some hotels and large estates.

Cuba and the Soviets encouraged Bishop with large grants of money and technical support. Between 1979 and 1983 Grenada, with its 100,000 inhabitants, received $126 million for a laundry-list of projects and became the fifth largest receiver of foreign aid in the world.

The construction of a 10,000 foot-long airport at Point Salines received millions of dollars and hundreds of workers from Cuba. It became an international issue when Bishop refused to rule out the possibility of the airstrip being used by Cuban and Soviet military.

The PRG spent all the foreign aid money and borrowed lavishly. Mismanagement and the decline of private enterprise, foreign investment and tourism moved Grenada to the verge of bankruptcy. Coard retired from both political parties in 1982, leaving Bishop solely in charge. The Central Committee decided that Bishop did not have the financial administrative skills to get Grenada out of its economic quagmire, so it proposed a joint leadership between Bishop and Coard. Bishop agreed, but changed his mind after a trip abroad.

The Central Committee and Politburo did not go along with Bishop's decision and placed him under house arrest on October 13. The following day they announced his dismissal as Prime Minister.

3000 of Bishop's followers marched up the hill from market square to Bishop's house and freed him. Bishop then led his supporters to PRG headquarters at Fort Rupert and captured it.

The Central Committee refused to negotiate with Bishop and instead, sent armored personnel carriers to retake the fort. They succeeded.

Maurice Bishop died in front of a firing squad on October 13, 1983 by order of the Central Committee. General Hudson Austin announced that the Revolutionary Military Council would rule Grenada.   These actions, especially Bishop's murder, were widely condemned, even by strong PRG supporters.

Operation Open Fury

It has been called an invasion, intervention and a military exercise, but "stabilization" might be the best term to describe the action President Reagan directed the U.S. Marines to undertake in Grenada on October 25, 1983.

Several conditions sparked the decision for action. After the Revolution Military Council (PMC) had taken control of the island upon Bishop's assassination, general chaos existed in the streets. U.S. leaders became concerned about the safety of the 1000 plus U.S. medical students attending St. George Medical School. There was a rising concern about the potential military use of the Cuban-built Point Salines airport and Grenada becoming a missile base.

A request for U.S. assistance by the OCS (Organization of Caribbean States) left the U.S. with little alternative. It stated in part:

". . . the current anarchic conditions, the serious
violation of human rights and bloodshed, and the consequent
unprecedented threat to the peace and security of the
region by the vacuum of authority in Grenada."

About midnight on October 20, 1983 an amphibious task force headed by Captain Carl R. Erie, USN, bound for the Mediterranean, received orders to turn south and take a station about 500 miles north of Grenada. No reason was given.

None of Erie's ships possessed maps of Grenada. One ship had nautical maps drawn in 1936. One officer, an amateur yachtsman, had sailed Grenadian waters in 1977 and taken notes on some coastal configurations. Lieutenant Colonel Smith had recently attended an Armed Services college and written a term paper on a hypothetical invasion of Grenada. These were the only resources available at the time for Erie to plan an assault, if directed.

The naval commanders believed their being stationed 500 miles north of Grenada was to be a warning to Grenadian leaders and to stand by in the event the evacuation of U.S. citizens became necessary. An officer wrote in his journal, "It is doubtful that we'll be called upon to carry out the mission." Plans for an "evacuation in a hostile environment" began.

On October 22 Erie received orders to sail towards Grenada. Estimates of the Grenadian fighting force numbered 1200 PRG members backed by 2000 to 5000 militia and 500 armed police. Post-landing documents revealed a force of only 500-600 PRG and 2000 to 2500 militia.

Around 11:00 p.m. on October 23, Colonel Smith announced, "It's on!" A contingent of intelligence officers had been flown in by helicopter from Antigua that night with orders to assault the island. Admiral Metcalf designated October 25 as D-Day.

At 2:00 a.m. on October 25 navy SEALS (sea-air-land), the navy's unconventional task force, landed and reported the beach near the Pearls Airport to be "Walking Track Shoes"--meaning, a marginal landing area. Erie decided the initial landing would be entirely by helicopter.

The night before the assault, the Marines aboard the aircraft carrier Guam were shown the movie, "The Sands of Iwo Jima" starring John Wayne.

Few of the helicopter pilots and none of the crew chiefs had battle experience, but a good number of senior noncommissioned officers had served in Vietnam. The officer in charge parceled out the experienced men so each helicopter had one to help the inexperienced through the early battle jitters.

Twenty-one helicopters took off in total darkness at 3:15 a.m. for the landing zone "LP Buzzard", just south of Pearls airfield.   The force came under erratic and inaccurate antiaircraft fire, but Cobra 20 mm cannon and 2.75 mm rockets quickly silenced them. Another landing near Grenville met with little resistance and shortly the Marines had Pearles and Grenville under their control.

The locals waved at the pilots as they approached their landing area and welcomed them as liberators. Local citizens voluntarily pointed out PRG members who had changed into civilian clothes and led the Marines to caches of PRG arms and ammunition. The Marines received this kind of welcome throughout the island during the mission.

The Marines gained complete control of Grenada on D-Day plus 3 and the entire fighting force was back on the carrier Guam on October 31.

The Command received word that many of the PRG and their supporters had fled to Curacao and on November 1 Marines landed there to find even more local support than they received on Grenada.   They found large stores of military supplies, but encountered no resistance.   PRG members, dressed in civilian clothes, surrendered voluntarily.

By late afternoon on November 2 the task force resumed its interrupted journey to the Mediterranean.

A thorough documentation of the   military stabilization of Grenada can be found in the publication: <u>U.S. Marines in Grenada, 1983</u> by Lieutenant Colonel Ronald Spector, published by the History and Museums Division, Headquarters, U.S. Marine Corps, Washington D.C., 1987. This document was used extensively in the preparation of this book's presentation of Operation Open Fury.

<u>Post Operation Fury</u>

The rigid economic restraints imposed by the PRG have been relaxed and many state owned enterprises are now in private enterprise hands.   The Cuban-built Point Salines Airport now welcomes tourists, now a major industry. Roads, telephone service and health care facilities are improving.

Hopefully the days of Grenada being known as the "Island of Conflict" are over.

Your island contact:

Mr. G.R.E. Bullen
Director of Tourism
The Grenada Board of Tourism
P. O. Box 293
St. George's, Grenada, W.I.
or
Ms. Regina Henry
Trombone Associates, N.Y.
Phone: (212) 223-2323
Fax: (212) 223-0260

CHAPTER 17

HISPANIOLA

(Dominican Republic & Haiti)

SIZE
Haiti: 10,715 sq. miles
Dominican Republic: 18,816 sq. miles

GEOGRAPHY
Haiti: Mountains and valleys--like a crumpled sheet of paper.
Dominican Republic: About 25% fertile valleys, 25% pasture
and 50% forests. 75% is mountainous up to 10,400'.

CLIMATE
Haiti: Temperatures range from a very hot and humid
82 degrees in the valleys to pleasantly cool temperatures in
the mountains. Hurricanes are rare before August.
Dominican Republic: Temperature around 78 degrees in lowlands, with frost above 3600'. Little change during
the year.

CAPITALS
Haiti: Port-au-Prince
Dominican Republic: Santo Domingo

INTRODUCTION
It is best to begin this Chapter by untangling the name changes
this island went through to get to what we call today the Dominican
Republic and Haiti.

Columbus first named the island Espanola. In the 17th century
the Spanish began to refer to it as Hispaniola. Later, after the
establishment of the city of Santo Domingo, the Spanish referred to
the island as Santo Domingo, following their practice of naming
islands after their major cities.

In 1659 the French assumed arbitrary control over the western
half of Hispaniola and it gradually became known as St. Dominique.
The Treaty of Ryswyck, signed by Spain in 1697, officially awarded
St. Dominique to the French. In 1805 Jean-Jacques Dessalines

defeated Napoleon's armies in St. Dominique and proclaimed himself the emperor of the new republic of Haiti. The Arawaks originally named the island Haiti which meant "high ground."

Spain lost interest in Santo Domingo because of the mortality rate due to Yellow Fever and the colony's high maintenance costs. Santo Domingo declared itself independent from Spain in 1821 and named itself the Dominican Republic. Haiti gained control in 1822 and held it until 1844 when, after continual squabbling, the Dominican Republic regained its independence. Efforts to annex the Dominican Republic to the United States failed in 1865. The name Hispaniola will be used until the time the French began to settle the western half of the island. From that time forward the island will be referred to as Haiti and the Dominican Republic, to avoid confusion.

AMERINDIANS

There is only disputed evidence that a small Ciboney settlement once existed on the southwestern shore of Haiti.

The population of Arawaks inhabiting Hispaniola at the time of discovery is also under dispute. The estimates range from 1 to 3 million. It is agreed that 25 years after discovery only a handful of Arawaks had survived European disease and starvation caused by over consumption of the food supply brought to bear by new Spanish mouths to feed, (the Arawaks only planted what they needed from year to year and made no attempt to store a surplus).

Columbus found the island divided into 5 kingdoms ruled by strong-willed caciques (chiefs). One search party reported finding an Arawak village with over 1000 huts. He found them lazy, dancing, smoking and drinking until they dropped and then sleeping. A stone axe and pointed stick comprised their tool kit.

A search party encountered some Indians on the northeastern coast of the Dominican Republic who talked a different language and painted their bodies with a black substance. When asked if they were Caribs, they pointed to the East. The Arawaks had complete control of Hispaniola.

DISCOVERY

Columbus first landed at the bay of St. Nicholas on December 4, 1492 on his first voyage. He made his second landing at Concepcion where a lone female Arawak met him on the beach. Here he erected a cross and claimed the island in the name of the King of Spain. The Arawaks gave Columbus a cordial greeting. They exchanged gifts, Columbus being most interested in any artwork set with gold.

The Santa Maria had only one apprentice seaman on watch the night of January 8 who carelessly allowed the ship to be grounded on a reef. They could not refloat the Santa Maria so the crew, with the help of the Arawaks, moved everything to the shore, dismantled the ship and built a small fort with the lumber.   Columbus became anxious to return to Spain and announce the news of his discoveries. On January 4, 1493 he departed, leaving a small party with a year's provisions at a settlement he named La Navidad.   Upon his return, he found La Navidad in ruins, established the town of Isabella, near a mosquito-infested swamp, which he soon abandoned for the harbor of Santo Domingo.

Details of this return to Hispaniola and La Navidad on his second voyage are also given in the description of Columbus' second voyage in Chapter 3.

Columbus returned to Santo Domingo after a two year's absence. He had left his inept brother, Bartholomew, in charge of building Santo Domingo and to explore the Jania River for gold.

Details of the Columbus brothers' administrative disaster at Santo Domingo are given in the description of Columbus' third voyage in Chapter 3.

SPANISH QUEST FOR POWER AND GOLD

Bartholomew Columbus directed the beginnings of the first construction of the great city of Santo Domingo, today the capital of the Dominican Republic, on August 4, 1496.

Upon his return to Hispaniola from Spain in 1498, Columbus found Santo Domingo to be a growing city, some gold being mined, unrest among the highly-taxed settlers and outright war with the Arawaks.

Impatient with the colony's administrative failures as reported by Columbus' mutinous mayor, Roldan, Queen Isabella sent Francisco de Bobadilla to "investigate" conditions on Hispaniola. He arrived in 1500 and immediately exceeded his authority by taking total command which included throwing Columbus in prison and then sending him back to Spain in chains.

When news of Bobadilla's actions reached the Queen she replaced him with Nicholas de Ovando on April 15, 1502, and made him governor of the island and all of the Indies.

Ovando pursued the Arawaks with his superior military might and soon brought the entire island under Spanish control. The Spanish experienced a short period of luxury while they swung from hammocks supervising the Arawaks who performed laborious tasks in the mines and fields. Columbus returned to Spain after his 4th and last voyage and Queen Isabella died the same year. Out of respect for the Queen, King Ferdinand ordered Ovando to free all Arawaks. Ovando ignored this royal order because it would upset the economy, so enslavement continued.

Sugar cane came on the scene in 1506. The Spanish increased the workload of the Arawaks so severely that suicide became commonplace and the disappearance of their workforce became evident.   Ovando secured some Amerindian labor from the Bahamas, but the number did not meet the need.

King Ferdinand became disenchanted with Ovando and in 1506 replaced him with Don Diego Columbus, Christopher's son. Oppression of the Arawaks continued and in 1508 their number had diminished to 14,000. The African slave trade began in 1510. In 1533 the Spanish made a peace treaty with the remaining 600 Arawaks and set aside a parcel of land for them to cultivate.

EUROPEAN POWER STRUGGLE AND SETTLEMENTS

The time is now approaching to begin to divide the island's history into that of the Dominican Republic and Haiti.   Santo Domingo grew to be a beautiful city financed by sugar crops and gold mining profits. Undisturbed by the Spanish, huge herds of wild cattle developed on the savannas of Hispaniola. Hispaniola reached its zenith in the mid-1500's and thereafter began a dismal decline.

One major cause of decline, over-governing, began with the establishment of a council in Spain which wrote a code of laws titled: "The Collection of the Laws of the Kingdoms of the Indies." It loosely delegated duties to a variety of government officials who felt the need to show their importance through public display of pomp and circumstance in the streets and halls of the courts. Internal bickering and conflict led to inefficient and ineffective administration. Much to the dismay of the colonists, the King levied an across-the-board 10% tax on everything from milk to sugar. Government officials, in their effort to promote their importance, deeded themselves large tracts of land, which went uncultivated, providing no income. The Church also received large tracts of land and leased out small plots to persons too poor to buy their own. Taxes extracted from these plots provided a major source of income for the Church, but often the lessors could ill afford to pay.

The Inquisition imposed additional hardships on the settlers in 1524. The inquisitors confiscated property, banned the sale of books and greatly discouraged settlement by Jews and citizens of any country other than Spain. They enforced the Crown's policy of imposing heavy duties on all goods going into or coming from Hispaniola.

After the conquest of Jamaica, Cuba, Peru and Mexico the treasure fleets abandoned the harbor of Santo Domingo and made Havana their major port on their way to Seville.

The blow that virtually depopulated the island was the discovery of gold and silver in Mexico and Peru. Young adventurers who came to Hispaniola for riches and found themselves barely able to survive, became lured to new lands holding more promise for wealth.

As a part of Cromwell's "Western Design", Admiral Penn led an English attempt in 1655 to invade Hispaniola by capturing the decaying city of Santo Domingo. It met with defeat. A failed night invasion occurred when the English abandoned the attempt when they heard what they thought to be the sound of oncoming Spanish calvary. What they really heard was the clatter of land crabs scrambling over leaves to escape to their dens upon hearing approaching footsteps.

Admiral Penn and his partner, General Venerables left Hispaniola in disgrace, but went on to successfully take Jamaica.

THE MOLD OF HAITI BEGINS

The settlement of the western part of Hispaniola, Haiti, came about as a result of a series of historical incidents.

The English and French became interested in the Indies and both occupied St. Kitts in 1628. Some English and French survivors of a Spanish attack on St. Kitts found their way to Tortuga, an island off the north coast of Haiti. Control of Tortuga changed hands several times between the French, English and Spanish, with the French finally becoming dominant in the 1660's.

The French settled Tortuga in earnest. In 1665 Governor D'Ogeron arranged to transport a number of women, described as the dregs of Paris' "ladies of the night", to engage in marriage with his lot of rough, tough and uncouth buccaneers.

Hazard's book, "Santo Domingo, Past and Present", published in 1873 quotes the courtship/marriage vows. They read in part:

"I take thee without knowing, or caring to know, who thou art. If anybody from whence thou comest would have had thee, thou wouldst not have come in quest of me. But no matter . . . Give me only thy word for the future; I acquit thee of the past."

The gallant suitor would then place his hand on the barrel of his gun and add: "This will revenge me of thy breach of faith; if thou shouldst prove false, this will surely be true to my aim."

While this ceremony lacked even a small degree of romance, it did the job; thereafter, the increased population and agricultural potential caused France to give Tortuga and "Haiti" increased attention.

The permanent separation of Haiti from Hispaniola came about through the Treaty of Ryswyck in 1697. Spain conceded the western part of the island to France.   Haiti (St. Dominique) prospered under French control for the next 92 years. Santo Domingo began to decay.   And it is here where we separate the historical dramas of these two nations.

HAITI

"Damn sugar! Damn coffee! Damn colonies!"
Napoleon Bonaparte, 1803

BUCCANEERS, PIRATES AND PRIVATEERS
Haiti and Tortuga were the birthplace of the Buccaneer. Haiti's role in Buccaneering is detailed in Chapter 6.

THE SUGAR ERA
French agricultural efforts began with the cultivation of indigo (a plant native to India providing a blue dye). The indigo success led to experimentation with sugar, coffee and cocoa. Haiti's fertile soil and ideal climate brought success in all these ventures.

The use of slaves began in 1720 when the French government granted the West India Company a contract to bring 3000 African slaves to Haiti each year.   Haiti's growth in sugar production from 1720 to 1791 was nothing short of astronomical. Haiti supported 600 sugar plantations by 1754.

The following table compares sugar production and slave population in Haiti and some other major sugar producers.

Island	Year	Sugar in Tons	Slave Population
HAITI	1720	10,500	---
	1791	78,696	480,000
BARBADOS	1792	9,025	64,300
JAMAICA	1789	59,400	250,000
GUADELOUPE	1790	8,725	85,500
CUBA	1792	18,571	85,900
ST. CROIX	1786	12,100	2,850

Source: F. W. KNIGHT, The Caribbean, Page 365.

The French planters dealt with their sudden accumulation of wealth in the same manner as planters on other islands. They built some of the most luxurious mansions in the world and spent half their time parading their wealth in their home city, Paris. Absentee ownership became a common practice.

When news of the gross mistreatment of the slaves reached Paris, a faction developed that promoted slave rights and even the suggestion that they be freed.

A series of tragic revolts began in 1791 which had a significant impact on the sugar and coffee plantations.

The revolutionaries devastated the plantations, killed the proprietors, and left the country in economic ruin.

When Toussaint L'Ouverture came into power in 1793 he brought peace to Haiti and invited the plantation masters to return. The former slaves worked for pay and for a while the plantations flourished.

In 1801 the French re-conquered Haiti with the intention of re-introducing slavery and sent Toussaint into exile. The occupation lasted until 1804 when Dessalines, Toussaint's second in command, malaria and yellow fever succeeded in routing the French troops.

In 1820 the Haitian government established the policy of dividing the great estates into small peasant plots. Sugar production, which had been 78,696 tons in 1791, dwindled to 800 tons by 1836.

Haiti's great plantations collapsed into a collection of subsistence truck gardens. Schoelcher wrote in 1841, "The fields of Haiti are dead. Cactus covers with its spines the cane fields deserted by the hand of man; it invades the towns, flourishing amid the ruins."

SLAVERY AND SLAVE REVOLTS

Haiti was the stage for a series of revolts that revealed to the world atrocities and cruelties performed on slaves that were so terrible they were almost beyond belief. At the outbreak of the French Revolution in 1789, the Haitian whites wasted no time in forming an Assembly to work for independence. They excluded mulattos and slaves. When a mulatto submitted a petition to include mulattos he was publicly executed in front of the entire Assembly.

The Crown reacted to the establishment of this colonial Assembly by seating their own Governor and commissioners along with a new constitution. This new constitution did not include the recognition of mulattos as active citizens.

Open warfare took place between supporters of the Colonial Assembly and the French Assembly. Both the mulattos and slaves engaged in minor rebellions against the Colonial rebels, seeing their only chance in the long run to be with the French loyalists.

During all this internal upheaval, England, France and Spain decided to invade Haiti. Napoleon's losses in Haiti exceeded those at Waterloo. The revolutions reduced Haiti's population by 50%.

In 1792 a French Royal Crown decree gave political freedom to all free people, regardless of race. Slavery remained.   The rich colonists had been eyeing and envying the freedoms the United States citizens had been enjoying since their succession from England. Many had rejoiced at the advent of the French Revolution, seeing their opportunity to break away from the Crown.   Mulattos and freed colored, while permitted to own property and employ slaves, had not been allowed to enter the political arena in spite of royal decrees. They, too, saw a chance for political representation at the onset of the French Revolution.   Neither the whites, freed colored or mulattos considered any change in the slaves' status.

This decree dashed all the slaves' hopes for any improvement in their status. It sparked a series of slave uprisings led by a creole slave, Toussaint L'Ouverture, of a magnitude never before seen at any time in the history of the world. When the revolts ended, virtually all whites in Haiti were exterminated.   These revolts struck terror in the hearts of plantation owners in the entire Caribbean and provided ammunition for those promoting legislation to abolish slavery.   Slavery ended in Haiti in 1794 when Toussaint began his reign.

POST-SLAVERY ERA

The last major European influence in Haiti ended in 1804. Jean-Jacques Dessalines, one of Toussaint's lieutenants, routed the French troops and killed all the French men, women and children. On April 22, 1804 there were no French left in Haiti. Dessaline exalted, "If I die at this moment I will go to my grave happy. We have avenged our brothers."

Haiti had gained its independence, but in the process killed off all who had a talent for governmental administration and alienated the rest of the world with their brutality.

Some preposterous leaders emerged. In 1849 Soulouque was proclaimed Emperor, the result of a supposed dictate by the Virgin Mary who made an appearance to him from atop a palm tree. After being crowned with a crown made from cardboard, he immediately installed a batch of 400 titled persons including 4 Princes, 59 Dukes, 2 Marquises, 90 Counts, 215 Barons and 30 Chevaliers.

In 1859 President Geffard started his term with a 2 million gourde deficit. The debt quadrupled by 1865. His solution was to print sheaths of paper money. In 1866 Haiti was broke. Pastor Bird accused Geffard of ruling the country for personal gain, being master rather than servant of the people.

Between 1843 and 1915, Nissage-Saget was the only ruler of 22 in Haiti to leave office alive at the end of his term. Four died in office. One was blown up in his palace. One had been overthrown and executed. One had been torn to pieces by his subjects. Thirteen had been ousted early by coup or revolution.

The United States sent warships to Haitian waters 28 times between 1849 and 1915 to protect American citizens and property. The U.S. Marines landed in July, 1915. The U.S. Assistant Secretary of State declared Haiti to be "a public nuisance on our doorstep."

Francois Duvalier (Papa Doc), physician and voodoo folklorist, came on the political scene in 1956. After he won the election in 1957 and gained the support of the military, he assumed the role of a dictator, declaring himself president for life. He perfected terror and bribery, always forgot his friends, but never forgot his enemies. He established the secret police, the Tonton Macoutes, who spied on and terrorized the cities. In his lust for power he closed the labor unions, press and boy scouts. He expelled white Catholic priests and compelled the Pope to appoint 5 Haitian priests he selected.

Papa Doc died in April, 1971. Before his death he appointed his 19 year-old playboy son, Jean-Claude (Baby Doc) to succeed him to be President for life. In 1980 Baby Doc married the arrogant and greedy light-skinned Michele Bennett. During a severe food shortage in 1985 Michele went on a $1.7 million shopping spree in Paris. Baby Doc lost support from the U.S. and massive Haitian demonstrations forced him and his wife to flee to France on February 7, 1986. In 1989 Haiti remained the poorest country in the Western Hemisphere with a yearly per capita income of $400, a 40% unemployment rate and only a 20% literacy rate.

Jean-Bertrand Aristide, a former Catholic priest, won election by a wide margin in the December 1990 election--said to be the most honest election in Haitian history. His reign lasted less than 8 months. He had support from the rural populace, but did not win the majority in the National Assembly or achieve the support of the army.

Aristide left Haiti in September 1991 to address the United Nations. In his absence the army subdued his personal security force. Upon his return he found the military in control and took the path of exile in October 1991.

Lieutenant General Raoul Cedras became Haiti's military dictator. His rule followed the stereotype of military dictators and his oppressive policies led to a mass exodus of Haitians by anything that would float to the coast of Florida in 1994.

Once again the U.S. saw it proper to intervene in Caribbean politics and President Clinton assembled a fleet of warships and 20,000 men in preparation for an invasion of Haiti. He issued an edict to Cedras that he should leave Haiti on October 15, 1994.

Cedras seemed to be making no move to leave so, in a last moment move, Clinton sent a negotiation team headed by former President, Jimmy Carter and including General Colin Powell, former chairman of the Joint Chiefs of Staff and Senate Armed Services Committee Chairman Sam Nunn to talk with Cedras. The team left no doubt about the consequences of a Cedras decision to remain.

Cedras left Haiti unceremoniously and Aristide returned to what might be described as an economic "basket case"--the poorest country in the Western Hemisphere.

VOODOO

No writing that discusses Haitian history would be responsible if it ignored the mention of Voodoo. The subject is, to say the least, complex and mysterious.   Voodoo is a melding of Catholicism and African beliefs which came mostly from the Dahomey region on the west coast of Africa. It evolved over decades after the revolts that began in Haiti in the 1790's.

Followers believe that there is a God, but God is too busy to help each person through the trials and tribulations of life; therefore, He works through an army of lesser cabinet gods called, "loas." Loas, which would take over 100 pages to catalog, are believed to have power over the forces of nature, health, wealth and happiness of all mortals. Loas are classified into two families, good (Rada) and bad (Petro). The price paid for the services of a Petro loas are high. A Voodoo follower will enlist the services of a Rada to derive protection or relief from the evils cast on him/her by a Petro.

The houngan (Voodoo priest) and mambo (priestess) have the power to be the contact person between his/her societe (following) and the appropriate loas. They hold special ceremonies in their own houmfort (cult center).

The followers of Voodoo in Haiti are found mostly among the poor, illiterate peasants who pay a price for the services of the hougan or mambo to give assurance or to tend to their sickly loved ones--there are few organized medical services in Haiti.

Voodoo also provides its followers with entertainment, displayed during ceremonies by accomplished drummers and dancers, moral guidance and a temporary escape from reality, which in Haiti is all too sordid.

Rituals (ceremonies) that involve initiation to the cult or those tainted with black magic are held in secret; otherwise, the rituals are held in public. Observers are welcome to watch and for a few gourde (worth $0.20 in the 1950's) a loas will be called on to give the donator a favor.

A houngan or mambo may perform the ritual. While they are allowed a fair amount of originality in conducting a ritual, they must keep within the theme and see that certain traditions are followed. For example, Metraux writes in his book, "Voodoo in Haiti":

"How, for instance. does a hunsi (assistant mambo) greet a mambo? Facing her squarely, she will turn first to the right, then to the left and then again to the right. After each turn she will drop a deferential curtsy bending her knees and leaning slightly backwards. She will then prostrate herself before the mambo and kiss the ground three times." The mambo replies with a similar sequence of salutations.

Sacrifice is a part of the ritual because it is believed that the loas needs to be fed. Chickens, pigs, bulls, snakes, turkeys and goats are carefully selected for proper color and prepared especially to appeal to a particular loas.   The procedure for sacrifice is meticulous. Only a few remote cases of human sacrifices have been recorded.

Black magic spells are initiated by "bad" Petro loas or by one voodooist wishing to impose evil upon another. Included in the Black magic repertoire are "expeditions of the dead" into a living body, "possession", the walking dead (Zombies), and evil spells cast on a person by sticking pins into a doll stuffed with the victim's hair or nail parings.

Observers/historians have witnessed persons in convulsions approaching death because their body had supposedly been entered by spirits from graves with the intent to kill and seen Zombies, the dead who have supposedly left their graves and wander about aimlessly or work on farms in a state of stupor.   They have witnessed ceremonies where followers enter a state said to be "possessed."

These historians/observers believe that the houngans and mambos are masters of the art of administrating drugs to produce a particular desired effect or state such as that seen in Zombies. They believe that it is quite possible that the pre-ceremony practice of dancing and chanting for hours is enough to exhaust anyone, particularly the undernourished voodooist, putting him/her into a state of exhaustion; therefore, their stupor gives the appearance of them being "possessed."

Both the Voodooist and historian each have their explanations for these most unusual events. It will be left to the reader to research Voodoo in depth, if desired, and come to his/her own conclusions.

DOMINICAN REPUBLIC

BUCCANEERS, PIRATES AND PRIVATEERS

Santo Domingo city fell to the infamous pirate, Sir Francis Drake in 1586. The Spanish rejoiced when Drake's 18-ship force sailed by the city on January 10, but dismayed when they learned he had landed at the mouth of the Jaina River and was marching on Santo Domingo.

Drake captured and held the city for 25 days while he negotiated a ransom. Each day the ransom went unpaid he burned buildings. By the time the residents paid a $30,000 ransom, Drake had burned one-third of the city. The Spanish went on to complete Santo Domingo city's fortifications which discouraged Buccaneers and repelled invaders. Seventy years later William Penn and his 9000 men attacked Santo Domingo city and experienced a disastrous defeat. He then headed for Jamaica where he met with success.

In the early 1600's the Spanish adopted a policy that attempted to close commerce in the Caribbean to all nations and limit new-world trade to the single Spanish port of Seville. This policy sparked brisk contraband and privateering operations by the Dutch, English and French and contributed much to the increased activity of the Buccaneers.

To counteract the contraband and privateering, the Spanish closed down and destroyed all the port cities on Santo Domingo's north coast. This left the country of Santo Domingo devoid of any meaningful trade relations.

THE SUGAR ERA

When Haiti began its prosperity period after the Treaty of Ryswick in 1697, Santo Domingo experienced decline for three reasons:

1. Spain eliminated trade by closing all ports on the north coast.

2. There was a mass exodus to Mexico and South America by those who came to the Indies to seek fortunes.

3. In those years Spain directed their interest to Mexico and South America in a quest for gold and silver. Santa Domingo's gold deposits had played out.
   While some did engage in producing sugar, the supply barely met local needs. Cattle ranching became the main support for the economy. The Santo Domingo people climaxed a series of revolutions against Spain in 1861 and established themselves as the independent nation of the Dominican Republic. The sugar industry in the Dominican Republic did not participate in the Caribbean sugar boom until 1875. Wealthy Cuban emigrants began arriving with funds, the desire and a knowledge of modern sugar-growing and milling methods. The price for the land offered the Cubans seemed like a fortune to Santo Domingo peasants, but only a pittance for the Cubans compared what they had to pay for land in Cuba.
   The Cuban investments did not last long. By the end of the century, United States and Puerto Rico operators had assumed control over the entire Dominican Republic's sugar industry.
   The foreign domination of the sugar industry continued until 1948 when Rafael Trujillo, then President and international playboy became aroused by an increase in sugar prices. After building two mills which operated inefficiently, he bought most of the U.S. and Puerto Rico interests. Profits from these operations found their way to Trujillo's Swiss bank accounts. When officers in Trujillo's army assassinated him in 1961, the sugar operation fell into a succession of inept governmental supervisors. After surviving many economic hills and valleys, sugar became the main export crop in the 1980's, but many moral and economic issues remained to be resolved.

SLAVERY AND SLAVE REVOLTS
Santo Domingo began its import of African slaves in 1520 at the rate of about 1000 a year until the mid-1500's. The need for slaves waned with the trade policies Spain invoked on Santo Domingo, along with other factors mentioned in the previous section. Slave masters gave many slaves their freedom during the 17th century because they could not afford to feed, clothe or house them. One historian estimates that during this period the slave population dropped 89%. Santo Domingo did not follow the sugar boom growth characteristic of other Indies islands during this period. A period of freedom for slaves came between 1793 and 1801 with Toussaint L'Ouverture's reign. Santo Domingo suffered the ravages of wars

with the Spanish, French and Haitians, all vying for the country's control. Spain restored itself to power in 1809. Spain administrated Santo Domingo until 1821, with the usual bungling parade of incompetent governors and self-defeating policies.

Slavery disappeared when the colonists rebelled and declared independence in 1821. In 1822 the Haitians once again swept across and conquered Santo Domingo and held it until 1844. In that year Juan Duarte, with assistance from Venezuela, successfully revolted against the Haitians and declared their independence as the nation of the Dominican Republic.

POST SLAVERY ERA

The new Republic sank into bankruptcy by 1861 because of corruption, mal administration, disastrous trade policies and continuous harassment by the Haitian military. In mid-1861 the Dominicans voluntarily re-united with Spain and became a Spanish colony. Once again Spain's administrative policies "blew it" and once again the colonists revolted. In 1865 the Dominican Republic regained its independence,

Ulises Heureaux, a dictator of sorts who believed in law and order, progress and economic modernization, came to power in 1882 and for 17 years directed the Dominican Republic down the road of economic growth. He built roads, canals and telephone lines. The stability of the country attracted investors from the United States, Puerto Rico and Cuba. The longer he held control, the more repressive he became. One of his opposition assassinated him in 1899, leaving no competent person to inherit the leadership role.

In 1907 the Dominican Republic was facing bankruptcy. U.S. President Theodore Roosevelt stepped in to introduce influence and guidance to protect U.S. business investments. They struck an agreement whereby the U.S. would oversee and distribute export revenues—45% going to the Dominican Republic to pay current expenses and 55% to pay off their debt Ramon Caceres, Heurbaux's assassin, gained the presidency and the country, with U.S. help, things ran smoothly for 5 years until he was assassinated. It is interesting to note that as of 1982 surviving members of the Heureaux and Caceres families still live in the Dominican Republic--but they do not speak to each other.

In 1916 and the advent of World War I, U.S. President Wilson feared a German invasion of the helpless Dominican Republic. He sent a military force, which gained control, and for 8 years the U.S. occupied the country. During these 8 years the U.S. financed and completed a number of public works projects and modernized factories and sugar plantations. The presence of the U.S. generated considerable opposition, resulting in some armed attacks.

The Dominican Republic wanted for leadership when a hurricane swept through the country in 1930 destroying cities and killing thousands. Generalissimo Rafel Trujillo stepped up to become the country's dictator. He set about rebuilding, gaining confidence of the populace and eliminating his opponents.

In his second term he succeeded in the massacre of all illegal Haitians and the elimination of borderline skirmishes with Haiti. They renamed the city of Santo Domingo, Ciudad Trujillo. He wooed the U.S., being one of the first to declare war on Japan after the Pearl Harbor bombing and set himself up as the hemisphere's foremost "anti-communist."

In 1947 Trujillo signed a check for $9 million, paying off their foreign debt and freeing themselves from U.S. supervision. Trujillo remarked, "We are absolutely free, absolutely sovereign and absolutely independent."

On the surface, the Dominican Republic appeared to be politically staple and prospering. Underneath, so was Trujillo. He ran a tight dictatorship that controlled the military and all government endeavors, directed organized terror squads to keep the opposition in line, censored and directed education and intellectual thinking and maintained control over all socioeconomic groups. By the 1950's he had amassed a personal fortune approaching $1 billion and had he and his family in control of 60% of the country's economic assets and labor force.

A seven-man assassination team, acting on their own and not a part of any organized movement, killed Trujillo on May 30, 1961.

The country struggled with a series of dictators until 1978 when the democratic process elected Antonio Guzman president. His human rights stand and the allowance for his opponents to speak out publicly made the Dominican Republic the most free and democratic country in Latin America.

Movements still exist to maintain democracy, return to dictatorship or invoke socialism. A large middle class has developed and historians feel that, with recent history still in many middle-class memories, it will be hard to move them very far from democracy. The middle-class fear is that movement away from democracy might result in a loss of the possession of their tangibles and the support of the U.S. that they now enjoy.

Rose Hall, Jamaica

Bauxite Mine, Jamaica

CHAPTER 18

JAMAICA

SIZE
4,411 sq. miles.

GEOGRAPHY
Narrow coastal plain. Mountainous interior.
Limestone plateau covers two-thirds of the
island.

CLIMATE
Upland tropical on windward side of mountains.
Semiarid on leeward side.

CAPITAL
Kingston.

AMERINDIANS

Although it is suspected that the Ciboneys inhabited the island at
some time, there is no physical evidence of their presence or cause
of their disappearance.   Spanish historical records cataloging the
period from discovery to English conquest are sketchy.   Some
mention of Carib presence is found in Spanish archives; however,
more detail exists about the Arawak.   The findings in refuse heaps
and pottery remains indicates that the Arawaks had villages all over
the island. Historians believe that more Arawaks settled on Jamaica
than on any other West Indies island.   Most of the Arawak villages
were along the coast because they were seafaring and fish was one
of their staples. The largest site, however, was inland on the present
road from Kingston to Spanish Town.   Repeated efforts by the
Spanish to settle Jamaica ended in failure. One reason for their
failure is the way the settlers exterminated their work force. They
abused the policy that gave them the right to use the Arawaks as
slaves by overworking them and providing them which such poor
food that they often died of malnutrition. Arawaks were frequently
executed for fun in the sport of seeing which Spaniard could most
expertly strike an Indian's head off with one blow.   Great numbers
died from this treatment.   Thousands more committed suicide by

hanging themselves or drinking the poisonous cassava juice. Mothers were known to have murdered their young so they would not have to survive Spanish slavery. Untold numbers also died from European diseases. By 1655, all traces of the Jamaican Arawaks had vanished.

DISCOVERY

Columbus set foot on Jamaica on May 5, 1494 during his second voyage and exclaimed that Jamaica was "the fairest isle that eyes have beheld; mountainous and the land seems to touch the sky." The Arawaks did not welcome Columbus' approach. They sent out a fleet of war canoes and he forced then to scatter with cannon shot. He tried a different location the next day and was met with the same reception. This time he did land and released his dogs which savagely tracked and bit the terrified Arawak. The following day six Arawaks appeared with peace offerings. Columbus was very disappointed not to have found a trace of gold. He returned to Jamaica on his fourth voyage, by necessity, not choice. Both of his ships became unseaworthy. He became stranded, faced mutiny, starvation and sickness. It was a year's experience of horror for him before help arrived.

SPANISH QUEST FOR GOLD

In the early days, having few economic assets, Jamaica was used by the Spanish mainly as a supply base to provide horses, food and arms. The terrain was suitable for grazing horses, pigs and cattle. Spaniards planted fruit trees, bananas and food plants. There was some trade with treasure-laden ships sailing from Cartagena to Havana, but this trade was not adequate enough to raise the settlers much above the poverty level, mainly due to the high cost of living. One Abbot said that their poverty was due to laziness. Jamaica was not known as a popular place to move to from Spain and many settlers made every effort to leave. Disease, earthquakes and hurricanes made living unpleasant.

EUROPEAN POWER STRUGGLE

May 10, 1655 was the date that began the end of Spanish rule in Jamaica. Thirty eight English ships were spotted entering Kingston Harbor. The settlers of Spanish Town had become used to pirate raids and were accustomed to packing their valuables and heading for the hills when unfamiliar ships were sighted. What the settlers didn't know was that this was not a pirate raid. Is was a part of Oliver Cromwell's "Western Design"--a plan aimed to take over all the Spanish possessions in the Caribbean. To make matters worse, this fleet, under the command of Admiral William Penn, had just suffered a major defeat at Santo Domingo and was attacking Jamaica to save face.

Penn arrived with 8000 troops. The Spaniards could muster a fighting force of only 500. Surrender terms were soon signed and the English took over. The settlers abandoned Spanish Town and fled to the North Coast where they departed for Cuba. In the process, they freed their slaves in the hope they would badger the English. These left-behind slaves became the infamous "Maroons."

THE BUCCANEERS

In 1657, in order to add to the protection from the Spanish, the Tortuga buccaneers were invited by the English to make Port Royal, Jamaica their headquarters. The move was made and lasted until 1682 when a new governor, Sir Thomas Lynch, convinced the Jamaican Assembly to oust the buccaneers. This was done and the buccaneers moved their headquarters back to Tortuga and other islands. Piracy went on. There was a violent earthquake in 1692 and Port Royal sank into the sea. A fitting end to a sinful city.

Some Famous Ones

Henry Morgan.

He was probably the most daring, successful and inspirational tactician of them all. Born a Welshman around 1635 it is guessed he first landed in Barbados as an indentured servant and found his way to Tortuga where he joined a pirate crew that was serving the Jamaican governor, Sir Thomas Modyford by attacking and spying on the Spaniards. When Mansvelt, the captain died, Morgan assumed the post.

Modyford's first assignment was for Morgan to investigate the rumor that the Spaniards were preparing to attack Jamaica. He ventured forth to Puerto Principe, Cuba where he captured the city with bloody house to house fighting. He tortured the rich who disclosed the location of their treasures and the fact that the Spaniards were planning to attack Jamaica. He began to fall out of favor with Modyford on his next raid. He attacked Porto Bello, Panama and seized a vast fortune in gold. The problem was that Morgan was commissioned to attack ships, but not cities. In spite of Modyford's cautions Morgan continued to raid cities, which brought great wealth to the English and tied up Spanish fighting forces. But these actions were not viewed with favor by the King.   Morgan was asked to retire, which he did to his country estate with his wife, Mary Elizabeth.

Times changed. The Spanish began to attack English ships and rumors spread of a Spanish invasion. The King called Morgan out of retirement, gave him the title of "Commander of all the Ships of War" and issued him orders to destroy all the Spanish ships and cities he could find.

This was Morgan's dream. He assembled a fleet of 36 ships and a force of 1200 men, landed on the east side of the Isthmus of Panama and hacked their way for 8 days through jungle to Panama City.   They were met by a force three times their size led by stampeding bulls. They valiantly fought through this. In a few hours, all resistance was crushed.   During this venture, Spain and England sealed a peace by signing the Treaty of Madrid.   To soothe the Spanish, Modyford was relieved as governor by Sir Thomas Lynch and sent to the Tower of London where he lived a life of luxury.   Morgan was also removed to London where he was celebrated as a hero and lavishly entertained by young English royalty.   Shortly, Morgan was knighted and returned to Jamaica as Lieutenant Governor and Modyford was given the post of Chief Justice.   Morgan died on August 25, 1688 at the age of 53 and was buried at Port Royal.

CALICO JACK.

Jack Rackman got his nickname for his fetish for wearing calico underwear. He terrorized the Caribbean for two years and was just another pirate until he met Anne Bonny who inspired him to climb the bloody ladder to pirating immortality.   He was a handsome desperado who swept women off their feet like the dashing Errol Flynn of the 1940's movie fame. He acquired a second female pirate, Mary Read, the only English-speaking bounty on a ship he captured. She agreed to become a member of the crew before she knew she would be a companion of Anne Bonny.

One day in 1720 he lingered too long in the harbor of Negril Bay sipping rum punch and a British warship which had been pursuing him caught him by surprise. Calico Jack and his crew retired to the hold quickly, leaving only Anne Bonny and Mary Read to ward off the boarders (which they did successfully for some time.)

It is reported that when all seemed lost, Anne turned on her crew mates, killing two and injuring eight.   Calico Jack and his crew were tried in Jamaica. On his way to be hanged, Anne yelled out to him, "If you'd have fought like a man, you wouldn't be hanged like a dog." According to historians, this was true.

After hanging, Calico Jack's body was pressed into an iron frame and hung on al islet off Point Royal as an example of what happens to pirates these days in Jamaica.

ANNE BONNY

Anne, born in Cork, Ireland, was the illegitimate child of her attorney-father's housemaid. Her father's infidelity was uncovered when his wife arranged for the maid to sleep elsewhere while she took the maid's place in bed. The events that followed resulted in a rude awakening for her father. After her father's divorce, her father and the maid began to live together unwed. The scandal ruined his practice and they moved to New England.

Anne became enchanted with the sea and began to frequent waterfront bars. This resulted in an affair with a no-good sailor, John Bonny, which led to marriage. Shortly afterwards, Anne met Calico Jack and they fell in love. Jack easily bought off John and Anne took off to sea with Calico Jack.

Anne stood trial in Jamaica with Calico Jack and was found guilty and sentenced to hang. When Anne disclosed the fact that she was pregnant, the sentence was dismissed, for English law forbid killing a pregnant woman. Anne disappeared without a trace. Some historians believe that her father, now a prominent New England planter, paid someone a ransom and she was released to his custody.

MARY READ

Mary was born in England. Her mother had married early and had a son. Her husband left on a voyage and never returned. A few years later the son died and Mary was born. Unable to explain who the father was, Mary's mother dressed Mary as a boy (disguising her as her son.) Mary's mother lost her financial support and at age 13, Mary went out on her on. She served as a foot boy for a French lady, crew member on a British warship and as a foot soldier, disguising herself as a man for a long period of time.

She fell in love with her roommate, Fleming and finally disclosed her sex to him. They married and they opened a restaurant called, "The Three Horseshoes" which was successful until Fleming died.

Mary once again disguised herself and joined a regiment of foot soldiers in Holland. She tired of this and boarded a ship for the Caribbean. It was on this voyage that she came in contact with Calico Jack. Mary was convicted in the same court proceedings as Calico Jack and Anne Bonny. She, like Anne, was pregnant and received the same clemency as Anne, but never returned to the sea.

She became sick, died and her burial was recorded in the "Parish Register of Burials of St. Catherine" on April 28, 1721.

BLACKBEARD

William Teach (Blackbeard) is widely recognized to be the cruelest and most ferocious pirate of them all. He relished torture--even on his own crew. He was a giant with a great appetite and possessed the ability to drink rum long after his drinking companions had passed out. Blackbeard would rage into battle wearing 12 pistols and several swords hung on a special belt. Just the thought of the legend of his fierceness often led to a quick surrender.

Blackbeard was killed in a battle off the North Carolina coast. It is said that he was still fighting after receiving 5 musket shots and 3 thrusts by a cutlass.

THE SUGAR ERA

Columbus brought sugar cane to Hispaniola on his second voyage and some found its way to Jamaica. At the time the English captured the island there were only a few small sugar works producing sugar for local use only. Eyes fell on Jamaica as a potential sugar producer after the success of the crop on Barbados. Profits had increased twenty-fold there in ten years and Jamaica was 26 times the size of Barbados.

Jamaica entered the Sugar Era and the plantation system in the late 1600's and it came into full bloom as a major crop in the 1750's. By the 1770's Jamaica, Barbados and the Leeward islands supplied 24 percent of all goods imported into Britain and took 13 percent of British exports.

Early efforts to encourage cane production were in the form of handing out liberal plantation acreage to prospective planters. They were hesitant at first to invest so heavily in slaves, equipment, the sugar mill, horses and mules. When it became clear that sugar was becoming the world's most profitable crop, planters were able to get favorable loans. Thus, the world's largest plantations were born.

The growth of sugar estates was rapid. There were 70 plantations in 1675, 455 in 1758, 775 in 1775 and 859 in 1806. Prosperity reigned until the 1820's. During the period 1766 to 1770, Haiti produced 38% of the world's sugar and Jamaica was second with 22%. A combination of events including the abolition of the slave trade in 1807, mismanagement by employees of absentee owners and severe overcropping, led to the beginning of the demise of the plantation. The major issue was labor. The plantation owner now had to pay wages, learn to cut costs and invest in ploughs and other equipment to do jobs formerly done by slaves. They tried to switch to other crops like rice, indigo, cocoa, cotton and silk, but these efforts failed. For sometime Jamaican sugar was protected by English tariffs. In 1846 the Sugar Equalization Act was passed that equalized sugar tariffs and eventually would eliminate all protection on Caribbean colony products. Jamaica now had to compete with slave operators in Cuba and Brazil in a market where prices were falling.

To add insult to injury, Jamaica suffered a series of droughts, earthquakes and an outbreak of Asiatic cholera in 1850 that claimed 32,000 lives. This was followed by an outbreak of smallpox in 1852. Plantations were abandoned or sold for whatever the owners could get. Some were bought by attorneys who sectioned them off and sold plots to settlers. The once-lush, productive plantations became the scene of vacant fields, rusted machinery, collapsing plantation estates and fallen-down fences.

SLAVERY AND SLAVE REVOLTS
Sugar plantations begat slavery. During the years 1601 to 1810, 747,400 slaves were imported to Jamaica. This compares to 4,059,900 to the total Caribbean region and 455,700 to British/USA and French Louisiana during the same time period.

During the "sugar years" the slaves considerably outnumbered the whites, as shown in the table below:

DATE	WHITES	SLAVES
1730	7,658	74,525
1758	17,900	176.900
1775	18,700	192,800
1800	30,000	300,000
1834	20,000	310,000

Source: Patterson, Slavery and Social Death, Pg. 477.

Slaves made up 93% of the population in 1834. The mortality rate of Jamaican slaves was astronomical. The slave population in 1703 was 45,000. In 1778 it was 205,261. Between 1703 and 1778 469,893, slaves were imported. By applying simple math, you will find that within a period of 75 years, 264,632 slaves had vanished. Jamaican slaves lived under a strict set of laws initiated by the Jamaican Assembly. They could not keep horses, mules, donkeys or cattle. They would be whipped if they sold meat, fish or handmade articles (except baskets) or worked for anyone else without the permission of their owner. There were strict limitations on how much white fathers could bequeath to their mulatto children or favorite slaves.

The Coromantees from the African Gold Coast and the Eboes from the Bight of Benin were two of the main tribes imported to Jamaica. They differed much in succumbing to slavery. The Coromantees were proud, strong warriors who did not readily accept the gang labor routines. They led most of the slave revolts and were the most numerous among the Maroons. The Eboes had been enslaved by other tribes in Africa and were rather docile; therefore, more readily accepted slavery.

The treatment of the slaves varied widely. There was Annee Palmer of Rose Hall who took pleasure in torturing her slaves and murdering her husbands. There was Charles Blagrove of Cardiff Hall who, upon his death, left each slave a gift along with a note thanking them for their service. Generally, the better the slaves were treated, the more successful the plantation. Even good treatment did not stop the slave who had the yearning to be free. Jamaica had a perfect place for the runaway to run to. It was the Cockpit, a desolate area which was occupied by other runways to--the Maroons.

The Maroons

It is suspected that the name Maroon came from the Spanish word, cimarron, meaning "wild" or "untamed". As mentioned earlier, when the Spaniards fled the island from the English, they freed their slaves in the Jamaican back country. These were the original Maroons. The Maroons managed to survive by growing plantain, corn and yams and hunting wild pigs. By 1662 the English saw them as pests and offered them land and full freedom if they would surrender. They refused this offer. Instead, as the plantations moved farther inland, they raided the plantations, setting fire to the fields and stealing cattle and stock. This warfare lasted for 76 years. Around 1690 a large number of slaves from Clarendon defected to the Maroons and came under the leadership of Cudjoe. Cudjoe was a short, squat hunchback Coromantee with a mission to conduct murder and robbery of the English.

The fighting strategy of the Maroons was nothing like the English had ever seen. The jungle the Maroons inhabited provided excellent cover for ambush, a tactic which the Maroons developed to perfection. The Maroons would coat themselves with leaves and conduct surprise attacks. They never fought in the open. They would make a quick attack, retreat, reform and conduct another. These battle tactics baffled the English.

The First Maroon War

The "First Maroon War" was waged from 1690 to 1734. In 1734, British troops, led by Captain Stoddard, successfully attacked and demolished the Maroon stronghold of Nanny Town. So complete was the destruction that it was never resettled.

The defeat at Nanny Town threw the Maroons into disarray. Shortly they were faced with the option of surrendering or facing starvation. The English did not know this and offered to meet Cudjoe to discuss peace. Cudjoe agreed to negotiate.

The peace terms included complete freedom for the Maroons, each Maroon being given 600 hectares of land, the right to hunt wild pigs within 3 miles of a plantation or town and complete power for Cudjoe to administer punishment for all crimes except those dealing with the death penalty. In turn, the Maroons promised no more raids and to turn back all runaway slaves to their owners for which they would receive a small reward. Two white men were to live with the Maroons to keep lines of communication open. The war ended and peace prevailed for more than 50 years.

The Maroons had settled in two high country jungle areas, the Trelawny Meadows on the Northeast section of the island and what was called the Windward Maroon area in the Southeast end. Cockpit country was a very densely wooded area within the Trelawny Meadows. By 1795 the Maroons had separated into five tribes. A comparatively trivial incident took place in July, 1795 which touched off the "Second (and to be the last) Maroon War."

The Second Maroon War

Two Trelawny Maroons were whipped in Montego Bay for pig stealing. The Trelawnys had no problem with this except that the black who wielded the whip was a runaway the Maroons caught. They had returned him and many other runaways to the English with the expectation that they would be punished. Instead, all were allowed to cheer and mock at the whipping. This outrage, along with ill feelings between the current Trelawny chief and the residing English superintendent, Captain Craskell and the long-standing disgruntlement over the land assigned them under the Cudjoe treaty led the Trelawnys to make wild threats against the English. They ordered Craskell to leave their settlement.

This incident came at a bad time. There had recently been major slave revolts on St. Dominique (Haiti) and the Jamaican plantation owners were living in terror that slave revolts might take place in Jamaica. The English overreacted by sending a detachment of soldiers to strengthen their force in the area.

The Trelawnys sent a message that they would like to meet and discuss their complaints. The English agreed and the outcome was that the negotiators agreed to lay their complaints before the governor and to return Trelawnys' favorite superintendent to the area. There were hopes that the matter would be settled peacefully. The Earl of Balcarres, a newly appointed governor and veteran of the American War for Independence, took a different view. He saw the Maroon threats to be the beginnings of a call to arms, incited by the slave revolutionaries in Haiti. He was convinced that the Maroons were just stalling for the right time and place to attack.

Balcarres called out the militia, declared martial law and recalled a fleet carrying soldiers to Haiti to return to Montego Bay. On his way to Montego Bay he met six Maroons who were carrying a list of grievances for discussion. He arrested them and had them imprisoned. Older settlers begged him not to be so impulsive, but to no avail.

He then notified the Maroons that they were surrounded by thousands of troops and ordered them to surrender within four days. There was sharp division among the Trelawnys whether to fight or surrender. At the end of the four days only 38 surrendered. The English immediately imprisoned them and dispatched a large military force to Trelawny country. This detachment was ambushed and massacred in typical Maroon fashion.

The "Second Maroon War" commenced with this battle. For about five months 300 Trelawnys fought off over 3000 English troops, helped by the Accompong Maroon tribe. General George Walpole was placed in charge of English troops. He established outposts that enabled patrols to fight and return without having to make long marches. He trained his men in jungle fighting. Once he wrote, "There is little chance of any but a Maroon discovering a Maroon."

Walpole soon saw the futility in fighting this kind of unconventional warfare and came up with the solution that dealt the death blow to the Maroons. He commissioned Colonel Quarrell to go to Cuba to secure some bloodhounds. Quarrell returned with 100 bloodhounds and 40 handlers, called "Chasseurs". The dogs immediately displayed their ferocity. When Walpole fired a musket in salute during an initial review ceremony, the dogs attacked him, dragging their Chasseurs. He narrowly escaped being torn to pieces. They did not have to use the dogs. The Trelawnys knew there was no escape from the dogs and agreed to surrender.

Acceptable surrender terms were negotiated, but a problem arose. The terms gave the Maroons only three days to appear--on

January 1. The Maroons were spread out over a wide area and only 21 managed to   meet the deadline.   Walpole understood the problem and extended the deadline until the end of January.

A joint committee of the Jamaican Assembly was formed to deal with the problem. They decided that the Trelawnys had broken the surrender agreement. The entire tribe was shipped to Halifax, Nova Scotia. Walpole spent years protesting this action, but his protests fell on deaf ears. The Trelawnys suffered a great deal from the cold climate and were poor workers. There became a dispute between Nova Scotia and Jamaica as to who was responsible for the support of the Trelawnys.

In 1800 the Trelawnys were transported to Sierra Leone, Africa. Descendants of these Maroons can be found today in Freetown.

Slavery Ends

The ending of slavery in Jamaica, and other English-held Caribbean islands, began in England in the late eighteenth century. Most Christians felt that slavery was wrong, but they rationalized: slavery is necessary for a working force to grow sugar; most slaves were slaves in Africa anyhow; and, their lot was improved because they were being exposed to civilized lifestyles and introduced to Christianity.   Slowly, influential religious, abolitionist   and philanthropist leaders became vocal enough to attract the attention of politicians and the public.   They exposed many incidents of cruelty. One ship's captain who had lost 60 of his 440 slaves at sea, threw 132 live slaves overboard because a clause in his insurance policy didn't cover the 60. However, the policy did cover those disposed of " . . for the good of the ship." He wanted to ensure that the owners made a profit.

Anti-slavery sympathy continued.   The Jamaican Assembly fought the efforts tooth and nail and especially resented Parliament making decisions that would eventually cause the destruction of the plantation system.

The Assembly tried an assortment of plans, including apprenticeship along with freedom.   All the plans met with varying degrees of failure and full freedom came on August 1, 1838.

THE POST-SLAVERY ERA

A civil government system was established in 1661 and continued until 1865. There was a governor, appointed by the Crown who appointed a Council of 12 to represent British interests. In addition, in order for the settlers to have input, there was the Assembly, (primarily plantation-owner oriented), elected by the settlers to represent colonial interests, which grew to 49 members by 1865. Rarely did the Assembly and Council ever experience a period without quarreling and bickering. The 1838 emancipation meant, in theory, that blacks would have the same rights as whites, which included the right to vote. But whites were in charge at the time and saw to it that they would remain in charge. Ways were found to limit the numbers of voters. Just before the system collapsed, 1457 voters out of a total of 1903 registered voters elected the Assembly. The population at the time was 400,000--half male.

The Morant Bay Rebellion

The Crown never laid much confidence in the Assembly as a body able to make responsible decisions. How to justify getting rid of this nuisance was a problem. A series of events brought about by Governor Eyre's ineptness, led to the October "Morant Bay Rebellion" and the demise of the Assembly.

There were three major figures in this rebellion. George William Gordon was a Jamaican-born mulatto. He was a bright, ambitious business operator who became a much liked political leader. He also started his own Baptist church. Edward John Eyre, after a short stay in Jamaica when he managed to make himself disliked by most, was appointed governor. This came as a shock, especially to Gordon. Eyre was stubborn, lacked experience in governing, only associated with whites, had no desire to deal with multi-cultural problems, and hated Baptists. Paul Bogle, a black from Stony Gut, was one of Gordon's deacons. He was uneducated, but an energetic and influential leader with the aura of an African chief. He became livid with anger over Eyre's indifference over the problems of unemployment, his refusal to grant good crop lands to small farmers and his posting of the "Queen's Letter."

The years leading up to 1865 were those of poverty, drought, heavy taxes and mismanagement by Eyre. Early in 1865 Bogle and others prepared a list of complaints and requests for action and presented it to Eyre to forward to the Queen. This he did, along with his own letter which showed no sympathy for them.

The Queen, being influenced by Eyre, wrote a letter stating that the colonials were in charge of their own fate and that they would just have to work harder. Eyre had this letter copied and posted 50,000 copies around the island. No one believed the queen could be so inhumane and all blamed Eyre for his influence on her.

On October 7, Bogle came to the town of Morant Bay with 200 followers to watch a trial of one of his flock. At the end of a trial just proceeding his, there was a disturbance when a friend of the person to be sentenced broke from the crowd to make certain demands on the court. When the police attempted to arrest him, he escaped into Bogle's group and Bogle took him back to Stony Gut.

Bogle returned to Morant Bay on October 11, stormed the police station, overwhelmed and killed a group of Eyre's Volunteers, burned the courthouse and other buildings and killed several officials.

Martial law was declared, regulars were called to the scene and Stony Gut was besieged. Bogle expected the Maroons to help them, but they joined the English. The retreat was disorganized and Bogle's followers scattered in disarray. Eyre was convinced that Gordon was solely responsible for urging Bogle to take the action he did. Actually, Gordon was a peaceful person and did not support Bogle at all. Eyre sent Gordon to St. Thomas Parish to be convicted of treason. He was and was hanged on October 21.

Bogle was found by the Maroons near Stony Gut the same day Gordon was hung. Officials convicted him after a short trial and hung him from Morant Bay's burned-out courthouse arch.

The Morant Bay incident aroused interest in England and a special commission was sent to investigate the matter in January, 1866. They found Eyre's actions excessive and brutal. The commission's report was so damaging that Eyre was returned to England and dismissed from public service.

The Arrival of Governor Sir Peter Grant

The Morant Bay Rebellion was to be the last major violent uprising in Jamaican history. Sir Peter Grant arrived as governor in August and, starting with his foresight and dreams, a new Jamaica began to emerge. He reorganized the courts and set up a district court system, modernized the police force, set up Boards to run the parishes to replace the self-serving appointed individuals. He withdrew governmental financial support of the Anglican church, established botanical gardens and installed programs to further science, art and literature. He developed a sewage disposal system and began to drain mosquito-infested swamps.

Education for slaves was approved of only when it served to improve their labor skills; therefore, at the time of emancipation there was a high rate of illiteracy. Beginning in 1865 with bequests being made by the wealthy, education began to spread and improve slowly until today when an elementary, secondary and college education are available to all.

Sugar cane production declined. In 1848 there were 500 plantations. In 1910 there were 70.

The Jamaican banana appeared as an important export crop in 1870. In that year, Captain Lorenzo Baker felt the good quality of the Jamaican banana deserved a trial in the American market. He sold a small cargo at a good profit and returned in 1871 for a full load. To protect themselves from giants like the United Fruit Company, the growers established the Jamaica Banana Producers Association in 1936, another bit of evidence that Jamaicans were working together to improve their lot.

Another economic boon came to Jamaica with the increase in the demand for aluminum after World War II. Jamaica had vast deposits of bauxite, the ore that is refined to make aluminum. By the mid-1950's 5 million tons a year were mined, with a target of 9 million projected. The strip mining operations took place on some of Jamaica's prime grazing land. The government and the three mining companies entered into an agreement that the land would be restored upon completion of the strip mining operations. The companies fully cooperated in this environmental effort.

There was little tourism in Jamaica until after World War II. The growth in the industry has been enormous and has recently overtaken bauxite mining to become Jamaica's #1 economic activity.

Independence

On August 6, 1962 Jamaica gained independence from the Crown. This was achieved by a seemingly endless number of political baby steps that took place over the previous 100 years. The constitution was revised, rewritten and updated countless times, opposing political parties vied for power and commissions and committees came and went. Princess Margaret opened the first session of Parliament on August 7, 1962.

Jamaican political leadership was narrowed in 1938 when two dynamic men, Alexandar Bustamante and Norman Manley formed the People's National Party (PNP). In 1940, under Manley, the PNP adopted a socialist platform and became affiliated with Socialist International.

Bustamante fell out with Manley and formed his own party, the Jamaica Labour Party (JLP). He was quoted as saying, "I am for the West. I am against Communism." He charged the PNP to be Communists and atheists and strongly supported private land ownership. He became Jamaica's first chief minister in 1953 and the JLP won two successive elections.

The JLP's successes led the PNP to modify their political philosophy. They expelled four Communists and became more conservative, but they still had socialist leanings.

The parties alternated being in power for several years. In the 1972 election the PNP promised social and economic reform. They won and this reform took the shape of establishing close ties with Cuba and the USSR and distancing themselves from the USA. A snap election was called in 1979 after the USA invasion of Grenada and the JLP won. They held power until the PNP won the election of 1989.

It was during one of Manley's terms, 1958-1962, that an effort was encouraged by the British for the formation of a West Indies Federation to increase government efficiency and cut expenses. There was strength in union. As it happened, Jamaica was experiencing a period of prosperity through its bauxite exports and Trinidad was prospering from their oil exports. Neither island was excited over the prospect that they might have to contribute support to the smaller islands who were less fortunate. Eric Williams of Trinidad and Norman Manley withdrew their support and the West Indies Federation was dissolved. It is felt by many historians that in the long-term a federation could have benefitted all.

Bustamante retired from political life in 1967. Manley passed away on September 7, 1969.

Your island contact:
Mr. Noel Mignon, Director of Tourism
Jamaica Tourist Board
2 St. Lucia Ave. Kingston 5,
Jamaica,
West Indies
Phone: (809) 929-9200
Fax: (809) 929-9375

DuBuc Castle, Martinque

DuBuc Castle, Martinique

CHAPTER 19

MARTINIQUE & GUADELOUPE

"The forest, what an inextricable chaos it is! The sands of the sea are not more closely pressed together than the trees are here: some straight, some curved, some upright, some toppling--fallen, or leaning against one another . . . You do not find here the eternal monotony of the birch and fir. This is the kingdom of infinite variety." Dr. E. Rufz. Source: Roberts: "The French in the West Indies."

SIZE
Martinique: 427 sq. miles
Guadeloupe: 585 sq. miles

GEOGRAPHY
Martinique: Predominately hilly. Highest point: Mt. Pelee, 4584 feet.
Guadeloupe: Gently rolling hills. Highest point: Mt. La Soufiere, 4813 feet.

CLIMATE
Strongly influenced by trade winds. Rainfall at higher elevations can be over 300 inches a year. Temperature varies with altitude.

MAIN TOWNS
Martinique: Fort de France.
Guadeloupe: Basse-Terre

AMERINDIANS
The islands of Martinique and Guadeloupe, with Dominica sandwiched in-between were strongholds of the Caribs who caused no end of trouble for the early French settlers. The Caribs provided the French with food for the last 9 months of 1635 after their arrival on Guadeloupe. In January 1636 the French governor attacked the Caribs and seized their provision grounds. This action provoked the Caribs and started a war that lasted until 1640 when the French defeated the Caribs in a 30 hour battle. Seeing the problems that developed in Guadeloupe with the Caribs, Martinique's governor, Du Parquet, extended a hand of friendship to them. The Caribs knew

of the Guadeloupe incidents and remained aloof.   Ill feelings escalated between the French and Caribs on Martinique in 1640 when the Caribs kidnaped two of their tribesmen from a plantation. Parquet arrested the chief and vowed to keep him until the two Caribs were returned. The chief escaped and died from an accident on his return home. Parquet was convinced the Caribs would blame the French for his death.   Fearing revenge, Parquet called the settlers to their fort and prepared for a Carib attack. The Caribs took this action as preparatory to a French attack on them and returned the two kidnaped Caribs. The island then entered a period of temporary peace.

A relatively minor incident provoked a major Carib uprising on Martinique in 1654. The Governor found eight Caribs guilty of killing five Frenchmen and had them executed. This enraged the local Caribs and they sent for help from Dominica. Over two thousand Caribs surrounded the Governor's mansion and in fear of attack he sent his wife to Fort St. Pierre for safety. She gave premature birth on the way amid a shower of arrows during the perilous journey. Both arrived safely.   The Carib attack came with great ferocity and it wasn't long before the Governor realized he lacked sufficient ammunition for an extended defense. He slacked his fire and the Caribs at once feared the French were about to turn their dogs loose. Some runaway slaves joined them and they decided to turn to the countryside and burn houses and kill settlers rather than face the dogs.   The French in outlying areas took to the woods in total confusion to hide.

In the midst of this impending French disaster, four Dutch ships sailed into the harbor and sighted what they thought to be either a slave revolt or Carib war. They decided to lend the French a hand and landed 300 men. The Dutch assaults drove the Caribs to the jungle. The French bought ammunition from the Dutch, caught up with the Caribs and put an end to the uprising.   The French began a concerted effort to remove the threat of Carib raids in 1654 with a victory over the Caribs on the island of St. Vincent. In 1658 the French virtually eliminated all the Caribs from Martinique and Guadeloupe.

In 1660 France signed a treaty with England which reserved the islands of St. Vincent and Dominica for the Caribs.

DISCOVERY

Columbus made landings on Martinique and Guadeloupe in 1502 during his fourth voyage. The Spanish showed no interest in the islands and they remained unexplored until 1631.   The lieutenant-governor of St. Christopher sent Guillaume d'Orange on a mission to survey Martinique, Guadeloupe and Dominica. He reported that of the three, Guadeloupe was the most promising for settlement.

SPANISH QUEST FOR POWER AND GOLD

Martinique and Guadeloupe, like most of the eastern Caribbean islands, were not on Spanish trade routes and held no deposits of gold or silver. In addition, they were inhabited by the warlike Caribs who did not submit easily to slavery as did the submissive Arawaks who inhabited other islands.

Consequently, these two islands played no role in Spain's lust for the riches to be found in their westward thrust.

EUROPEAN POWER STRUGGLE AND SETTLEMENTS

After d'Orange returned from his explorations of Martinique, Guadeloupe and Dominica and reported to lieutenant-governor L'Olive, he and L'Olive set sail for France to secure financial support for settlements. Their arrival in Paris in 1634 was timely. A new company, Company of the Isles had just received a patent to send four thousand French to the Indies. Soon after his arrival, L'Olive met Jean Duplessis, a likable experienced adventurer and the two formed a partnership. They received a grant which made them governors for ten years and five thousand francs to finance their venture. In return they were to build a fort, warehouse and transport 900 men, not including women and children, to the island of Guadeloupe over a ten-year period for three-year terms.

The first expedition experienced no end of misery. The merchants who had supplied them shorted the supplies, which were of very poor quality. Many died during the passage. Within two months after their arrival the food supply ran out.

Lack of experience living in the tropics also took its toll. Intent on clearing land as soon as possible, they worked long hours in the blazing sun, drank water to excess. Weakened from overwork and malnutrition, many easily succumbed to disease. If it were not for some foodstuffs being supplied by the Caribs, all would have perished. The entire colony was on the verge of insanity when a long-awaited supply ship arrived from France. Instead of bringing food for survival, the ship unloaded 140 half-starved men from France. Once again, the homeland merchants had fallen short with supplies. The captain disembarked the new arrivals and at once departed saying he had just enough food to get him back to France. L'Olive then made a desperate decision to declare war on the Caribs and seize their provisions. Dupleses opposed the move so L'Olive sought help from Belain D'Esnambuc, governor of St. Christopher, who thought the idea was despicable. When L'Olive returned from St. Christopher he found Dupleses had died; therefore, he had total control.

On January 26, 1636, on the pretext that the Caribs had stolen a roll of cotton cloth, L'Olive declared war. The "war" turned out to be only a minor skirmish. The Caribs got wind of the French change of heart and escaped to the nearby island of Dominica. From there the Caribs conducted continual guerrilla warfare.   Misfortune continued to follow L'Olive after his unwarranted attack on the Caribs. One ship loaded with supplies from St. Christopher was turned away by Spanish warships. Another sailed from Guadeloupe to St. Christopher, but never returned. The crew decided they had had enough of Guadeloupe and continued on to France.

Unable to secure direct help from France or the colonists who blamed him for all their problems, D'Olive turned to the clergy for help. After granting the Fathers a tract of land, they appealed to the Cardinal to use his influence to help D'Olive.   These efforts succeeded.   On December 12, 1637 the Company issued a proclamation continuing D'Olive as governor and a flow of supplies began to regularly come to the island.

The French Settle Martinique

D'Esnambuc had plans to extend his governorship of St. Christopher to Martinique, Dominica and Guadeloupe. When he realized D'Olive was becoming entrenched as governor of Guadeloupe, he wasted no time in organizing an expedition of experienced colonists in 1635 to settle Martinique. After landing the party, he left his lieutenant, Jean du Pont in charge and returned to St. Christopher. du Pont had immediate problems with the Caribs. They did not welcome the French as those did on Guadeloupe. After a few assaults on the French, the Caribs found they were too few in number so they sent to Dominica and Guadeloupe and amassed a fighting force of 1500 men.   du Pont got wind of the impending Carib attack and called his settlers to the fort. He loaded his three cannon with musket balls, nails and assorted metal pieces and waited. The Caribs took heart at seeing the French retreat and attacked in full force. The blaze and roar of the French cannons terrified the Caribs who felt all the devils in France were being unleashed upon them. They retreated in haste and rowed their canoes to Dominica.   This event ended Carib harassments and enabled the French to pursue the peaceful endeavors of clearing land to plant vegetables for their needs and tobacco for export.

The English Attempts at Takeover

In 1702 the Dutch and English declared war on France and Spain. St. Kitts had been jointly occupied by the French and English at the outbreak of the war and the English decided that the time had come to gain sole possession of the island. The English effort succeeded and they next turned their attention to Guadeloupe and Martinique.

A hurricane and excess demands for exports from the homeland drove many Martinique settlers to piracy just to get food for survival. The English were not aware of Martinique's problems and thought them to have formidable defenses. But Martinique was strategically a more desirable plum than Guadeloupe, so the English dispatched a fleet of six warships and ten transports carrying 4000 men to join the victorious commander over St. Kitts, Sir Christopher Codrington, for a Martinique attack. This force arrived at Barbados to rest before the engagement. Over a thousand men died there as a result of disease and overindulgence in "wild parties." With his force reduced, Codrington decided to switch his attack to Guadeloupe, supposedly the weaker of the two in defense. At 5:00 p.m. on March 5, 1703 Codrington set sail from Antigua to attack Guadeloupe.

Upon arrival, Codrington made several probes at landing sites to determine the French strength and commitment to defense. Satisfied that he had the superior force, he attacked and battles began on March 24. Being out manned, the French retreated to their fort at Bassaterre and prepared for a siege. Just at the time the French feared all would be lost, 12 French transports and 3 warships arrived on April 3 with Jean Gabaret, Governor of Martinique, in charge. Codrington was so intent in preparing for his attacks, he failed to post lookouts and Gabaret landed with no resistance. Rather than attempt to face a frontal attack from the English, Gabaret decided to abandon the fort at Bassaterre and adopt the Fabian strategy--that of using a cautious strategy of delay and avoidance of battle. To his credit, Gabaret was very concerned about protecting the inexperienced and inept colonists from engaging in fighting the professional English military. He also felt that the English could not sustain themselves without supplies and ammunition forever. Around the first of May Gabaret gained information from English deserters that their ammunition and supplies were indeed running low. Gabaret's strategy was working.

The English held a council of war on May 5. Disease and the battles had taken a heavy toll. They had run out of bread and were low on other foodstuffs and ammunition. In addition, Codrington had become ill and taken to St. Kitts. They decided to evacuate the island and abort the conquest. The English completed their evacuation on May 15 by burning 7 towns, 8 churches and 5 convents. They left the island in shambles. While there was considerable material loss during the 2-1/2 month siege, the loss of Frenchmen's lives (27 killed and 50 injured) was small due to Gabaret's brilliant tactics.

BUCCANEERS, PIRATES AND PRIVATEERS
Neither Martinique or Guadeloupe played a major role during the Pirate era. Historians have not recorded any major raids, but the island certainly experienced occasional visits by the Brethren. Father Labart of Martinique did record a meeting with the buccaneer, M. Pinel in March 1694. The Fathers spent the day confessing Pinel's crew. In return, Pinel left generous amounts of supplies as a gift.

THE SUGAR ERA
Guadeloupe joined Barbados as the first exporters of sugar through Dutch merchants in 1647, but tobacco was the major agricultural export until the 1660's. Sugar investments in St. Dominique (Haiti) had overshadowed all other opportunities in the French West Indies. Seeing the success in Haiti, in 1672 the Crown instructed the Governor of Martinique to persuade the planters to establish their own sugar refineries. By 1679 two refineries were in operation in Martinique and three in Guadeloupe. In 1698 Martinique boasted 18 refineries.

A major conflict arose between the refineries in the islands and those established in France. While less product was lost during shipment when sugar was refined before shipment, considerable unemployment resulted in France where refineries had been in operation to process the raw product from the Indies. The Crown issued a ban on West Indies refined sugar and when the planters ignored the proclamation, the Crown reduced the duty on unrefined sugar by 50% and increased the duty on West Indies refined sugar by 220%. This brought about the death of the French West Indies refining business.

The abolition of slavery brought a dramatic reduction in sugar production. Between 1836 and 1848 production fell from 25 million kilos to 12 million in Martinique and from 35 million kilos to 12 million in Guadeloupe.   The geographical location of both islands during the sugar years made them more desirable as trading posts and first ports of destination for slave ships than for promotion of the sugar industry.

SLAVERY AND SLAVE REVOLTS

Slavery was introduced to Guadeloupe when 50 Hollanders entered the island in the 1600's from Brazil bringing around 1200 slaves to help them in establishing sugar plantations. By the end of the Seven Years War in 1763 slavery had become commonplace on both islands due to the expansion of the growing of sugar.   Not all the sugar plantations operated on the same scale, employing the same number of slaves.   The historian, Raynal, described the plantation proprietors as falling into four categories:

(1) One hundred first class plantations are operated by the rich, employing 12,000 slaves. They are able to enhance the birthrate by allowing women of child-bearing age comparative leisure to bear and rear their children.

(2) One hundred fifty second class plantations operated by men of modest means, employing 9000 slaves.   Their expansion is limited by the capital needed to invest in additional slaves and equipment.

(3) Thirty-six third class plantations operated by men of limited means, economically struck by the Seven Years War, employing around 2000 slaves. They will not survive without no-interest loans from the government.

(4) Uncounted, the fourth class grows coffee, cotton and other less-important crops than sugar.   They are small growers who employ around 12,000 slaves.

Neither island escaped slave revolts. Guadeloupe experienced revolts in 1737 and 1802 and Martinique in 1762 and 1822.   The emancipation and humanitarian movements in England had spread to France and the "writing was on the wall" that the era of slavery was coming to an end.

The first Martinique black leader, Bissette, and 37 of his followers emerged and were deported to Sengal in 1827 for spreading racial propaganda.   Bissette was sentenced to life imprisonment.   He received amnesty in 1830 and became a recognized spokesman for his race in France.   Victor Skulker, a French istocrat, traveled around the world and became an authority on slavery.   His efforts resulted in a proclamation in 1842 that all masters could voluntarily free their slaves.   This sounded like a noble effort, but the slave owners only freed their concubines and illegitimate children, keeping their able-bodied workers. When England took the final step in emancipation in 1838, more serious attempts to free slaves began in French colonies. Slaves did everything they could to escape from Martinique and Guadeloupe to Dominica and St. Lucia where they would receive asylum. Some even attempted to swim and were caught and punished.

In 1845 France's new Government attempted a different approach to eliminating slavery. Slaves ceased to be property. The only right the master had over the slave was the right to require him to work. Slaves could purchase their freedom at a price set by the courts. Each slave would have one day each week to his own to do what he pleased, which included working for a profit. The planters were outraged by this policy, but the revolution in 1848 that established the Second French Republic swept it away. In its place, this new Government abolished slavery without qualifications. This act was rushed through in March 1848 in the midst of the cane harvest. To help the planters, they postponed the date of emancipation until July. The jubilant slaves refused to work and the entire crop was lost.

THE POST-SLAVERY ERA

The new republican government in France overhauled the entire administration of the colonies. Both Martinique and Guadeloupe received 32 seats in Parliament. Bissette, Skulker and a gentleman named Pory-Papy won seats for Martinique.   What seemed to be a new democratic era in the islands was short-lived. Louis Napoleon Bonaparte III won the presidency in 1848 and by 1851 had restored the Empire with himself in total control. Bissette and others who supported him disappeared into obscurity. Napoleon III went through the Franco Prussian War with a disastrous ending at Sedan. A new republic was formed in 1875 and Martinique and Guadeloupe once again enjoyed political recognition. Towns were allowed to elect mayors and councils to make laws to fit local needs.

Some interesting stories arose about Martinique's early elections. In one case, a council member was elected by only 42 votes being cast in a district with an electorate of over 5000. He received all 42 votes. In another case, no votes were cast in a district for any council member on election day. The polls reopened again a week later.   On that day a candidate met 9 of his employees on his way to the polls and encouraged them to vote. He won by 10 votes--only 10 votes were cast.   As time passed, the black population grew and with it control over land and politics. Blacks intermarried with whites and both Martinique and Guadeloupe, with the demon of racial warfare reduced, became happy communities. While a low standard of living existed, starvation and impoverishment were unknown.

The cataclysmic eruption of Mont Pelee in 1902 brought this period to an end.

The Eruption of Mont Pelee

Four thousand five hundred foot Mont Pelee, which towers over the Martinique town of St. Pierre, had remained a dormant volcano from discovery until 1851. In that year the mountain rained ashes over St. Pierre, then Martiniques's largest town, and created a lake in its summit. Some rumblings took place about 20 years later, but no one thought much of them. Pelee gave unheeded warnings in April 1902 when a series of earthquakes occurred and gas, mud and ashes were emitted from fissures near her summit. Residents began to pack and move from the area. Governor M. Mouttet tried to calm them by moving his family to St. Pierre and placing guards to prevent emigration. Election day had been set for May 8 and for political reasons he did not want to change the date.

Morning broke calm and clear on May 8. About 8:00 Pelee announced its eruption with a deafening thunderous explosive clap and followed with an expulsion of fire, gas, mud and ashes. Within one minute Pelee cremated all life in St. Pierre and turned the town into a burning inferno. The waters in the harbor receded, then returned led by a tidal wave. One-fifth of Martinique had been devastated. About 30,000 St. Pierre residents lost their lives within Pelee's first eruptive minute. An additional 10,000 souls in the surrounding area also died. Rivers had changed their course and much of the island's topography changed. Fallout of ashes were reported a thousand miles away. Pelee continued to erupt throughout the day, pelting the few surviving ships in the harbor with fiery coals the size of walnuts. There was, remarkably, one survivor in St. Pierre on that fatal day. A black, named Monat, was doing a short term in the city jail. He had come down with a fever and had been removed to the dungeon the evening of May 7 where it was cool. The next morning he arose, went to the jail yard to look outside and on his return, as he related, "It was though all the thunder that ever roared and all the cannon in the world had been set off at once. I fell on my face, knocked down by the shaking of the earth." Monat related how he stumbled out into the street after the jailhouse walls collapsed, saw the devastation and sought the safety of the waters in the harbor to gain relief from the heat and sight of the dead. He broke his leg in his effort and passed out after crawling along the beach. He awoke aboard a ship the following day.

Help came from all over the world. President Theodore Roosevelt requested congress for immediate aid in the amount of $500,000. Congress appropriated $200,000. Mr. Hemenway, acting Chairman of the Appropriation Committee said Roosevelt's request was reduced because of the large amounts being donated by private parties. He cited one sizable donation by a citizen of Maine in the amount of $500 alone.

Post Pelee

Mt. Pelee's eruption brought significant social and economic change to Martinique. St. Pierre was the commercial center for both Martinique and Guadeloupe. Rum had been the major export and all the distilleries were located in St. Pierre. When they were rebuilt the new owners scattered them throughout the island and after a short depression, trade resumed. Over the years there had been a gradual exodus of whites from Martinique back to France by those who had gained wealth and wished to enjoy it in the homeland. Insurance did not begin to cover the losses, so rather than reinvest to rebuild, many whites decided to return to France. This upset the racial balance and it wasn't long before blacks and mulattos gained social prestige and political power.

By 1914 Martinique and Guadeloupe were the last two French controlled islands in the Caribbean and while there was a healthy economy, public receipts did not cover public expenditures. The islands had ceased to be important strategic outposts, but the government continued to subsidize them out of sentiment. Martinique and Guadeloupe both sent around 15,000 men to France to fight in World War I while the islands' economies flourished through sales of rum and sugar. Both islands suffered with the rest of the West Indies in the decline of the sugar industry after the War, but rum sales helped to support the economy. With the exception of a hurricane that swept through Guadeloupe killing over 1500 in 1928, nothing of historical significance occurred between the ending of World War I and World War II. Martinique, along with other Caribbean islands became a defensive base during World War II to protect the Panama Canal.

Independence movements began after World War II. Communist and Socialists parties made a play for power, but elections in 1978 led political analysts to conclude that there was little support for them, except in Fort-de-France, and no public desire for independence. Both islands are currently politically classified as French Overseas Departments.

Your island contacts:

<u>Martinique</u>:

Mr. Jacques Guannel, Director
Office Departmental du Tourisme de la Martinique
B.P. 520-97206
Fort de France Cedex
French West Indies
Phone: 011-596-7-21850
Fax: 011-596-7-36693

<u>Guadeloupe</u>:

Mr. Erick Rotin, Director of Tourism
Office Departmental du Tourisme de la Guadeloupe
5 Square de la Banque
BP 1099
Guadeloupe, French West Indies
Phone: 011-590-8-20930
Fax: 011-590-8-38922

Typical Aruba Scene

Typical Aruba Scene

CHAPTER 20

THE NETHERLANDS ANTILLES

SIZE
ARUBA: 75   Square Miles
BONAIRE: 111   "   "
CURACAO: 171   "   "
SURINAM: 63,037 "   "

GEOGRAPHY
ARUBA: Flat. Highest point is Haystack Hill, elevation
500 feet. Divi Divi trees, cactus and brush dominate the
landscape.

BONAIRE: Hilly in northern section, flat in the south.
Landscape similar to Aruba.

CURACAO: Gently rolling hills with landscape similar to Aruba.

SURINAM: Forested hills over 4/5 of the country.   A narrow zone
of savanna grasslands lies behind a coastal plain.

CLIMATE
All the islands and Surinam have a similar climate. They
are arid, averaging about 17 inches of annual rainfall;
warm, averaging 80 degrees; and out of the hurricane
region.

CAPITALS

ARUBA: Oranjestad
BONAIRE: Kralendijk
CURACAO: Willemstad
SURINAM: Paramaribo

AMERINDIANS
The Dutch began their archaeological digs in their Islands (Aruba,
Curacao and Bonaire) and Surinam in the early 1800's. Their
findings led them to the conclusion that the Arawaks had many
long-established villages throughout the Islands and that their sheer
numbers enabled them to ward off the waves of Caribs that followed

them from the South American mainland. The exploration of Arawak village sites uncovered their unique ability to survive. The Dutch almost gave up settlements on Curacao for lack of water in 1654 when they discovered wells dug by the Arawaks and notches cut in cliffs, not 60 yards from the sea, which led them to caves containing spring water. It is suspected the Arawaks made fire by striking two pieces of flint together, igniting a pile of bird feathers. They made tools from coral and shells. Archaeologists found a large Boar's tooth among a cache of tools on Curacao, which was a mystery to them because no Boars ever existed on the island.

Arawak population in the post-Columbus period is guessed by historian, Dr. J. Hartog to have been between 700 and 800 on each island after Diego Salazar carried off 2000 of them to work the mines on Hispaniola in 1515.   Both Arawaks and Caribs inhabited Surinam in pre-Columbus times and were in a continual state of war with each other. When the Europeans first arrived the Amerindians confronted them in battle but soon found it a better strategy to retreat to the jungle for protection. It is in the jungles where they gradually dispersed and escaped the tragic fate of other Caribbean island Amerindians.

DISCOVERY
It is only by piecing together a letter written by Amerigo Vespucci and depositions presented in a lawsuit in 1508 which challenged Columbus' discovery of the island of Margarita that the discoverer and date of discovery of the Netherlands Antilles can be surmised.

By 1499 Ferdinand and Isabella had become concerned over Columbus's administration of his discoveries. In May of that year they sent an expedition including Alonso de Ojeda, who was hostile toward Columbus and Amerigo Vespucci, who remained a friend of Columbus to the end, to assess conditions.   As the two approached the coast of South America, they split up, Ojeda heading for Hispaniola and Vespucci taking a southward course.

On September 5 or 6 Vespucci landed on an island presumed to be Bonaire. Later he sailed to an island he called "The Land of the Giants." This name came from the sight of large human footprints found in the sand and a meeting with some unusually large Arawaks. The Spanish changed the island's name to Curacao, after the name of the resident Arawak tribe.   Although Ojeda later claimed to have discovered all the Netherlands Antilles, historians feel he never saw Aruba and, if anything, merely sighted Bonaire and Curacao.   There are no substantiated records of the discovery of Aruba. The Crown appointed Ojeda the governor of the three "Islands of the Giants" in

1501 and records showed some habitation of the islands shortly afterwards.   King Phillip II of Portugal claimed the region of Surinam on the "Wild Coast" in 1593.

SPANISH QUEST FOR POWER AND GOLD
The islands remained virtually unnoticed by the Spanish until 1513 when Diego Colon proclaimed them to be without precious metals.   At this time the Spanish rounded up the Arawaks and shipped them to the silver mines on Hispaniola.   The Spanish returned the Arawaks when the silver deposits ran out and made attempts on Curacao to raise cattle and a variety of agricultural commodities. The agricultural efforts were not successful, but cattle, sheep, goats and pigs multiplied quickly and their hides, not their meat, became the economic base for Curacao and Bonaire.

Prior to the arrival of the Dutch in 1634, Curacao and Bonaire were major exporters of leather goods, cheese, wool and brazil wood.   The salt pans of Bonaire remained virtually untouched. Some Spanish made feeble attempts to colonize Aruba by engaging in raising cattle and producing agricultural crops, but nothing significant ever came of their efforts.

EUROPEAN POWER STRUGGLE AND SETTLEMENTS
When King Phillip II closed all Portuguese ports to the Dutch in 1580, the Dutch began to search the Caribbean for salt, used in the preserving of their Herring.

This need and the need to establish bases for their growing trade in Brazil and the Caribbean led to the Dutch West India Company's seizure of Curacao and Bonaire from the Spanish in 1634. When the Dutch learned the Spanish were making plans to retake Curacao, they occupied Aruba to prevent it from being used as an enemy base.

By 1634 the Dutch had driven the Spanish from all three islands and placed Joannes Van Walbeek, who had a distinguished military career in Brazil, in charge. Curacao became a major naval base and they built a triangle of fortresses so impressive it discouraged the Spanish from implementing a plan to retake the island.   Van Walbeek went through a period of continual friction with his military commander, strikes by the soldiers, shortages of supplies from Holland and general unrest by the settlers.

The Peace of Munster in 1648, which ended Spanish threats, changed Curacao's role from that of a naval base to a center for slave trading and smuggling ventures. The islands gained the interest of England and in 1805 they invaded Curacao, retreated and re-captured the island again in 1807.   This occupation, which included Aruba and Bonaire, lasted for 14 years and introduced some lasting English culture.

On August 13, 1814 the Treaty of London permanently returned the Netherlands' Leeward and Windward islands to the Dutch.

BUCCANEERS, PIRATES AND PRIVATEERS

Aruba's cattle and horses were attractive prizes to pirates and privateers and the island's lack of defense was an open invitation to raids. Fifteen soldiers provided the island's defense in 1678 and a force of one commander in charge of two horsemen and two soldiers defended the island in 1701.   Assaults by privateers became so common in the Islands that Curacao established a Privateering Fund to aid the victims.   In addition to Island raids, Privateering was disastrous to Dutch shipping. Between 1734 and 1776 the Dutch lost 73 vessels; 37 to the English, 32 to the Spanish and 14 to the French.

Not all privateering activities resulted in losses to the Dutch. They outfitted privateers of their own. In 1628, Holland's Admiral Piet Heyn became a national hero when he captured an entire Spanish flotilla during its return to Spain.   Heyn's loot included 177,357 pounds of silver, 135 pounds of gold, 37,375 hides, 2,270 chests of indigo, 7,961 pieces of logwood, 735 chests of cochineal (a red dyestuff consisting of the dried bodies of female cochineal insects), 235 chests of sugar and an assortment of pearls and spices. Heyn's success was Sir Francis Drake's dream but it was England's Admiral Blake who duplicated Heyn's glory 27 years later when he captured a Spanish flotilla off the coast of Cadiz, Spain.

THE SUGAR ERA

It was the inspired Dutch who gave birth to the sugar era. During their occupation of Brazil they learned the techniques of planting sugar cane and processing it into a product the world was waiting to consume with unimaginable zeal—sugar.   Their own Islands (Aruba, Bonaire and Curacao) never became major agricultural exporters. The soil was rich, but ample rainfall could not be depended upon. In times of war many refugees came to Curacao and caused a food crisis, accentuated when the enemy threw up blockades. In 1819 only 81 plantation owners reported their lands produced the majority of their income. Of these, only 38 relied solely on income from their plantation.

Cattle, goat and sheep raising produced most of the income on Curacao. Horses and donkeys abounded on Aruba and Bonaire, but ran wild and were caught only when the need arose.   An 1817 report suggested that Cochineal production might be possible. The Cochineal insect, which produces a red dye, feasts on cactus plants, native to the islands. In 1841 an additional 50,000 cactus plants became available through the government and an experiment in Cochineal production began, with the backing of Governor Van Rader. The project did not receive an enthusiastic support from the planters and outright rejection by some government officials who had other priorities.   After a peak production of 20,000 pounds of Cochineal in 1848, harvests plummeted to 4000 pounds in 1851 and Cochineal plantations disappeared--but the cactus remains to this day.

When the Turk Islands salt fields were destroyed by a hurricane in 1832, the Dutch turned to the prospect of developing the salt pans on Curacao and Bonaire.   Between 1839 and 1849, Curacao exported 225,000 barrels of salt and Bonaire exported 255,000 barrels. The USA was the largest customer.

Cochineal production and salt farming were only two of Governor Van Rader's attempts to solve some of the Island's economic problems. While he had some minimal support from the homeland, the elite was more into developing trade than taking a fling at unusual projects that required enormous investments with little promise of success.

It was this lack of support and the marginal geological and climatic conditions not favoring agriculture that caused all of Van Rader's agricultural projects to end in failure. Trade, not agriculture, was to be the mainstay of Dutch commerce in their Antilles islands. Gold was accidentally discovered on Aruba in 1824 when a 12 year old sheepherder boy sat on a rock in a gully to pick a cactus thorn from his foot. Seeing a yellow-glittering piece of rock, he took it home to his father who recognized it as gold.   The boy had discovered a large deposit of alluvial gold--one piece ending up in the Museum of National History in Leyden, Holland which weighed over 6 pounds.   The settlers soon found that many of the gullies contained gold and the hunt was on. Seeing the potential for wealth, in 1854 the government proclaimed all gullies off-limits to all except government personnel.

Gold was discovered in the form of ore, which required technical know-how to extract the gold. The government made several attempts to license mining companies to extract the gold.   One of these companies was the Aruba Island Goldmining Company, Ltd. which installed a stamp mill and smelter and operated between 1878 and 1880 and extracted over 2000 ounces of gold.

The island became pock-marked with small enterprises digging shafts. The cyanide process introduced a new technology for gold extraction from the quartz ore and dynamite sped the recovery of ore from the shafts. Extensive operations continued until 1916 when they closed during World War I. Some Canadian, German and Curacao interests tried a revival of the industry in 1946, but recovery did not prove to be economic.

SLAVERY AND SLAVE REVOLTS

The Dutch West India Company (WIC) began establishing ports, forts and warehouses along the West African coast as early as 1598. By the middle 1700's the number of ports reached 29, stretching over 500 miles from the southern tip of the Gold Coast to the northern part of the Bight of Benin. These garrisons were, for the most part, poorly maintained and the disease-ridden west coast of Africa was the least popular station for applicants for jobs with WIC. A writer described the soldiers as "miserable wretches, looking as awkward as a company of old Spaniards" and the doctors as "ignorant barbers, who bring some unto the utmost danger of their lives." Many soldiers turned to desertion.   The number of men stationed at the forts varied widely. Around 1700, Fort Crevecoeur was manned with 3, Fort St. Sebastian with 10 and Fort Conradsburg with 130.

In the early days the Dutch focused on shipping ivory, salt, gold and hides. Around 1720 shipments of gold almost ceased to exist and the Gold Coast became known as the Slave Coast. The need for an increase in Caribbean slave labor   started with the extermination of the Arawaks by the Spaniards. Gold mining, growing sugar, tobacco and other products, even for local use, required labor. The Dutch signed asientos (contracts) with the Spanish and stepped in early to become Spain's major source   of black African slaves for their colonies.

The slave market boom opened up between 1640 and 1645 when growers from Barbados returned from a Dutch sponsored trip to Brazil where they learned the techniques of sugar production. Their enormous profits in a short period opened the sugar era.   The Dutch were at hand to meet the demand for labor. So were the English and French and a fierce competitive fight for a piece of the slave market broke out between the three nations.

Curacao and Surinam became Dutch slave emporiums.   The Dutch kept meticulous records.   The WIC recorded 227 slave voyages to the Caribbean islands between 1674 and 1791. Over 500 slave voyagers were recorded by other companies and sole proprietors. During the 64 years between 1731 and 1794, 610 slavers arrived at Surinam unloading 149,999 slaves.   Slaves were ordered by the "head" and the "ton." Between 1682 and 1689 the slave trader, Barroso, held a contract to supply 11,000 tons of slaves. It is estimated that the Dutch transported around 20,000 slaves to the Caribbean annually during the 17th century and around 100,000 annually during the 18th century.

The Dutch established two slave camps on Curacao. Their first priority was to restore them to good health after their arduous middle-passage journey. The slaves received medical attention, were gradually introduced to Curacao food and not required to do any heavy work.   High walls and heavy guards precluded any outright rebellions. In spite of tight security, some slaves did escape and joined those who had run away from plantations. Successful escapees found their way to the mainland. The island didn't offer many good hiding places and from time to time the Dutch would hold "roundups". Plantation owners were fined for any runaways found on their property.   The treatment of slaves on Curacao was milder than most other Caribbean islands.   Maybe it was because the plantations were smaller and there were proportionally more whites than blacks. Nevertheless, a slave uprising did occur in 1795. By this time the WIC had been dissolved and the governmental forces were weak. Toela, a field slave on the Knip plantation, planned the revolt and in August a troop of 40 to 50 left the plantation and marched down the road collecting firearms from estates and destroying barns and property. As they marched, they gained support and by August 18 over 300 were involved and the destruction level increased to burning estates and killing of some whites.

The government militia sent a small force to quell the uprising, but got a great surprise at the number of slaves who had become armed. Their first attack on the slaves resulted in a retreat. On August 20, the government sent a priest to offer them amnesty, but Toela countered with, "We want our freedom. We have suffered enough. The French slaves have been emancipated and Holland, conquered by the French, should follow." At this time the number of slave rebels had risen to over 2000.

A final attempt to escape Toela on Sunday, August 30 failed and the militia seriously took to the task of defeating the rebels by force. They brought field artillery into play, poisoned wells and conducted organized attacks on the rebels' camps and offered "free passes" to any who would quit the rebellion voluntarily and return to their plantation. Van Westerholt, the general in charge, returned to

Willemstad on September 15–mission accomplished.   Many rebels hid and refused to surrender in spite of Dutch efforts to entice them with such promises as no work on Sunday or Christian holidays, specified working hours, specified food, decent clothing and no unreasonable punishments. Still, enough continued in hiding to pose a threat to the planters which caused many to seek the safety of towns until the later part of the year when the last rebels were captured.

The rebellion failed in Curacao for two reasons, which were the cause of defeat of so many other Caribbean slave rebellions. First, the rebellion did not have the total participation of all the slaves and second; the island didn't offer adequate coverage and protection for them to hide for any sustained period of time.

The concept of emancipation did not receive wide support from the Dutch. It was the pressure from England's emancipation in 1834 that started Holland on the road to end slavery by taking a series of small steps. They allowed slaves to buy their freedom and in 1837 they let slaves marry freemen.   They eliminated the charge for manumission and prepared new regulations regarding the treatment of slaves.

The abolition of the slave trade and finally the emancipation of slavery in the Caribbean by other European powers put the entire region into a period of depression. In spite of the unfavorable economic impact emancipation would bring and the opposition from planters and merchants, the new King of Holland, King Willem III (who owed his gaining the Crown to England), threw his support behind emancipation and the Dutch government proclaimed July 1, 1863 to be the Day of Emancipation. Curacao freed 6,684 slaves on the Day of Emancipation and the former owners received 200 guilders from the government for each slave. The Day was one of happiness and the transition from slavery to freedom passed without incident.

POST-SLAVERY ERA

The oil refining industry came to Curacao in 1916 when a subsidiary of the Royal Dutch/Shell Company built an enormous oil refinery to process oil from Venezuela and Columbia. Curacao's economic base changed from agriculture to oil.   The Standard Oil Company introduced oil refining to Aruba in 1929. On March 15, 1945 Aruba processed its world record one billionth barrel of oil. Ever since Aruba's discovery, islanders lived under the threat of a water shortage. Water rationing was common and often residents lived on a day to day supply. In 1956 the Executive Council decided to build what was to be among the largest sea water distillery plants in the world. Work started in 1958 and the system began operations in 1959. In 1961, only four houses remained unconnected to the island's 440 miles of pipelines   The retail and tourist industries benefitted in the early 20th century when cruise ships began docking at Curacao to take on cheap fuel oil. Since the 1970's the ABC (Aruba, Bonaire and Curacao) islands have enjoyed a tourist boom.

On December 15, 1954 all the Dutch islands and Surinam became an autonomous part of the Kingdom of the Netherlands. Aruba continued to seek total independence. In 1986 the Dutch granted Aruba's independence, to start in 1996.

Your island contacts:
ARUBA

Mr. Jan van Nes, Managing Director
Aruba Tourism Authority
P. O. Box 1019
L.G. Smith Blvd.
Oranjestad, Aruba
Dutch Caribbean
Phone: 011-297-8-23377
Fax: 011-297-8-3470

BONAIRE

Mr. Ronnie Pieters, Tourism Director
Bonaire Tourism Corporation
Kaya Libertador Simon Bolivar 12
Bonaire, Dutch Caribbean
Phone: 011-599-7-8322

CURACAO

Mr. Pieter C.T, Sampson, Director
Curacao Tourism Development Bureau
Pietermaii, P. O. Box 3266
Willlemsted, Curacao
Netherlands Antilles
Phone: 011-599-9-616000
Fax: 011-599-9-612305

Fort El Morro, Puerto Rico

Plaza de Armas, Puerto Rico

CHAPTER 21

PUERTO RICO

SIZE
3435 square miles.

GEOGRAPHY
Varied with coastal plains and mountainous Cordillera Central reaching 4357 feet. The Puerto Rico trench offshore plunges to a depth of 30,200 feet.

CLIMATE
Marginal-tropical. Temperature range between 74 and 81 degrees. Temperatures in the mountains can dip to 5 degrees. Annual rainfall on mountain slopes can be 100 inches.

CAPITAL
San Juan

AMERINDIANS
Archaeologist Ricardo Alegria explored Cueva Maria de la Cruz, a large cave on the northeast coast, in 1948 and discovered a considerable number of non-ceramic artifacts. Radiocarbon dating placed the age of these artifacts in the first century A.D., providing evidence that the Ciboneys were the first human settlers in Puerto Rico. Subsequent radiocarbon dating of pottery remains have revealed that the Arawaks arrived in 120 A.D. and by 1000 A.D. had adopted the Taino culture and named the island "Boriquen"--the land of the brave lord.

On Puerto Rico, as on other Caribbean islands, the Arawaks became the major labor force for the Spanish. They rebelled in 1511, but Ponce de Leon and his superior weaponry quickly subdued them. Some Arawaks fled to some small Carib camps and some villages lasted into the late 18th century. The Spanish paid little attention to the Indians as a labor supply when the importation of slaves from Africa began.

DISCOVERY
Columbus discovered this island, which he named "San Juan Bautista" during his second voyage on November 19, 1493. He

found a deserted village with a dozen huts surrounding a large one, which he presumed to have belonged to an Arawak chief. No Arawaks appeared, so Columbus concluded that the village served as an occasional recreational site. Columbus laid in port for two days and did little exploration before departing for Navidad. The Spanish left the island unsettled until Ponce de Leon founded the town of Caparra, not far from present San Juan, in 1508. After Ponce de Leon's death in 1521 during a battle with the Arawaks in Havana, Cuba the Spanish relocated the Caparra settlement to a new site with a more defensible port. They named it Puerto Rico, which later became the city of San Juan.

SPANISH QUEST FOR POWER AND GOLD

As the sixteenth century unfolded and Spain entered the era of transporting gigantic amounts of gold and silver from South America to Seville, Puerto Rico became the "key to the Indies." San Juan was the first port of call for ships headed for shores where great stores of wealth would become their cargo. Spain recognized the potential for raids by other European nations and by pirates, who began to infiltrate the region in the 16th century. They made some feeble attempts to build fortifications, but built nothing of consequence until 1541 when they began construction on El Morro to protect San Juan. While they protected San Juan, the Spanish did little to defend or encourage the settlement of the rest of the island. During the entire period that Spain had control of the island, the protection of the harbor of San Juan was the only major interest they showed in Puerto Rico--and they did little to support this strategic port.

EUROPEAN POWER STRUGGLE AND SETTLEMENTS

France, England and Holland began to serve notice that they would not be excluded from the West Indies in the late 16th century. Queen Elizabeth became a serious threat when she commissioned Sir Francis Drake to devastate Cartagena, St. Augustine and Santo Domingo, which he did successfully.

These events, the defeat of Spain's "Armada Invincible" and England's rise as a powerful naval power caused the Spanish to strengthen Puerto Rico's defenses and serious construction efforts began on forts El Boqueron, Santa Elena and El Morro. In 1590 General Valdes wrote to the Crown: " . . . (El Morro) when it is ended it will be the strongest that his majestic hath in all the Indies." Spain's concern over an English attack were warranted. In 1595 Queen Elizabeth learned that a Spanish galleon had wrecked and that its treasure had been stored in Puerto Rico's Fort La Fortaleza.

She ordered Sir Francis Drake and John Hawkins to take the island. The Queen provided the two with 6 royal ships, 21 others of different sizes and a detachment of 4500 men to accomplish the task.

Drake's plan to take the island "with all speed" did not materialize. Instead, Hawkins was killed in the beginning and the unexpected intensive bombardment by El Morro's cannon caused Drake to sail away in defeat, himself mortally wounded. Drake's defeat didn't quell Queen Elizabeth's desire to control Puerto Rico. On June 16, 1598 the Earl of Cumberland began his siege on San Juan. He managed to gain control of the city and when famine, shortage of ammunition and continuous bombardment plagued El Morro for 15 days, Governor Mosquera surrendered and the English raised their flag. Cumberland's occupation was short-lived. An epidemic of Yellow Fever and Dysentery killed over 400 of his men and there was no reason to believe that these diseases wouldn't continue to take its toll. This and continuous harassment by the locals led Cumberland to evacuate the island. In his departure he burned crops and most of the city, looted valuables and left San Juan in ruins. The Spanish did little to improve El Morro's defenses. Cannon became under disrepair, the fighting force (with their pay reduced to 1/2), ammunition, food and supplies were minimal.

On September 24, 1625 a guard sighted seventeen Dutch ships approaching San Juan. They rang El Morro's alarm bells and shot cannons to gather townspeople to the fort. On the morning of the 30th, when the attackers felt properly prepared, a courier from the Dutch flagship arrived with a demand for surrender. The Spanish Governor responded with a demand that the Dutch fleet surrender--and a 3-day battle ensued. The Spanish conducted a surprise attack on the entrenched Dutch and in their frenzy to retreat, the disorganized Dutch invaders left 400 dead. The Dutch sailed away. A motley group of 300 poorly armed and supplied Spanish soldiers and farmers had repelled a large well-trained, supremely equipped Holland invasion force.

The King rewarded the Spanish commanders well with ducats and political assignments. It had become obvious that El Morro could be a bastion of Spanish security in the Indies if properly supplied and manned, but a parade of military problems demanded the Spanish King's attention. Spain suffered naval disasters like the defeat of the Armada, destruction of the fleet preparing to invade Ireland and the defeat of a fleet in Brazilian waters in 1630 by the Dutch. Land defeats in battles with the French and Portuguese and the spendthrift habits of the Duke of Olivares emptied Spain's treasury.

The 17th century ended with Puerto Ricans having to find their own defenses against the Europeans and Buccaneers. They experienced a series of attacks in the 18th century, but with earnestness, bravery and on occasion, some help from Mother Nature—in 1768 a hurricane destroyed a large English fleet while it was preparing an invasion—succeeded in driving off the invaders.

In February 1797 over 6000 English troops under the command of Sir Ralph Abercrombie conquered Trinidad. March found the fleet at the doorstep of San Juan. By this time construction on El Morro had been completed and 376 cannon, 35 mortars, 4 howitzers and 3 swivel guns were in place. Their fighting force included 200 veteran soldiers and 4000 militiamen plus a few supporting French privateer ships. Abercrombie landed 3000 men on March 18 and more or less serious battles took place for 13 days. On the morning of the 14th day of siege the Spanish poised for a general attack. But, lo! Daybreak found no Englishmen in sight. Abercrombie had determined that the fort was invincible.

The English followed this assault with a blockade of the island and made repeated small attacks. In spite of the lack of every kind of help and support from Spain, the Puerto Ricans remained loyal to the mother country, even when they saw other Indies islands declaring independence from Spain. To survive, they released the militia to farm and left the few remaining soldiers, still only receiving ½ pay, to defend the fort. Although Puerto Rico had fine soil and a well-located harbor in San Juan, Spain continued to ignore the island. The populace fell into a lethargic state, most inhabitants cultivating just enough land to maintain a minimal survival existence.

Gradually, educated emigrants from Columbia, Venezuela and other South American countries experiencing revolutions began to settle in Puerto Rico. These new immigrants awakened the docile locals to Spain's indifference to them. A succession of revolts began in 1868. In 1898 Spain watched a glorious island slip from its grasp—Puerto Rico became a territory of the United States of America.

BUCCANEERS, PIRATES AND PRIVATEERS
While the majority of the buccaneers had their beginning in western Hispaniola, small numbers had made their home and sold "boucan" in Cuba and the western part of Puerto Rico. When buccaneering became popular and more and more English, French and Dutch ships appeared in the Caribbean, the Spanish took to supporting privateers. Privateer Miguel Henriquez won the favor of Spanish King Phillip V by his attack on Crab Island in 1718.

Phillip gave him the title: "Captain of Sea and War and Provider of Cosairs of Puerto Rico." This title gave him more power than the governor. The privateers targeted English ships. In February 1734 alone, the Spanish privateers ushered six English ships into Puerto Rican harbors. The harsh treatment of the English by Spanish privateers led to the War of Jenkins Ear in 1739. In return for Spanish atrocities, buccaneers and privateers harassed Puerto Rico throughout the 17th and 18th centuries.

In 1780 the Spanish outfitted a fleet composed of 500 of Puerto Rico's finest well-armed soldiers and 50 cannon. The objective was to seek out foreign buccaneer and pirate nests and destroy them. The fleet sailed away never to return. Everything was lost in a hurricane.

THE SUGAR ERA

Early efforts to introduce sugar in Puerto Rico got a jump-start around 1550 and ended with a bang around 1647. Sugar cane production required a large capital investment in machinery, slaves and property. The settlers had plenty of desire and initiative, but few economic resources. The Crown provided loans to help establish the industry. Fraud became widespread in the loan-granting process. Many borrowers didn't repay their loans and lost their property and slaves to indifferent royal subjects.

To compound the problem, the Crown didn't supply the needed number of slaves and didn't provide the required ships to carry the product to Seville. Eleven sugar plantations existed in 1582. The number of plantations dropped to seven in 1647 and many planters switched to growing ginger or cattle raising. During the time following this meager effort by the Spanish to improve the economy, the settlers migrated to the countryside. They literally became hermits, establishing small farms on property they did not own and away from each other and towns. Subsistence farming became the way of life in Puerto Rico until increased immigration in the late 17th century brought capital to the island. Sugar production became a commercial enterprise by the 19th century. Between 1820 and 1896 the land devoted to sugar increased three-fold and production increased from 17,000 tons in 1820 to 62,000 tons in 1896. By 1832 the trend was away from peasant farming and toward the hacienda. The crisis in Puerto Rico's sugar industry closely followed that of other Caribbean islands in the closing years of the 19th century and planters converted their land to growing coffee. By the end of the century, coffee had replaced sugar as the main agricultural crop.

SLAVERY AND SLAVE REVOLTS

Puerto Rico found itself in a unique position with regards to a labor force as sugar re-entered the commercial scene in the 1800's. The large number of peasants, many being freed runaway slaves from other islands subsisting on small plots, had no title to their land. The Crown enacted legislation to force these farmers to enter the work force as wage earners on the plantations. Planters continually called for more slaves to work on their sugar plantations than the government would import. In 1820 Puerto Rico, unlike other Caribbean islands, had a slave population of only 10% of the total. In that year England applied pressure on Spain and forced the Spanish to sign a treaty to abolish the slave trade. Governor Torre found a loophole in the treaty. Instead of importing slaves from Africa, he imported them from St. Thomas and other neighboring islands "in view of the need of hands to work in agriculture and to replace those who die annually." The treaty allowed this. Even though the slave population was small, the uprisings in Haiti and other islands concerned the planters. In 1843 the government issued a decree listing punishments for participants in rebellions. No significant rebellions seem to have occurred. A strong anti-slavery movement began in Madrid in 1865 and 33,000 slaves became free in 1873.

POST SLAVERY ERA

Napoleon's near-conquest of Spain and the struggles by many Spanish American colonies to free themselves from Spanish rule had an impact on Puerto Rico's political agenda. Spain began losing their West Indies colonies in the 1800's and turned to Puerto Rico to provide a showcase of their intent to reform their colonial administration. They over-administrated and always favored the colonial elite at the expense of the laboring class.

Some examples of their decrees included:

1. Anyone may be fired or arrested for any reason at the will of the Governor.

2. A 10:00 p.m. curfew and a ban on reunions after dark.

3. Anyone found to be without work or income would be punished.

4. No mustaches or goatees were to be permitted.

5. Puerto Ricans could receive no foreign visitors.

6. No horse racing or collective petitions are allowed.

7. Everyone over 16 and not a property owner must carry a passport in which is recorded the workers place of work, salary and conduct.

8.People could not change their place of residence, travel throughout the island or give parties without prior governmental permission.

Puerto Rico rebels tired of these oppressive decrees and began to get notions about separating from Spain. By the 1830's Spain had lost the Spanish Main and became so beset with domestic problems that their attention to Puerto Rico began to wane again.

In 1868 a series of revolts brought about important changes in Spanish rule. Military leaders in Spain forced Queen Isabella to give up her throne. Cuban leaders, citing lack of liberties, corruption in government, unfair taxation and poor education began their 10 Year War in this year. Ramon Betances, a French-educated Puerto Rican physician and political activist, issued his "Ten Commandments for Free Men" in 1868 and led a short revolt. While the revolt did not succeed, it became a symbol of resistance and of Puerto Rican's desire for self-rule. Spain declared itself a republic in 1873 and in 1897 Spain's Prime Minister, seeing the war being lost in Cuba and the growing anti-Spanish sentiment in the United States, granted Puerto Rico a charter of autonomy.

While this was taking place, tension between Spain and the United States grew. The United States had already engulfed Texas, California, Florida and parts of Louisiana and had their eyes on Cuba and Puerto Rico. The United States feared that England could threaten their commerce if they gained control of Cuba and Puerto Rico. In February 1898, General Manuel Casado was inaugurated governor of Puerto Rico's new autonomous government and efforts to establish a political system began. One week after a new legislature had started to address their tasks, the United States invaded Puerto Rico. Puerto Rico's long sought after self-government died during birth.

On July 28, 1898 3,400 U.S. troops stormed a beach close to Columbus' landing site. After a few skirmishes, with no support from the Puerto Rican people, the Spanish surrendered. This surrender became an issue during the December 1898 Treaty of Paris in which Spain ceded Puerto Rico, Cuba, the Philippines and Guam to the United States in return for $20 million from the United States. Puerto Ricans looked forward to an even more democratic controlled self-government than that given by Spain. Such was not to be. The U.S. felt they could govern Puerto Rico better than the Puerto Ricans and proceeded to try to mold their culture to that of the United States.

The Puerto Rican legislature became a mere figurehead and felt treated like some sort of inept stepchild. U.S. Representative

Joseph Cannon, visiting Puerto Rico in 1919 typified U.S. feelings with his statement, "Why are you worrying about statehood or independence? You will get either or both   as soon as you are ready."

Relations continued to be strained through the 1920's when significant U.S. investments, particularly in sugar, reaped huge profits which left the island and ended up in the States. The population had increased, but wages remained low, in spite of the fact that the cost of living was higher than in New York.   Puerto Rico did not gain much during the U.S.`s affluent 20's, but did share the economic disaster of the 1929 U.S. stock market crash and the depression that followed. In 1935 the U.S. Secretary of the Interior described Puerto Rico in a letter to Senator Fletcher which read in part, ". . . There is today more widespread misery and destitution and far more unemployment in Puerto Rico than at any previous time in its history." During the 30's the average per capita income was $118 a year.

Munoz Marin emerged as Puerto Rico's most effective and influential leader. In the 30's he established the Popular Democratic Party, organized to represent the mass of the rural population, with the motto, "Bread, Land and Liberty."   Munoz hit a windfall during World War II. Puerto Rican rum became a big seller in the U.S., and its sale included a sizable excise tax--the money being added to the Puerto Rican treasury. The Puerto Rican budget increased from $22 million in 1938 to $150 million in 1945.

In 1941 Rexford Tugwell, (the last Anglo-Saxon to be a Puerto Rican governor) became governor and quickly showed himself to be on Puerto Rico's side by becoming an effective mediator between Munoz and the U.S. government.   In 1943 Tugwell succeeded in getting President Roosevelt's permission for Puerto Rico to elect their own governor. In 1945 Munoz's party won an overwhelming majority in the legislature.   In 1946 Tugwell left office and Jesus Pinero replaced him. For the first time in Puerto Rico history a Puerto Rican occupied the highest post in the land.

A considerable amount of wrangling between Munoz, his political party and the U.S. Congress produced an acceptable Puerto Rican constitution. On July 25, 1951 in San Juan, near the eve of the fifty-fourth anniversary of the U.S. invasion, Governor Munoz Marin raised the Puerto Rican flag to fly alongside of the "Stars and Stripes" of the U.S. and Puerto Rico became a Commonwealth of the United States.   The political status of Puerto Rico remains an issue to this day. In 1993 Puerto Rican voters had their choice to elect: 1. To remain a U.S. Commonwealth, 2. To apply for U.S.

Statehood or, 3. Become an independent nation.   The voters elected to remain a U.S. Commonwealth.

Your island contact

Mr. Louis Fortuno, Director
Puerto Rico Tourism Company
P. O. Box 4435
Old San Juan Station
San Juan, PR   00902-4435
Phone: (809) 721-2400
Fax: (809) 725-4417

Government House, Nevis

Hamilton Mill Machinery, Nevis

CHAPTER 22

ST. KITTS & NEVIS

SIZE
ST. KITTS: 68 square miles
NEVIS: 37 square miles

GEOGRAPHY
St. Kitts: Shaped in the form of an Indian paddle
with gently sloping hillsides rising to the top
of a mountain range. Highest peak is 3792 foot Mt.
Misery, renamed Mt. Liamuiga, the original
Amerindian name, in 1983.

Nevis: Mt. Nevis. elevation 3232 feet, is
surrounded by a gently rolling landscape.

CLIMATE
Rainfall varies between 40 and 150 inches, depending
on altitude, but the average is around 60 inches.
The wettest months are from September to November.
The driest months are January and April. Average
temperature is 80 degrees.

CAPITALS
St. Kitts: Basseterre
Nevis: Charlestown

AMERINDIANS
Archaeological digs have uncovered evidence that both the
Arawaks and Caribs inhabited the islands in pre-Columbian times.
In keeping with the history of the migration of these two cultures, the
Arawaks arrived first, followed by the Caribs who dominated on the
battlefield.
St. Kitts and Nevis were among the Leeward islands the Spanish
designated as useless for settlement because of the lack of precious
metals and geographical location. They did, however, find a use for
the resident Caribs. The profits from their pearl diving venture on
the island of Cubagua, off the coast of South America, was being
threatened because of the high mortality rate of divers.   The

Spanish turned to St. Kitts and Nevis to replenish their labor supply. They forced the Caribs to dive 16 hours a day to depths ranging from 20 to 70 feet. The divers would caress an armful of rocks to their chest to carry them down. The death rate was high and in 1520 a large contingent of Caribs arrived in canoes from the mainland and killed all the Spaniards. This event and the near depletion of the oyster bed ended the pearl diving project on Cubagua. When Englishman Thomas Warner arrived at St. Kitts in 1624 the Carib population numbered only in the hundreds. Warner had made a short stay in St. Kitts in 1622 and befriended the Caribs; therefore, the Caribs welcomed the Warner party. As time wore on and the French arrived and the Europeans began dividing up the island with disregard of the Caribs, the Caribs became concerned about their own security.

In 1625 several canoe loads of Caribs arrived from nearby islands and skirmishes took place between November 1625 and August 1626. According to local legend, Barbe, a Carib woman, warned the English of an imminent Carib attack. Wasting no time, the English and French joined forces and conducted a nighttime massacre on the Carib encampment, now known as Bloody Point. This attack, which killed the Carib king, Tegreman, ended future Amerindian threats to the Europeans on these two islands.

DISCOVERY

Columbus anchored overnight during his second voyage at Nevis on November 11, 1493. He named the island San Martin because he sighted it on St. Martin's Day. By 1540 the island appeared on maps as "Santa Maria de las Nieves" (nieves meaning snow). It is said the name change coincided with an unusual summer snow (nieves) storm in Spain. Later, map makers shortened the name to Nevis. The following day, November 12, Columbus sailed by St. Kitts. He did not land on the island, which he named St. Christopher after himself. The locals shortened the name to St. Kitts in the 18th century. The Caribs had named the island Liamuiga, meaning "Fertile Island."

Captain Barthomew Gilbert of Plymouth, England made the first written report of landing on Nevis on June 1603. He and his work party of 20 harvested over 20 tons of lignum vitae wood in two weeks. This wood is so dense it will not float and has to have guide holes drilled before it can be nailed. A writer reported that the sea abounded with tortoises which tangled their fishing nets, often causing them to break, releasing the fish. He wrote, "This day in the Evening some went with the Boate unto the shore, and brought on boord a Tortoyse so big that foure men could not get her into the Boate but tied her fast by one legge unto the Boat, and so towed her to the ship, when they had her by the ship, it was no easie matter to get her on board. . This day at night we opened our Tortoyse, which had in her about 500 Egges, excellent sweet meat, and so is the whole fish."

Hubbard, Vincent K. Swords, Ships and Sugar

SPANISH QUEST FOR POWER AND GOLD

When the Spanish extracted all the assets of interest the islands had to offer, namely the Caribs for pearl diving, they let the islands be.   While they claimed St. Kitts and Nevis to be theirs by right of discovery, they put up no resistance to Warner and company when they arrived to settle in 1624.

EUROPEAN POWER STRUGGLE AND SETTLEMENTS

Thomas Warner was one of two Englishmen in charge of establishing an English settlement on the "wild coast" of South America in the early 1600's. When the attempt failed in 1622 he stopped at St. Kitts for a few months on his return voyage to England.   Warner fell in love with the island and returned in 1625 after securing financing and a handful of hopeful settlers to start a colony. Upon his return he found a few Frenchmen had established a settlement. More French came when a pirate ship, badly battered in a fight with the Spanish, put in for repairs.   The English, French and Caribs coexisted for awhile until the aforementioned battle took place at Bloody Point, eliminating the Caribs.

The English and French signed a treaty after the Bloody Point incident which divided the island, the French getting the northern section, the English the central part and the southern third, including the salt flats, to be left as neutral territory. The agreement included a clause that they would remain neutral in the event England and France went to war.   The treaty seemed to work as far as drawing lines of possession, but not in cooperation. In 1629 a Spanish fleet attacked St. Kitts in their continuing attempt to drive invading foreigners from the West Indies. The French and English failed to cooperate in defense and, as a result, the Spanish easily demolished their colonies.   Once the Spanish left, the English and French quickly rebuilt and the two sides tolerated each other until 1666.

The 17th century saw a virtual continual state of war between England and France.   In 1666 the French invaded the English section of St. Kitts, but the Treaty of Ryswick in 1697 divided the island as written in the 1627 treaty.   Somehow, the two sections managed to survive during the period of warfare between the two homelands until 1713. In that year the Treaty of Utrecht ceded all French claims on St. Kitts to England.   One explanation for the English and French being able to tolerate each other as well as they did on a divided island is that the island had become known as the "mother of the Caribbean" to each country. Each settlement had become a home base for settlers who formed expeditions to other islands.   From St. Kitts, the English settled Nevis, Antigua and Montserrat. The French launched expeditions to settle Martinique, Guadeloupe, St. Martin, St. Bart and St. Eustatius.

Captain John Smith, on his way to establish a colony in Virginia, North America, anchored his three ships for a five day rest on Nevis in 1607. He wrote that his men became greatly rejuvenated from their journey, especially after bathing in the hot sulfur waters of Bath Stream. Sulfur baths were to become very popular on Nevis. There are reports of occasional visits to Nevis by adventurers, but the first serious attempt to settle Nevis happened when Thomas Warner sent Captain Anthony Hilton to establish a colony in 1628. Hilton proved to be more of a pirate than a governor and ended up as Governor of Tortuga, the notorious buccaneer island. He died there during a raid by the Spanish. The Earl of Carlisle took over management of the colony, but the Crown replaced his authority and established a colonial office in 1664. The tiny island of Nevis did not escape the wrath the European powers laid on each other during the 17th and 18th centuries.

A major sea battle took place in 1667 when 10 British ships faced a force of 30 French and Dutch frigates. The victorious British saved Nevis and the Leewards for England. Nevis became a naval base for the British while they raided St. Martin and Martinique and it was from here that the British recaptured St. Kitts from the French in 1690. The French took revenge for their loss of St. Kitts through a siege on Nevis in 1706. Their purpose was to devastate, not conquer, the island. This, they did, burning all records and buildings and leaving the island in such a total state of destruction that it never recovered to become the major settlement that it was previously destined to be.

BUCCANEERS, PIRATES AND PRIVATEERS

Nevis became earmarked as the center for trials and executions of pirates and enemy privateers in the 1670's. This came about through an English agreement with Spain that granted English Caribbean possessions to England if England would agree to call off English privateers who were raiding Spanish shipping, and would endeavor to help Spain to rid the region of pirates. The English complied in part, but did keep three privateers on standby just in the event of the resumption of hostilities.

In 1683 Nevis Governor Stapleton ordered Captain Carlileto take his frigate, patrol the area and destroy any pirates he found. One night they sailed into the Danish-owned harbor of Charlotte Amalie on St. Thomas and anchored beside the 32 gun ship owned by the pirate Jean Hamlin. Carlile boarded the ship, killed the skeleton crew and burned it. The Danish governor was enraged, because this harbor was declared neutral and all ships were invited to lay in for repairs, trading or carousing. In spite of the English diligence, pirates remained a problem in the area until the middle of the 19th century.

THE SUGAR ERA

Much land became available when the French relinquished the island and many acres were given away or sold at auction in 1726. Instead of selling some parcels which small farmers could afford, the plots auctioned exceeded 200 acres and sold at prices only the wealthy could afford. This firmly established the sugar economy and when the small farmer moved to other islands, the planters replaced them with slaves.   St. Kitts became the richest of England's colonies in the 18th century as sugar plantations stretched from the water's edge to half-way up the mountains. Sugar production rose from 1000 tons in 1710 to 10,000 tons in 1770. Income from an average plantation was about 100 pounds per year, which calculates to approximately $70,000 U.S. dollars. Sugar production began to eclipse during the American War for Independence when prices for supplies needed by the planters began to rise. Prices rose even more in 1778 when France declared war on England and invaded the island twice. More and more plantations came under absentee ownership management and the end of the heyday of sugar was seen with the forthcoming of the emancipation of slavery and growth of the sugar beet industry.

When emancipation came, only one estate was sold for housing. The former slaves were forced to live on the estates during the 4-year apprenticeship program imposed by the Crown. Many former slaves left the island and an attempt to enlist 1500 Portuguese indentures failed when they returned home, instead of staying on after their period of indenture.

By 1890 St. Kitts was in a bad way. Roads were in disrepair, housing almost nonexistent, except in Bassaterre, and working conditions were pitiful.   St. Kitts then experienced a series of catastrophes which started with a disastrous earthquake in 1841. This was followed by a wave of Cholera 11 years later which claimed 4000 lives, 1/6 of the population. In 1867 a great fire, which started in a bakery, destroyed 500 houses in Bassaterre, leaving 5000 persons homeless. A great flood struck in 1880 when 36 inches of rain fell in central St. Kitts one day in January. Whole houses were washed out to sea and the event claimed another 300 lives. Historians find that the homeland did little more than wring their hands and complain about the expense of the tragedies. The poor received the least help.   One wonders about the circumstances that gave birth to the field names used to identify the various estates on St. Kitts during the sugar era. Some names were: Jumbie Hole 9, Upper Dung Pit, Big Runaway Grave, Ten-Penny Garden, Upper Jack Spaniard, Twelve and Salt Water, Banky-Banky, Monkey Jar and Little Nanny Coffin.

Sugar production on Nevis started during the second half of the 17th century with the establishment of a few plantations of from 100 to 200 acres. The number increased rapidly until, at the height of the industry, Nevis sported 41 windmill powered plants, 20 steam-powered mills, and 22 animal-driven mills and by 1774 Nevis was considered a more important commercial entity than New York.

Nevis entrepreneurs continued efforts to produce sugar cane long after those on other islands abandoned the industry. Six windmills were in operation at the turn of the century and production continued through World War II. The last mill, government-owned New River, closed in 1958.   The present-day Hamilton Museum and Nevis House of Assembly building is the reconstructed house where Alexander Hamilton was born on January 11, 1757.

Hamilton was the illegitimate son of divorcee Rachel Levine (who was forbidden to remarry) and Scottish aristocrat James Hamilton. He lived on Nevis until the age of nine when he was moved to St. Croix. Since he was illegitimate, he could not be educated in the Anglican Church School on Nevis; therefore, he was enrolled in the Jewish School. From St. Croix, he ventured to NewYork to study. He signed the Declaration of Independence, became a Colonel in the American Revolutionary Army and served as the first Secretary of the Treasury.

SLAVERY AND SLAVE REVOLTS

The introduction of sugar ended the era of tobacco farming and with it came the need for an increased labor supply. When the indentured Irishmen ended their term of indenture, they found little reason to stay on the islands. Small plots of land were not for sale and they didn't have the funds to invest in a large estate. Continuing to work on the plantations at the low wages offered was unthinkable. The "great clearing" of land for cane growing began around 1650 and with it began the importation of slaves from Africa. Many hundreds of ships arrived at St. Kitts to satisfy the insatiable thirst for slaves until the slave trade became illegal in 1807.

Marked in the annals of St. Kitts history is the tragedy that took place on the ship, the <u>Prince of Orange</u> one day in March 1737. While the ship lay in Bassaterre's harbor preparing their slaves for sale, some potential buyers came to visit. During this visit one of the buyer's slaves, with a warped sense of humor, told the slaves to be sold that the next day they were to be taken ashore and eaten. In panic, over a hundred slaves jumped overboard in an attempt to commit suicide. Thirty-three did drown themselves, but the rest were rescued and sold. The proportion of black slaves to free whites on St. Kitts rose considerably during the 18th century. In 1707 there were 1,416 whites and 2,861 slaves. In 1774 there were 1,900 whites and 23,462 slaves, a ratio of 12 slaves to one free white. The ratio of blacks in Nevis was 3 to 1 in 1707 and 10 to 1 in 1774.

The largest slave revolt on St. Kitts took place in 1639 when 60 slaves escaped and built a fort atop a hill, with entry to be gained only through a narrow pass. A force of 500 English militia stormed the bastion and only the leader survived the day. The following day he was cornered and shot. The English uncovered a slave revolt plot on Nevis in 1725 and killed two suspected leaders before the plot could unfold. Both denied their charges to the end. The planters on Nevis generally treated their slaves well by abiding to certain rules of conduct by consensus. But there were exceptions. Edward Huggins, the richest and most powerful planter in Nevis during the 18th and 19th century owned 900 slaves which he mistreated and got away with by influence and intimidation. For example, he worked slaves by moonlight spreading manure the fields. Planters agreed that no work would be performed after nightfall. The planters had an unwritten law that no slave would receive more than 39 lashes for punishment. One day in 1812 he marched 32 slaves he felt were lazy to the Charlestown town square. There he had them flogged in public. One slave received 241 lashes and another 292. One woman died after her flogging, but the coroner recorded her death was due to natural causes.

This event horrified the Nevis Assembly and they brought Huggins to trial for the incident. He was found not guilty by a jury of his peers and a newspaper was fined 15 pounds for carrying the story. In 1817 Huggins was charged with forcing a father to flog his son. Again, he was found innocent. Some good did come from these terrible acts. Those leading the movement for emancipation back home picked up on Huggin's actions and used them as ammunition to support their view of the inhumanity of slavery.

The planters on St. Kitts did not accept emancipation with grace. They owned the land and would not part with it. Freed slaves had no place to live except in the squalid conditions on the plantations or in tiny congested areas where they had to rent. The work they could do was limited. In order for them to do work in occupations other than field work, such as porter, driver or lighterman, freed blacks had to secure licenses--which were sparingly issued. As a result, many took the first opportunity to leave the island.

POST-SLAVERY ERA

In 1698 all the British colonies in the Leewards from the Virgin Islands to Trinidad were placed under the administration of a Governor-General who lived on Antigua. A lieutenant-governor was appointed for each island who worked through a Council and Assembly. Wealthy planters composed the Council, while the Assembly were freeholders elected in the various parishes. The Assembly seldom agreed with the lieutenant-governor and the council and neither worked well with London's Governor General.

In 1882, with no input from the island residents, the Crown eliminated the representative form of government and placed St. Kitts, Nevis and Anguilla under the rule of a Crown-appointed Administrator, Council and Assembly. This form of government lasted until 1937 when the Crown again allowed elections; however, the income and property ownership requirements making persons eligible to vote limited the number of voters to 1500.

It wasn't until 1952 that governmental reform appeared in a significant way. That year saw universal suffrage for St. Kitts and Nevis and Legislative and Executive Councils with elected members. The newly-formed St. Kitts-Nevis Labour Party became a political power.

In 1967 St. Kitts, Nevis and Anguilla became an "Associated State" with full internal self-government with an elected Governor, Senate and House of Representatives. Income and property requirements for voting had ceased. Anguillans violently opposed being governed by a St. Kitts based government and after several referendums, various political maneuvers and outright rebellions spaced over a period of 15 years, Anguilla gained severance from St. Kitts. The island finally became a British colony with their own

British governor in 1982.   Nevis wasn't happy with the Associated State concept either, but took a less aggressive route to change than Anguilla. Nevis waited for their opening for self-government which came when both St. Kitts and Nevis gained independence from England on September 19, 1983. The St. Kitts-Nevis Parliament now meets in Bassaterre. Oddly enough, Nevis representatives have a say about the internal affairs of St. Kitts, but there is no reciprocal right for St. Kitts. While sugar cane production ended on Nevis in 1958, over one-half the work force on St. Kitts was employed in the industry as we entered the 1990's.

    Bassaterre opened a deep water port in 1981 and cruise ship and other vacationers rose in number from around 7000 a year to a projected 100,000 in 1988.   Nevis seriously entered the tourist industry in 1991 when the Four Seasons Hotel opened. Its 18-hole Championship golf course replaced Nevis's original which boasted one hole and four tee boxes.

Your island contact:

St. Kitts and Nevis Tourist Board
Pelican Shopping Mall
Bay Road
Basterre, St. Kitts
West Indies
Phone: (809) 465-2620
Fax: (809) 465-8794

Altos de Chavon, Dominican Republic

The Pitons, St. Lucia

CHAPTER 23

ST. LUCIA

SIZE
238 square miles

GEOGRAPHY
Northern section relatively flat. Central section mountainous. Island famous for its twin inverted rock cones (pitons) on the south end of island: Grand Piton, 2681' and Petit Piton, 2415'.

CLIMATE
Temperatures average 75 degrees. Lowest humidity is between December and June. Rainfall varies between 47 and 150 inches, depending on altitude.

CAPITAL
Castries

AMERINDIANS
Archaeological digs in the 1940's revealed a considerable number of axes, artifacts and other findings that indicated the island once hosted a large population of Caribs.   Whether the Arawaks settled here is one of conjecture. Digs in St. Vincent, 30 miles to the southwest and Martinique, 20 miles to the north have uncovered Arawak relics. In spite of the lack of concrete evidence, historians believe that the Arawaks must have included St. Lucia during their island-hopping ventures prior to the appearance of the Caribs. The St. Lucia historian, Reverend C. Jessie, admitted in 1968 that many digs have been cursory and many findings are left without explanation or conclusion.

DISCOVERY
Columbus is supposed to have discovered St. Lucia in 1502, during his 4th voyage. The problem is that his son, Fernando, recorded the discovery of Martinique and Dominica--but not St. Lucia. It is possible that when he landed on Martinique and continued north, he never looked south to see St. Lucia. Someone discovered St. Lucia, because the King of Spain ordered war against the Caribs in 1511 and a map of the island dated 1512 exists.
 The first account of Spanish contact with the Caribs on St. Lucia came through a Captain Gilbert in 1603. When he stepped ashore

he thought he had landed on Bermuda. The Caribs showed no aggression during his short stay.

Two years later the ship, Olive Branch, ran aground on St. Lucia with 67 passengers. What started out as a friendly relationship turned into a pattern of Carib ambush and treachery. Shortly, the 19 Olive Branch survivors escaped for South America in an open boat. Approximately 400 English settlers from St. Kitts made the second attempt to settle St. Lucia in 1638. Everything went well for 18 months. Then, one day, some friendly Caribs boarded an English ship in the harbor, thinking it was French. The English primed them with brandy and attempted to capture them as slaves. Some Caribs jumped overboard and swam to shore. They notified other Caribs on Martinique and Dominica and in acts of revenge virtually exterminated the English settlement. The few survivors fled to Monserrat and for a time abandoned thoughts of settling St. Lucia.

This abandonment by the English, real or supposed, opened the door to the French. The French Crown claimed St. Lucia and ceded the island to the French India Company who, in turn sold St. Lucia, Grenada and Martinique to one of its shareholders, a certain de Parquet in 1650.

No country cataloged official documentation of St. Lucia's discovery on any specific date by any specific person. By 1650 Spain, England and France all felt the island belonged to them because of their settlements.

SPANISH QUEST FOR POWER AND GOLD
St. Lucia held nothing of interest for the Spanish. A few Caribs might have been taken for slaves, but beyond that the island offered no promise for gold and was certainly off the trade routes between South America and Seville.

EUROPEAN POWER STRUGGLE AND SETTLEMENTS
By 1663 both England and France had experience with settling St. Lucia. For the next 140 years the island became a political football with the number of governmental changes bordering on comedy, as described in the following paragraph. In 1663 English settlers from Barbados captured the island. In 1669 epidemics of malaria and yellow fever forced them to evacuate the island and the French took it over. In 1700, Governor Grey of Barbados claimed the island, but their invasion attempt failed. In 1722 the King of England claimed the island and sent a military force to invade it. This time the invasion succeeded without a shot being fired. War between England and France broke out and in 1723 the island

became neutral territory by treaty. A large influx of French settlers between 1748 and 1756 caused the island to be considered French. Another war and another treaty returned the island to England in 1762, but the Treaty of Paris gave St. Lucia to France in 1763. After a major island invasion, the English captured St. Lucia in 1773. Although the English defeated the French in battle in 1783, France regained control under the Treaty of Versailles in 1784. General warfare broke out again between England and France and Queen Victoria had the English flag raised on St. Lucia in 1794. Disorder, massacres and burnings directed by French revolutionaries temporarily defeated the English in 1794. The English regained power in 1796. In 1802 the Treaty of Amiens restored the island to France.

On June 19, 1803 Lieutenant-General Grinfield of Barbados set forth on the last military attack on St. Lucia, then also known as the "Helen of the West." Grinfield succeeded and the struggles for the island ended. St. Lucia changed hands 14 times in 140 years before becoming an English Crown colony under another Treaty of Paris in 1813. This volatile little island came under the administration of 84 governors in 192 years (1651-1843), the average term being 2.3 years.

BUCCANEERS, PIRATES AND PRIVATEERS

St. Lucia, not being on the Spanish trade route from South America to Spain and lacking any significant booty to sack, did not attract the sea-going Brethren; therefore, it did not become a major player during the pirating Caribbean era.

THE SUGAR ERA

There appears to have been no cultivation of any kind on the island until the middle of the 17th century. The settlers introduced tobacco, ginger and cotton in 1651. Adventurers from Martinique arrived in 1736 and introduced the more lucrative crops of coffee and cocoa. Sugar appeared on the scene in 1765. By 1780, thirty plantations were in operation and twenty more had neared the production stage. A violent hurricane occurred in that year that destroyed most of the sugar operations, and the French Revolution that followed produced a period of political and economic instability. Resumption of sugar enterprises took place when the English took control in 1803, but by then the English had abolished the slave trade and only allowed the plantation owners to operate with the slaves they already owned.

Economic conditions forced the planters into a partnership with English merchants. The merchants provided the financing and the planters did the work.   Few laws protected either the planter or merchant. The merchants fell to the temptation of charging usurious interest rates and extracting large profits. In retaliation, the planters sold the same crop to 3 or 4 merchants and allowed liens to be filed on their plantations by any creditor wishing to have one.

When foreclosure took place the owners sold their slaves separately or took them to other plantations.   This led to litigation and in the end the lawyers alone triumphed financially.

SLAVERY AND SLAVE REVOLTS

Three factors had an influence on the slave population in St. Lucia: 1. St. Lucia entered the sugar era about 100 years after Barbados and other Caribbean producers; 2. The 1780 hurricane devastated the island plantations as they began to grow in number; and, 3. The English shut off the slave supply in 1803 by freezing their importation.   The major import of African slaves occurred between 1772 and 1789 when the slave population increased from 10,000 to 18,000. The black population increased somewhat in the 1830's when a considerable number fled slavery in Martinique to seek refuge in St. Lucia. British law gave any slave from a foreign colony freedom the moment they set foot on British soil.

A major slave uprising was incited by a shipload of French revolutionary artisans and other "humble orders" of the French populace who arrived at St. Pierre in the late 1820's. "Respectable" St. Lucians shunned them, so they formed friendly relationships with the blacks, who were delighted to be treated with equality by the whites. Upon hearing of the past inhumanities these newcomers encouraged the willing former slaves to plan a rebellion to kill white plantation owners and destroy their property. They designated December 24, 1830 as the target date, but a problem arose that would have spoiled the plan, so a new date, February 9 of the following year was set.   The chiefs of the uprising learned that the whites had wind of their plan and ordered another delay. The order did not reach the rural regions in time and the revolt began as scheduled. By noon on February 10 the totally disorganized revolt had been suppressed, martial law declared and over 500 revolutionaries taken prisoner. They hanged 21 organizers on May 19, 1831.

Emancipation came in 1834, along with the installment of the apprenticeship   program,   supposedly   designed   to   provide skill-training for former slaves.   Soon after Emancipation Day,

August 1, 1838, they eliminated the apprenticeship program, which only served to prolong slavery and provided little training. Apparently all made the transition to complete black freedom peacefully.

POST-SLAVERY ERA
Available historical writings don't indicate that many major events occurred from 1838 up to 1927 when a fire burned most of downtown Castries. Castries became a major coal-bunkering station in the 1800's; a heavy rainstorm in December, 1877 did much damage to Castries; an Agricultural Society was started in 1882; improvements in docking facilities started in 1886.

World War II came to St. Lucia in 1942 when a German submarine entered Castries harbor and torpedoed two ships. Subsequently, the U.S. built airfields on the island as a part of their Caribbean defense effort. Another catastrophic fire destroyed most of Castries in 1948. The fire, started in a tailor's shop and fanned by brisk winds, enveloped most government buildings including the library and archives and virtually all businesses in downtown Castries. Eight hundred families found themselves homeless; however, no one lost their life. The loss amounted to over nine million 1948 dollars.

St. Lucia joined the West Indies Federation in 1958 along with nine other islands with the expectation of improving their economic status. The Federation failed in 3 years after Jamaica and Trinidad withdrew. Land ownership became a problem for the peasants in the later years because of the "family land" law. Under this law all descendants of the original owner have an equal share in the ownership of his land. Thus, there can be as many of 80 equal owners of 10 acres of land; therefore, no one plants a crop because he can't be sure if he will be able to even share in the harvest. Bananas replaced sugar as the major crop in the 1950's and now account for about 83% of the island's exports. The last sugar factory closed in 1963. Tourism, now ranking second in economic importance behind the banana industry, recorded 18,000 tourists in 1964, 49,000 in 1969 and around 200,000 in the early 1990's.

St. Lucia gained her independence as an English Commonwealth in 1979.

Your island contact:

Ms. Agnes Francis, Director
St. Lucia Tourist Board
P. O. Box 221
Castries, St. Lucia
West Indies
Phone: (809) 452-4094
Fax: (809) 453-1121

Mountain Stream, St. Lucia

CHAPTER 24

SINT MAARTEN/SAINT MARTIN

SIZE
34 Square Miles
French part: 21 sq. mi. Dutch part: 13 sq. mi.

GEOGRAPHY
French part: Covered mostly by dry forests
with highest point, Mt. Paradise, 1391 feet.
Dutch part: Lowlands with salt flats.

CLIMATE
Average temperature is around 79 degrees. March is
the driest month, November the wettest.

CAPITALS
Saint-Martin: Dutch, Phillipsburg
Sint Maarten: French, Marigot

> *NOTE; The name St. Martin will be used in this chapter
> when referring to the island as a whole.*

AMERINDIANS
It is supposed that the Arawaks once passed through the island,
but the only relics found in refuse dumps and around the island are
of Carib origin. Father Jean-Baptiste Labat, a French missionary
from Guadeloupe visited St. Martin around 1700. He described the
Caribs as careless, stubborn, hard to take orders, unreliable, haughty
and unwilling to be converted to Christianity. He found them to be
very jealous of their wives, to react violently to insults and much
addicted to alcoholic beverages. Father Labat politely refused to eat
a tasty arm of a recently-killed Englishman. He reported that the
Caribs liked the taste of human flesh, but this is contrary to the
writings of other historians. Six former Carib settlements have been
located. Relics and artifacts, dated from 800 to 1300 A.D., have
been removed to the Florida State Museum.
  Historical writings that document the early Spanish occupation
and the events that took place during the settlement era describe the
squabbles between the French and Dutch, but make no mention of

major difficulties with the Caribs. It is therefore assumed that the Caribs somewhat quietly emigrated to nearby islands.

DISCOVERY

To say that confusion surrounds the identity of who discovered the island, and when, is an understatement. Columbus' ship's log did not document discovering St. Martin. Alvarez Chanca, his ship's doctor, wrote a travel story that told of sighting St. Martin on November 12, 1493 after docking at Redonda on November 11. This was accepted for some time until detailed mapping of the area showed that it is more likely that Alveraz sighted Nevis instead.

In a 1931 study, historian Lucius Hubbard concluded that there was a chance that Columbus sighted St. Martin after passing Saba on November 13 if it was a very clear day—but who knows what the weather was like on November 13, 1493? A historical document written in 1668 states that some French occupied the island in 1638, but this isn't possible since at that time the entire island was under Spanish control. So, no verified documentation exists that positively identifies the discoverers. In 1959 the French and Dutch settled on November 11 as the day of discovery. The day also marks the opening of the tourist season and anniversary of the World War I armistice in 1918.

SPANISH QUEST FOR POWER AND GOLD

Early Spanish interest in St. Martin had to do with keeping the English, French and Dutch from settling in the region. Spanish interest in St. Martin intensified when King Phillip IV decided to raise the price of salt to increase revenue. Salt was a Crown monopoly. The development of the salt pans on St. Martin by the Dutch posed a problem as a ready source of black-market salt. To deal with this problem, King Phillip sent a fleet of 53 ships and a force of 1300 men to St. Martin and they took possession of the island on July 3, 1633 after a week of fierce battles. Once the threat of black-market salt disappeared, the Spanish maintained their military post, but made no attempt at settlement.

The Spanish occupied the island for 15 years. During this time the garrison suffered from neglect. Failure to pay the men and increasing reductions in rations led to mutinies. Manpower dwindled from 250 in 1636 to 120 in 1644. The Dutch were aware of the weakness of the garrison and on March 20, 1644 Peter Stuyvesant, Director of the Netherlands, arrived with approximately 1000 men and launched several unsuccessful attacks. They left the island on April 17 when their attempt at a starvation siege failed. The

Spanish Governor was so proud of his victory that he wrote the King requesting he and his men be reassigned. Four years later he got his wish when Spain decided to abandon the island. They brought workers from Puerto Rico to dismantle the fort and in March 1648 the Spanish left their interest in St. Martin behind.

EUROPEAN POWER STRUGGLE AND SETTLEMENTS

The first to occupy St. Martin was a group of 14 Frenchmen who had fled from the 1629 attack on St. Kitts by the Spanish. They engaged in growing tobacco and farming some of the salt pans. The Dutch made St. Martin their first Caribbean settlement when they arrived in 1631. Their original purpose was to establish a naval base in the Caribbean to protect their merchant ship ventures, but they immediately identified the promise of profits from the salt pans. One observer noted 25 ships entering their harbor during 3 weeks in June 1632. These initial settlement efforts ended with the 1633 invasion by the Spanish, as described in the previous section.

The French returned after the Spanish evacuation in 1648, not as refugees from St. Kitts, but to establish a base to help protect their other interests in the region. The Dutch, no longer needing St. Martin as a naval base, returned so it could serve along with St. Eustatius (St. Stat) as a trade center.

How the Dutch and French Divided the Island

The romantic legend--and it is a legend--goes like this. The Dutch and French met each other in 1648 and agreed that the island had to be divided. To do this, they conducted a walking match, which began at Oysterpond, to determine the boundaries. The French walked around the island in a northerly direction and the Dutch walked in a southerly direction. They agreed that they would draw a line from where they met to Oysterpond. The Dutch were presumed to have walked less distance than the French because they consumed a jar of gin along the way and stopped for a short catnap. They met at Cupecoy Bay and when they drew the boundary line, the Dutch catnap gave the French a larger slice of the island. They actually divided the island by a vaguely-worded partition treaty signed on March 23, 1648. The first three articles read:

1. That the French shall continue in that quarter where they are established at this present, and that they shall inhabit the entire coast (actually: side) which faces Anguilla.

2. That the Dutch shall have the quarter of the fort, and the soil surrounding it on the South coast.

3. That the French and Dutch established on the said island shall live as friends and allies, and that, in case of either party molesting the other, this shall constitute an infringement of this treaty, and shall therefore be punishable by the laws of war.

It took until 1772 for the line of demarcation to be clearly identified. It is assumed that the stone wall, part of which exists today, dates back to 1772 and traverses that boundary.   While agreed upon in principle, neither side took the 1648 treaty seriously. Ignoring this one, new treaties were negotiated in 1703 and 1774. Treaty violations were recorded by one side or the other in 1672, 1676, 1703, 1781, 1793 and 1795.

The period from 1715 to 1750 was one of growing prosperity on the Dutch side. By 1750 the population included 400 whites, and 1500 slaves. Thirty-five sugar plantations contributed to the economic activity. During that time the French side experienced a depression and in 1750 had a population of only 40 French.

The Period of Changing Administrations

John Phillips, a strong Dutch governor seeing the prospect of overpopulation on the Dutch side, proposed the Dutch buy out the French. Other governors supported the idea after his death even to the point of a Dutch governor making an offer of 100,000 piasters to the governor of Martinique.

In 1793 a Dutch Commander of Civil Defense took it upon himself to capture the fort at Marigot. This led to the French governorship being transferred to three French merchants who wooed some French from Guadeloupe to St. Martin. The French invaded the Dutch part in 1795 and held it until 1801 when the English took control. English occupation lasted until 1803. Then, the Dutch returned only to lose control to the English again from 1810 to 1816. Finally, in 1816 the Dutch and French returned permanently to their respective portions of the island. In 1867 the Dutch made a final attempt to secure the French portion by offering to swap it for St. Stat, but nothing happened.

BUCCANEERS, PIRATES AND PRIVATEERS

Smuggling was big business for the Dutch in the Caribbean. The Crown monarchs of Europe and influential producers set the stage for this. Each Crown endeavored to establish a monopoly on their economic activity in the West Indies. Their monopolistic policies limited the sale of products through the Crown which established prices, controlled production and invoked various types of duties. It was only natural for an English merchant to try to do business with an illicit Dutch trader if he could undercut his costs and avoid the English duties.

The English reacted to Dutch smugglers by seizing Dutch ships with their naval forces and employing privateers to intercept them. For example, during the first few months of 1758 St. Stat reported the loss of 19 ships to the English with many Dutch crews and passengers suffering the indignation of being brought to St. Kitts and sold into slavery. Dutch ships also became marks for French and Spanish privateers during this period and these conflicts lasted throughout the 18th century.

Dutch smugglers held allegiance to no one, including the Dutch government. A situation arose on St. Martin in 1884 that brought out the human instinct to circumvent anyone's law whenever possible.

The Dutch on St. Martin served traders in the region by providing them with warehouse facilities. The Dutch government imposed an export duty for products passing through these warehouses. When they found that merchants were transporting merchandise overland to the French side and exporting from there with no duty, they enacted a law that required all exports to be made by sea.   It so happened that the Van Romondts owned a plantation, half of which being on the Dutch side and half on the French. A public road ran through the center of the plantation along the border and down to a French port. Trucks leaving the plantation could not be checked as to from which side they came. Dutch smugglers took advantage of this opportunity and the effort to collect the duties disappeared and ended legally in 1939.   The Dutch smuggling industry and the privateering of their ships ended in the 19th century with the emancipation of slaves and the adoption of kleine vaart by their competitors. Frustration at being unable to control Dutch free inter-island trade (smuggling), called kleine vaart by Dutch historians, caused European powers to relax their monopolistic practices and join the Dutch.

THE SUGAR ERA
More money was to be made for the Dutch on St. Martin through smuggling than agriculture. In 1792 St. Martin had 92 estates with only 35 growing sugar (compared to 800 in operation in Jamaica at that time) and the rest devoted to food crops and cattle breeding. Salt production exceeded sugar with 30,000
barrels of sugar being shipped in 1703 compared to 200,000 barrels of salt shipped in the 1790's.

The French in Marigot concentrated their economic activities by warehousing goods (probably smuggled out of the Dutch half of the island) for the Dutch.   The prohibition of the slave trade in 1830 began an economic depression on St. Martin.   Plantation owners either went bankrupt or limited their maintenance.   Rats took over many plantations and the owners would offer a reward of one bottle of rum for every 100 rat tails turned in.   By the end of the century only 3 sugar mills in the French part and 11 in the Dutch part still operated.   Farming in the salt pans ended around the same time when salt from Iberia proved to be too competitive.

SLAVERY AND SLAVE REVOLTS

The Dutch in the Leewards were more suppliers than users of slaves. The Heren X, the administrative arm of the Dutch West India Company (WIC) was committed to the business of slavery from its beginning in 1675 to its demise in 1815.   Between 1722 and 1726 records show that St. Stat processed 8,268 African slaves. The total number of slaves delivered to the Caribbean, mostly to Curacao by WIC is estimated to be 101,000 between 1675 and 1775.   The number distributed to the Dutch Leewards during that time is described as "trifling."   The Dutch side of St. Martin recorded a population of 648 whites and 1,795 slaves in 1750.   Neither the Dutch or French entered the era of slave emancipation with enthusiasm.   No strong abolitionist movement ever existed in Holland.

Historians don't record any major organized slave revolts on St. Martin.   The reason for this could have been the lack of concentration of large numbers of slaves and the small number of plantations, which enabled the masters to "keep an eye on them."
When the French abolished slavery in 1848, it was a simple matter for a Dutch slave to cross the border and become free.   But the problem existed as to how to survive in the French part, once there. No jobs or housing awaited the escapees.   When a small revival in salt pond farming took place around 1850 many former slaves returned to the Dutch part, bringing friends, to seek employment.
The whole island went into economic decay when slavery ended in the Dutch part in 1863.   Seasonal emigration took place to the Dominican Republic, Puerto Rico and Cuba to work the sugar plantations, to the island of Sombrero to work in the phosphate mines and later to Panama to toil in the digging of the Panama Canal.

POST-SLAVERY ERA

A glance through the chronological history of St. Martin doesn't uncover any significant economic, cultural or political happenings until the 1970's.   A pier opened in Phillipsburg in 1876, post office in 1881, and a passable road opened from Phillipsburg to Marigot in 1906.   A hospital opened in 1907, the Juliana Airport received its first airplane in 1943 and disembarked 307,504 tourists in 1983.   The islands of St. Stat, Saba and Sint Maartin became self-governing Dutch territories in 1951.   St. Maartin finally got a drug store in 1960.   The 1970's saw St. Martin readying itself for the tourist industry. An explosion of 19 hotel and guest house openings took place between 1970 and 1979.   Some have creative names like Mary's Boon, the Naked Boy (named after a mountain), Devils Cupper and the Red Lobster.   The Mullet Bay Resort and Casino introduced gambling and golf to St. Maartin in 1970.

Your island contact:

Ms. Bernadette Davis
Director of Tourism
Office du Tourisme de St. Martin
Port de Marigot
Marigot, 97150
St. Martin, French West Indies
Phone: 011-590-8-75721/23
Fax: 011-590-8-75643

Steel Band Museum, Trinidad

CHAPTER 25

ST. VINCENT

SIZE
150 sq. miles

GEOGRAPHY
A very hilly volcanic island. Mt. Soufriere, one of the Caribbean's most active volcanoes rises to 4000 feet. A major eruption occurred in 1902 and killed 2000 persons.

CLIMATE
Temperatures range from 77 degrees in January to 81 degrees in September with tropical humidity. Rainfall varies from 3 inches in March and April to 12 inches in December.

CAPITAL
Kingston

AMERINDIANS
St. Vincent's rugged terrain and dense forests provided the Caribs with a natural formidable bastion for defense against the newly-arriving Europeans. The shores abounded with fish, the forests were plentiful with fruits and the fertile soil ideal for growing cassava and other staples. Both St. Vincent and Dominica became Carib strongholds and because of their warlike nature and the promise of fortunes to be found elsewhere, the early European immigrants to the Caribbean region designated these islands as belonging to the Caribs.

The first infiltration of "foreigners" to St. Vincent came by the accident of a shipwreck. In 1675 a vessel carrying a cargo of African slaves ran aground on the coastline of Bequia. The survivors found their way to St. Vincent where they were warmly received by the Caribs. The yellow-skinned Caribs generously offered their daughters in marriage and the offsprings, whose skin color was closer to the father, formed a new race which became known as the "Black Caribs." Differences arose between the Yellow and Black Caribs around 1718 and the two began to war. The Yellow Caribs, who had established some friendship with the French in Martinique, sought help. The French saw this as an opportunity to gain a foothold on the island by accelerating the war which would hopefully reduce the Carib numbers and eventually eliminate them as a threat to settlement.

A small number of French military arrived but several yellow Caribs feared becoming allies with such potentially dangerous comrades and defected from the battle. The French withdrew and the Black Caribs were victorious. In a peaceful gesture, the Black Caribs invited the French to buy land and share the island with them. The French accepted and several planters arrived with their slaves and established the first plantations. Fearing they might suffer an eventual fate of becoming slaves, the Black Caribs retired to the countryside for a generation. They gradually moved back to the leeward coast and adopted some of the French culture, including the use of firearms. War broke out again between the Yellow and Black Caribs and the knowledge of the use of firearms enabled the Black Caribs to drive the Yellow Caribs to the Windward side of the island where some fled to Honduras and Tobago. The Black Caribs became masters of the island and continued to sell land to the French. By 1743 800 French and 3000 slaves inhabited St. Vincent plantations.

The British landed and took occupation of the island in 1763. The Crown made it clear that the Carib lands should be preserved for them; however, much of this land was fertile and the planters couldn't resist ignoring the Royal decree. The Caribs rebelled at the English encroachments and the first Carib War began in 1772. The Caribs surrendered within a year and signed a treaty, which ceded the island to England, forcing them to swear allegiance to the Crown and designated specific very desirable lands for Carib "reservations." A force of 450 French took the island in June 1779 and the French flag flew over St. Vincent until the Treaty of Versailles returned the island to England in December 1783. The English planters continued their encroachment on Carib lands and early in 1795 the Caribs began to burn sugar cane fields and murder planters. French forces from Martinique supported their effort and soon the English feared the entire island would be lost.

English reinforcements began to arrive in March with two warships, followed by the main fleet which arrived during April. As the English received support from the homeland, the Caribs continued to receive French support from Martinique and St. Lucia. The tide began to turn in 1796 when English General Abercrombie re-captured St. Lucia, cutting off the major flow of Carib reinforcements and supplies. After finishing business in St. Lucia, Abercrombie headed for St. Vincent and landed on June 3 with a force of around 4000 men. On October 26, 5080 Carib men, women and children surrendered and the Carib's dominance of St. Vincent ended.

The English transported most of the Caribs to Roatan in the Bay of Honduras. A few were allowed to remain and settle on the northwest coast.

DISCOVERY

Columbus recorded the discovery of St. Vincent during his third voyage on January 22, 1498. This was the day St. Vincent of Spain was martyred in 305 A.D. He found the coastline rugged and the island mountainous with dense forests. He did report contact with the Caribs who had established small villages close to the beaches. Being anxious to find the route to the land of the Khan, Columbus didn't want to take the time to deal with Caribs in order to explore the island, so he decided to sail on.

SPANISH QUEST FOR POWER AND GOLD

There is no evidence that, after discovery, the Spanish ever considered settling St. Vincent or using it as a base for supplies.

EUROPEAN POWER STRUGGLE AND SETTLEMENTS

The Europeans pretty much ignored St. Vincent until 1627 when English King Charles I granted the island, along with several others, to the Earl of Carlisle. The Earl did nothing with the island. King George I, ignoring Carlisle's grant, granted the island to the Duke of Montague in 1722. The Caribs drove away Montague's attempt to land.

The European struggle for St. Vincent was more with the Black Caribs than with other European nations. These struggles, and the eventual English success in gaining control of the island were discussed in this Chapter's heading, "Amerindians". After Abercrombie's defeat of the Caribs, St. Vincent became an English Crown Colony.

BUCCANEERS, PIRATES AND PRIVATEERS

Historians make no reference to pirate activity on St. Vincent. While not a pirate, exactly, it seems appropriate to note here, the landing of the infamous Captain William Bligh with a cargo of Breadfruit plants.

After Captain Bligh's famous mutiny on the H.M.S. Bounty which aborted his efforts to deliver Breadfruit to the Caribbean in 1787 the Crown re-commissioned him to make a second attempt in 1793. He successfully delivered Breadfruit to St. Vincent and St. Thomas and received noteworthy recognition from the Jamaica Assembly.   The Breadfruit was to be a cheap source of starch for the field labor slaves; however, the slaves preferred yams and plantain and refused to eat Breadfruit. Pigs enjoyed the harvest of Breadfruit for 50 years before it became recognized as fit for human consumption.

THE SUGAR ERA

The sugar industry blossomed after the end of the Carib wars. St. Vincent rose to be ranked fourth in sugar exports in 1828 when it exported over 14,000 tons. Between 1827 and 1829, 1,162 ships left St. Vincent for foreign ports.   A survey taken in 1777 showed that out of 84,000 acres, 28,000 acres had been granted to the Caribs and 35,000 acres were under the control of estates.   The survey designated 21,000 acres as "Impracticable Land." The land granted the Caribs didn't remain in their possession long when large profits from the sugar industry began to unfold.   When 6000 Carib acres were found to be very fertile, they were recovered and divided between a Colonel Thomas Brown, an English hero during the American war for independence and other English notables.

St. Vincent sugar exports declined along with other West Indies islands after emancipation and in 1894 exports had dropped to 2727 tons.   Arrowroot began to replace sugar as a major crop in 1850 when 60,000 pounds were produced.   The figure rose to over a million pounds by 1857.

SLAVERY AND SLAVE REVOLTS

Ninety-seven sugar estates, ranging in size from 116 to 1600 acres, were reported in operation between 1827 and 1829. They employed from 18 to 900 slaves, the average estate being around 300 acres and employing around 150 slaves. A census report issued in 1820 ranked St. Vincent fifth among 13 islands in slave population with a count of 24,282. Jamaica ranked first with 341,812.

St. Vincent passed the Slave Act on December 16, 1825, and it remained law for seven years. It contained 83 Articles. Among them, slaves were to become real estate, could not leave their estate without a ticket and were denied the right to attend church. The Act classified practicing Obeah (Voodoo), striking a white, learning the use of firearms, stealing more than 6 pounds or stealing cattle as felonies and ordered the only method of execution to be by hanging.

The slaves did receive some protection under the Act. The Act made the wanton killing of a slave a felony, exempted slave mothers having more than 6 children from hard labor, ordered diseased slaves "not to be suffered to wander" and encouraged marriage. Historians mentioned a few incidents when the slaves murdered their masters on individual estates.   The Slave Act did address punishments for runaways; therefore, it is assumed runaways were a problem.   No mention is made of any organized major slave uprising and descriptions of estate life on St. Vincent during these times is very sketchy.   The Day of Emancipation came on August 1, 1834 and the Lieutenant-Governor proclaimed all churches to be open for Thanksgiving on that day. The to-be-freed slaves began to gather at churches just before midnight and at the stroke of midnight services began and those freed sprang to their feet and sang with joy.

POST SLAVERY ERA
There was some apprehension as to how the freed slaves would handle their freedom, but when they showed a real desire to improve their condition, this apprehension disappeared. Only a few accepted the low wages paid for their work on the sugar estates. Some managed to pool their funds and buy estates which they turned into small villages. Along with religious freedom, the government began to provide medical services and to establish schools.

St. Vincent tried to fill the labor gap on the sugar estates by importing Portuguese and East Indian indentures, but the general decline in sugar prices caused so many estates to close, the immigration efforts were short-lived. The 1880's found the island in a deep depression and the government sold land cheap to small farmers who began to produce Arrowroot and Cocoa. A great hurricane in 1898 destroyed all the island's crops and many of the buildings and houses. A relief fund from other Caribbean islands helped and a new plan, which provided agricultural education and land for the peasants, pumped hope into the economy.

The island suffered another disaster in 1902 when Mt. Soufriere erupted in May, killing over 2000 people. St. Vincent's crops, buildings and houses were destroyed for a second time and once again a relief fund provided aid for rebuilding The island went through another depression era, but was blessed with a series of apt governors and with the introduction of the growing of cotton, and continued agricultural education, the island once again recovered.

St. Vincent gave support to England during the two World Wars. The late 1940's saw the government address social problems such as slum clearance, the construction of new hospitals and schools and training teachers and nurses. St. Vincent's population grew from 60,000 in 1946 to 80,000 in 1960. Agriculture in the '60's remained the main pursuit with arrowroot, cotton, rum, sugar and coconuts being the major exports.

St. Vincent became an independent British Commonwealth in 1967.

Your island contact:

Mr. Andreas Wickham
Department of Tourism
P. O. Box 834
Kingstown
St. Vincent & the Grenadines
West Indies
Phone: (809) 457-1502
Fax: (809) 456-2610

CHAPTER 26

TOBAGO

"There is only one island in the world that rightfully can claim to be Robinson Crusoe's island, and to have been his lonely place of abode and the site of his strange adventures. It is Tobago . . . "
Lou Lichtveld, Crusoe's Only Isle. 1974.

SIZE
116 square miles

GEOGRAPHY
The Main Range runs across the island, the highest point being 1890 feet. A forest reserve running northwest features rain forests and tropical flora.

CLIMATE
Temperature ranges fro 75 to 85 degrees. Rainy months are from July to December. The island is out of the path of hurricanes.

CAPITAL
Scarborough

AMERINDIANS
Early historians wrote that the Amerindians used Tobago as a stepping stone on their migration to other Caribbean islands. Recent archaeological findings in Amerindian middens (refuse dumps) have convinced historians that both the Arawaks and Caribs made permanent settlements in some of Tobago's ideal village sites and apparently managed to coexist on the island. Tobago's food supply enabled the Amerindians to enjoy a standard of living superior to that on many other West Indies islands.   In addition to the abundance of fish offshore, the island offered deer, wild pigs, armadillo, turtles, iguana and cassava roots. Up to the time of the coming of the Europeans, the Amerindians were described as a lazy lot, swinging in hammocks and only exerting the necessary effort to thatch their roofs. They had been subjected to attack by mainland tribes from time to time and did not welcome the persistent European probes.   During the 16th century they watched the Spanish, English and pirates from the bushes as each landed for a quick look and foraged for food supplies, water and ballast.

Serious efforts by the Dutch to settle Tobago began in the 17th century and while the Amerindians succeeded in thwarting the initial efforts, most decided to give up the struggle and migrate to other islands. By 1750 only a few Caribs remained in isolated villages and they eventually left only to return on occasion for a festival or to take revenge on some old enemy tribes.

DISCOVERY

It cannot be positively determined whether or not Columbus discovered Tobago. Some historians say his chronicles indicated that he came within 200 miles of Tobago and could not have seen it to name it. He did sight an island in August, 1498 which he called Belladona, but didn't bother to explore it. This could have been Tobago or just a mountainous part of Trinidad or an outlying cape.

In 1580 an English ship, on its way to Barbados, stumbled on Tobago. Some sailors landed, took on some water and affixed a Union Jack to a tree. No one made note of this "discovery" as being anything significant until the 17th century when all of Europe began vying for sovereignty of West Indies islands.

SPANISH QUEST FOR POWER AND GOLD

While the Spanish were among the first visitors to Tobago, they never followed through with any significant effort to settle there or even to claim it. Trinidad showed more promise than Tobago as a supply depot for Spanish inland explorations to find El Dorado, the king of a gold-rich region in South America. It is there that they focused their settlement efforts; thus, Tobago played little role in Spain's westward ventures.

EUROPEAN POWER STRUGGLE AND SETTLEMENTS

The 16th century passed with Tobago receiving only passive attention by anyone. The losses sustained by Spain as a result of the Thirty Years' War (1616-1648) were crucial in opening the door to other nation's efforts to colonize the "new world." The Dutch and other small Baltic countries were recovering from this war at the turn of the century and were seeking opportunities for expansion. The substantial number of unoccupied islands in the West Indies lying there "just for the take" seemed like plums ready to be plucked.

Tobago interested Duke Jekabs, the ruler of the small country of Courland, in the Baltic Sea region. He had received the promise of a Dutch banker to finance a colonizing enterprise and heard details about the island from an English explorer. Jekabs had political connections which paid off in 1641. In that year King Charles I of

England granted Tobago to Jekabs. Prior to 1641 the Dutch and English made several attempts to settle Tobago, but had been driven off by disease and the Caribs.

Jekabs sent a few ships to Tobago in 1642. The Caribs drove them off and Jekabs tried again a few years later, with the same results. His third effort succeeded in 1654, for by this time the Caribs had tired of fighting off newcomers and were in the process of emigrating to other islands. Jekabs' settlers retained possession of the island until 1658 when the Dutch seized the island and a long series of changes in the island's rulership began. The Dutch held Tobago until 1664. In that year King Charles II of England agreed to regrant Tobago to Jekabs in spite of the fact that King Louis IV of France had granted the island to the Dutch in 1662. At this point Jekabs temporarily lost interest in settling Tobago. Matters really got confusing in 1666 when four English vessels arrived and ran off the Dutch. Soon after the French arrived from Grenada and ran off the English. The Treaty of Aix-la Chapelle in 1684 made Tobago neutral and for the next 25 years abortive settlement attempts were made by England, Holland, France and even Jekabs who, thinking the island belonged to him, had sold it to England in 1683.

The English gained control in 1762 and won possession of Tobago in the 1763 Treaty of Paris. The Treaty of Amiens ceded Tobago to the French in 1802 but the English recaptured the island again in 1803. The long history of takeovers ended when England once and for all regained recognition as rulers of Tobago in another Treaty of Paris signed in 1814.

BUCCANEERS, PIRATES AND PRIVATEERS
Turmoil in the island in the 1600's caused by internal strife over Tobago's control by the Europeans left little resistance for pirates to use the island's harbors as bases of operations and locations for their rendezvous with each other. The island was frequented often enough to have harbors named Pirate's Bay, Man-o-War Bay and Bloody Bay.

Their haven ended in 1723 when the British sent warships to drive them away.

THE SUGAR ERA
The first sugar was exported in 1770. Tobago recorded shipments of 1549 tons in 1774. The island's sugar industry suffered an extreme setback in 1775 when the island became infested with ants that completely destroyed the canes, causing the planters to switch to cotton. Sugar did return and shipments of over 6000 tons

were made in 1815. The abolition of slavery posed a labor problem in Tobago as elsewhere.

Tobago's answer to the labor problem in 1843 was to follow a plan adopted by some other British colonies, the Metayer system. This was the West Indian version of sharecropping. Under this method of operation the landowner supplied the land, equipment for processing, horses and carts. The Metayer farmed a specific amount of acreage and supplied the labor in the field and factory. Often the landowner supplied the hogsheads (shipment containers) and the Metayer agreed to haul them to the ships. The Metayer received half the profits and one bottle of rum for each hogshead produced, and the landowner the other half plus the skimmings and molasses. By 1896 over 90% of Tobago's cane was produced by this system. The Metayer system did not prove to be efficient. The 6000 ton shipments made in 1815 fell to 599 tons in 1894.

SLAVERY AND SLAVE REVOLTS
Tobago's entrance into the sugar industry began in 1771 and ended with the emancipation of slavery in 1834, a period of only 63 years. By the end of the 18th century Tobago had over 100 sugar, indigo and cotton plantations and a population of around 11,000 slaves. Two slave insurrections occurred in 1771 and another in 1801 and were suppressed by a well-organized British Militia.

POST-SLAVERY ERA
The ending of the turmoil created during the colonization years with the final conquest being gained by England and the demise of the plantation system and slavery, brought an era of relative peace and tranquillity to the island that remains today. The island experienced a number of economic difficulties during the early years of the 19th century and when some of the largest sugar companies collapsed in 1888, the English government made Tobago a subordinate to Trinidad in January 1889. From that time forward the governments have been referred to as T & T.

By 1969 sugar cultivation had completely disappeared from Tobago. Agriculture remained the major industry, however, with coconuts and cocoa becoming the main crops. Tobago somewhat rode the coattails of Eric William's indifference to the development of tourism and awaits development through a T & T master plan being developed in the early 1990's.

CHAPTER 27

TRINIDAD

SIZE
1864 square miles

GEOGRAPHY
The Northern, Central and Southern ranges run
across the island, the highest point being 3000'.
Fertile valleys and rivers are between the
ranges. All ranges contain extensive rain
forests.

CLIMATE
Temperature ranges from 75 to 85 degrees. Rainy months are
from July to December. The islands are out of the path of
hurricanes.

CAPITAL
Port of Spain

AMERINDIANS
    Some confusion existed in the early years as to whether the
Amerindians on Trinidad at the time of discovery were Arawaks or
Caribs.   Recent research has led to the belief that the   early
Spaniards identified the Amerindians as the warlike, cannibalistic
Caribs because of this convenient supply of Indians to be used as
slaves. The Crown had granted permission to enslave the warlike
Caribs, but not the more peaceful Arawaks. But, taking the evidence
of the location of the villages, pottery remains, word lists and lack of
findings of poisoned arrows into account, historians now conclude
that the Amerindians were predominately Arawak, with the Caribs
using the island as a stepping stone in their migration. For a time
the Spanish raided the island for slaves with the Crown's permission.
In 1520 the Crown appointed Rodrigo de Figeueroa to study the
warlike nature of the Amerindians on the West Coast of South

America and Trinidad. He reported the Amerindians on Trinidad to be "people of goodwill and friends of Christians" and the Crown forbid future enslavement.

The Conquistadors were far from Spain and made their own rules and the enslavement practices continued, for there was great need. For example, Columbus discovered the island of Margarita in 1498 and soon after extensive pearl-bearing oyster beds were found. The mortality rate for the local divers was huge and the Spanish replaced them with Trinidad Arawaks. While there is no evidence of a major disease epidemic, the continued enslavement practices by the Spanish and increased raids by the Caribs resulted in a dramatic decrease in population. Population estimates are 30,000 Arawaks at time of discovery, 15,000 in 1592 and 5000 in 1680. The normally peaceful Arawaks took up arms against their invaders.

In 1531 Antonio Sedeno, named Captain-General of Trinidad for life attempted a landing. The Arawaks met him with a large force and a two-day battle ensued. The Arawaks suffered huge losses from cannon fire, but retaliated with enough bow and arrow flights to compel Sedeno to withdraw. Sedeno returned in 1533, but a delay in the arrival of promised supply ships put him and his men on the verge of starvation. While he waited for supplies, the Arawaks gathered for a massive attack. When the attack came, Sedeno sent a few mounted soldiers into the battle. Having never seen a man riding a horse before, they assumed they were facing some sort of monster and fled.

Continual attacks by the Spanish and Caribs forced the Arawaks inland and diverted the male population from hunting, fishing and agriculture to military defenses.   Around 1686 Spain sent the Capuchin Fathers to round up the Arawaks and settle them in missions, miniature versions of Spanish towns, with the objective of converting them to Christianity. The Arawaks were comfortable with their own gods and became very discontented when forced into baptisms and Spanish "ways."   In turn, the Fathers became impatient with the Arawak's reluctance to accepting the Catholic faith and fell to the practice of punishing the recalcitrants.

The San Francisco de los Arenales mission was established in 1687. In 1699 the Fathers directed the Arawaks to build a church, an activity that turned their discontent into outrage. The Fathers sent for the Governor to come and impose punishments. The night before the Governor's arrival the Arawaks met and decided on a plan of revolt. The following day one-half of the Arawaks stayed at the mission and at an appointed hour killed the Fathers and threw their bodies into the church's foundation. The other half met the

Governor at a river crossing and slew the Governor and all in his party except one who escaped and brought news of the slaughter to the Spanish command post at San Jose.

The Spanish sent search parties who sought out and killed those responsible. This event, the most bloody encounter on Trinidad between the Spanish and Arawaks, became known as "The Arena Massacre." This ended activities at the San Francisco mission and in a short time all of the four main missions closed in failure for a variety of reasons.

The 18th century saw the continuing decline of Arawak population and a disappearance of their culture. An English observer in 1803 wrote describing how the men spent their time— ". . . swinging in hammocks, which slavery of their wives enables them to do, as all the work is done by women, planting the bananas, getting shellfish from the rocks and cooking for their lazy husbands."

DISCOVERY

Columbus set forth on his third voyage with six ships. When they reached the Canary Islands he sent three to Santo Domingo and sailed into the unknown depths of the Caribbean Sea with a crew more intent on seeking fortunes than adventure. After some anxious days, on July 31, 1498, they sighted land and three peaks arising from a range of mountains. He named the island La Trinidad, keeping his vow to name the first land he saw after the Blessed Trinity. He sent a landing party ashore on the following day. They found fresh water and human footprints. He set sail and spied what he thought to be another island which and named La Isla Santa (Holy Island). It was, in fact, the east coast of South America.

On August 2 they dropped anchor at Punta Arenal and were met by a canoe carrying 24 armed Arawaks. He noted some differences in appearance from other "Indians" and a shield they carried with a design he had not yet seen. As a welcome, Columbus ordered some of his boys to perform a national dance to the beat of tambourines. The Arawaks mistook this for a war-dance and let fly with a volley of arrows. The Spaniards responded with crossbows and the Arawaks took flight. A long parlay followed which ended in a peaceful meeting. Anxious to continue his explorations, Columbus pulled anchor and headed for a narrow passage with strong currents. When a mast-high wave struck one ship and tore away its anchor, he tried to find another passage to return to the Gulf. Finding no passage, he navigated what he called the Dragon's Mouth and on August 14 he again found open sea.

SPANISH QUEST FOR POWER AND GOLD

Spain felt that Trinidad had resources to exploit, but having no gold or silver, was not worthy of investments. It was an excellent base for expeditions seeking South America's golden "El Dorado", source of timber for repairing ships and labor supply for the oyster beds of Margarita island. Attempts by Sedeno, Ponce de Leon and Antonio de Berrio to conquer the entire island failed, but Sedeno did manage to build a fort and Governor Antonio de Berrio established the settlement of Caroni in 1593. With the exception of the attempt to Christainize the Arawaks, which ended with the Arena Massacre, Trinidad passed through the 17th century with few historical incidents. Cacao became the island's major export in the beginnings of the 18th century. The entire crop was lost in 1725, the cause blamed on the presence of a comet by the planters, but placed by the Fathers on the planters for not paying their tithes. The Council sent an appeal for help to the Crown, but by this time Spain had become overextended in their colonizing efforts and only aided colonies that held promise of providing gold and silver in return. Trinidad did not promise to be a profitable venture.

By 1750 the Spanish colonists had reached abject poverty, were facing a food shortage and had to post guards to prevent persons from the mainland who had become carriers of smallpox and other diseases from landing. Adding to this misery, a drought destroyed the entire Cacao crop again in 1772.

A political order by the Crown in 1776 ushered in a new era for Trinidad when this island and Margarita came under the Governorship of the Kingdom of Grenada. The new Governor sent an envoy led by the Captain General of Venezuela to assess conditions in the islands. Meanwhile, the Governor mentioned Trinidad to Mons. St. Laurent, a large French Grenadian planter, during a dinner conversation. This conversation led St. Laurent to visit Trinidad and he became so impressed with the island's agricultural potential that he visited King Carlos III in Madrid to try to influence him to initiate some plan to develop the island. St. Laurent's presentation and the Captain General's favorable report so encouraged King Carlos that he issued the famous Cedula proclamation in November 1783. The Cedula proclamation encouraged settlers by issuing land grants to new immigrants. The Crown issued extra-large land grants to immigrants who came to the island with slaves. The order opened the door to all foreigners as long as they were Roman Catholics. The Catholic stipulation ruled out the English and the Spanish showed little interest, having other islands such as Hispaniola and Puerto Rico to choose from. This left the French as the major immigrants.

Cedula created a land rush to Trinidad and because time became a factor, a tremendous increase in slave trafficking and theft quickly developed. Thirty-two acres were given to each owner and 16 additional acres given for each slave brought with them. In order to obtain large grants, smaller planters would steal slaves. Trinidad became so notorious for illegal slave activities that many islands, including Grenada, banned all trade with the island. The large influx of French created problems of administration.   Fortunately, Governor Chacon possessed the administrative skills necessary to deal with land ownership problems, implement an organized plan to explore and develop the island and invoke several compassionate regulations for the treatment of slaves.   The capital of Trinidad moved from San Joseph to Port-of-Spain in 1783.

1796 brought war between Spain and England and the beginning of the end of Spanish rule in Trinidad.   On February 15, 1797 English Commander of Land Forces Sir Ralph Abercrombie and Real-Admiral of the Navy, Henry Harvey sailed from Carricou with orders to attack and take the island of Trinidad. Their attack force included 17 ships and 10,000 men. Upon entrance to the harbor at Port-of-Spain, Abercrombie found only four Spanish ships manned by 1600 men, many of whom were recovering from Yellow Fever. He surrounded the ships with the plan to capture them for his own use, rather than to sink them.

The commander of the Spanish fleet, Don Apodaca, conferred with Governor Chacon who gave the order to fight to the end. Seeing his four ships in a hopeless position to fight, he set them afire so they would not fall intact to the English. Abercrombe found little resistance among the Spanish residents who feared the French planters more than the English. The French resistance amounted to some of them gathering in Port-of-Spain to sing the song of the French Revolution, the "Marseillaise" while others took their arms and fled to the forest.   Abercrombie saw the Spanish plight as hopeless and sent a messenger to offer Chacon an honorable capitulation. Chacon accepted and on February 18, 1797, 300 years of Spanish rule over Trinidad came to an end.

EUROPEAN POWER STRUGGLE AND SETTLEMENTS
Spain's Trinidad had several occasional visitors prior to Cedula and Abecrombie's conquest.   In 1593 the notorious Sir Walter Raleigh sent his advanced guard, John Whidden to scout Trinidad. One day, on his way to a feast hosted by the Arawaks, Spanish

Governor de Berrio's militia ambushed Whidden after de Berrio had promised Whidden he would not be molested. Whidden reported this incident to Raleigh who came to the island in 1595 with revenge in mind.

Raleigh first explored Trinidad's shores and found Pitch Lake, a huge deposit of asphalt very suitable for caulking ships. de Berrio refused to meet with Raleigh, so Raleigh stormed the island, took de Berrio captive and burned the city of San Joseph. After an unsuccessful South American search for "El Dorado" gold, Raleigh returned to Trinidad and released de Berrio. Both the English and Dutch attempted to settle in Trinidad in the 17th century, but the Spanish destroyed the settlements before they established a strong foothold. While a considerable number of French inhabited the island, the French Revolution split the residents into groups of royalists and republicans. The Revolution, and the political split it produced, eliminated the threat of a French takeover of Trinidad and any significant threat to Abercrombie's attack.

BUCCANEERS, PIRATES AND PRIVATEERS
Trinidad must have experienced visits from many pirates because Pitch Lake's asphalt deposits were so useful in ship repair, but only one visit resulted in an event noteworthy of reporting. In 1716 Edward Teach (Blackbeard) entered the Gulf of Paria and burned a ship loaded with Cacao. A Spanish frigate appeared and chased him away with volleys of cannon fire.

THE SUGAR ERA
Barbados awakened to the prosperity the sugar plantation brought in 1647. Jamaica entered the sugar era in the late 1600's and became a leading producer by 1790. Spain's lack of economic support delayed Trinidad's entrance into the sugar market. The large amount of investment capital just wasn't available. The complete failure of the Cocoa crop in 1725 sparked some interest in growing sugar, but only enough was produced to supply local needs. The advent of Cedula Proclamation in 1783 encouraged French settlers to bring their capital and slaves to glean the profits to be had from growing sugar. By 1793 sugar had become a major crop on the flat western shores of the island. The interior of the island had yet to be developed. When the British took over the island in 1797, 159 of the 452 plantations were growing sugar.

Trinidad's sugar explosion, using traditional production methods was short-lived, for the dawn of the 19th century saw the beginning of the end of slavery.   Most freed slaves were not about to work the plantations.

East Indians Come to the West Indies

A successful experiment that took place on the English-occupied island of Mauritius, 500 miles east of Madagascar in the Indian Ocean had a dramatic impact on Trinidad.   Mauritius had experienced the same labor difficulties as Trinidad after emancipation and had imported over 20,000 East Indians as indentured servants to fill their labor needs.   The planters extended the practice to British Guiana, but it ended in 1837 after reports of ill-treatment and contractual fraud there and on Mauritius.

Pressure against Parliament by influential planters reinstated the program with specific safeguards and regulations and the practice of importing East Indian indentured servants, with Calcutta being the major port of embarkation, continued until 1917.   The journey took 5 months.   During the period 1837 to 1917, 240,000 East Indians were imported to British Guiana, 143,900 to Trinidad and thousands more to other West Indies islands.

Interviews with descendants of the original immigrants revealed that they spent their first few years "crying" over how the recruiting agents, plantation owners and government had tricked and deceived them to emigrate by promising high pay for easy work "sifting sugar." However, conditions in India at that time apparently left the emigrants the choice between becoming an indentured servant and facing starvation.   The British offered the indentures two choices of earnings, one being 25 cents per day for 9 hours work, the other, being paid upon completion of an assigned task.   In practice, the planters applied the assigned task method and it was common for the overseer to judge that the indenture did not complete the task satisfactorily; therefore, the indenture would receive no pay for that day.

Few East Indians had any desire to remain in the West Indies after their 5-year indenture expired.   An initial condition of their contract included free passage back to India.   The planters tired of paying for the return passage and costly recruitment expenses. Guadeloupe passed an ordinance to keep the Indians in perpetual servitude and some planters eliminated the return passage clause in the contract.

Trinidad chose to entice indentures to stay by offering them land to rent or buy.   This policy worked to the advantage of both the planters and indentures.   The indentures gained their freedom to establish their own villages and worked when they chose on the plantations and the planters did not have to support them on a year-around basis. One term of the contract stated that no family was to be separated and this helped to encourage settlement on the lands they could buy.

The Chinese Immigration

Thomas Hislop took over the duties of Governor in 1804. He immediately became aware that many inhabitants had not taken the oath to the Crown or registered in the militia and were not contributing to the economic growth of the island. He employed several schemes to identify and deport the unwanted, but the need for immigrants with industry to augment the sugar economy remained. Hishop heard of the success in Java, Manila and Prince of Wales Island experienced by importing Chinese. They had proved to be hard-working and represented to be "inured to industry and anxious to become proprietors themselves."

In 1806 Hishop arranged for the immigration of 192 Chinese to Trinidad from Prince of Wales Island. When the transport ship Fortitude landed, authorities found unreported Indian goods aboard. The Navy seized the ship and future plans for Chinese immigration ended when this incident and an inquiry that revealed much dissatisfaction with Chinese who were charged to be "rebellious and troublesome." Interest in renewing the Chinese immigration effort came about in the 1860's when the planters tired of seeing so many East Indian indentures returning home at the planter's expense.

In 1862 the ship, Wanata, arrived from Hong Kong with 452 Chinese and brought another problem. The Government of Trinidad agreed to pay the passage for wives. The agent in Hong Kong seized the opportunity and paired each male with a female, calling them their wives and received the appropriate commission. The agreement with China included a clause that women would not have to suffer the indignity of indenture—the clause intended to be directed to wives. When the assigned females landed they either ran off from their male companions or were kicked out by the males. Thus, the Government paid passage for passengers they had to free, with no promise of their becoming productive citizens.

The Chinese immigrants did not fill the working slot that was intended. They became known as "a new, important and dangerous class" who were "laborious, industrious and persevering." They lived up to this reputation by not submitting to the slave-like treatment given by the planters and leaving the states as soon as possible to set up shops and engage in other enterprises. Their opium-smoking and playing whe-whe, a gambling game, kept the police vigilant.

The years of Chinese immigration brought only about 2500 to Trinidad. While they didn't serve as a valuable asset to the planters, their industriousness left an important economic impact on Trinidad.

The Close of the Sugar Era

The passage of the act which equalized duties on sugar forced Trinidadian planters to compete on the world-wide open market. This, coupled with their acute labor problem, caused over 140 estates to be abandoned by 1848, and ended the planter's reign of power. Sugar production in Trinidad remained an important export long after emancipation. Among the 12 leading West Indies sugar producers, Trinidad was 3rd in production in the period 1890-1894 and 2nd in the period 1925-1929.

SLAVERY AND SLAVE REVOLTS

In 1702 Spain contracted with the French-owned Royal Company of Guiana to provide 4800 slaves per year for a period of ten years to Spanish West Indies colonies. Trinidad   received several shiploads of slaves under this agreement and used them mainly on the Cocoa plantations. The Cedula proclamation in 1783 brought the French and the first significant number of slaves. In 1797, 10,000 of Trinidad's 17,000 population were African slaves. Lieutenant-Colonel Thomas Picton assumed the Governorship of Trinidad after Abercrombie's conquest. While he had little regard for the slaves personally, he sensed the anti-slavery movement gaining strength at home and enacted slave laws that were less harsh than on other islands. But the laws did not satisfy Colonel Fullarton, one of three Commissioners appointed to govern Trinidad in 1803. He was a strong anti-slave supporter and publicly voiced the rights of man. The blacks, both freed and enslaved, who were somewhat resigned and happy with their fate, took notice of Fullartron's stand and rumors of slave revolts surfaced.

In 1805, Governor Hislop announced that he had discovered a slave plan, following Haiti's rebellion pattern that killed off all the whites, to revolt on Christmas Day. He captured the ringleaders and suppressed the rebellion. The slave owners felt this would damage the anti-slavery movement, but the British Parliament passed the bill to abolish the slave trade in January 1807 and to abolish slavery in 1834.   The transition to freedom, which included a period of apprenticeship, did not take place peacefully. The freed blacks formed protest mobs that left the estates and marched through Port-of-Spain. The protest lasted for a week before the unarmed protesters were forced into submission. The Port-of-Spain Gazette reported, "We are happy to say that tranquillity has been restored ."

POST-SLAVERY ERA

On August 30, 1854 a newspaper reported, "It is our painful duty to announce the existence in this town (Port-of-Spain) and its vicinity of an epidemic which there is too much reason to believe is the same disease which afflicted some of our neighboring colonies. ." The disease referred to was Cholera.

By September 13 the death toll had risen to 50 a day and by the 20th caused a 1000 deaths and had filtered into the countryside. The epidemic lasted into November with the deaths numbering over 4000. The remedies, first a mixture of diluted sulfuric acid and tincture of cardamum and later, powdered chalk together with ammoniated tincture of opium gave no relief. Causes for the epidemic have been pointed to either the filth in the streets and polluted water supply or from ships' passengers coming from other islands. For whatever reason, the epidemic not only sparked interest in bettering sanitation, including the installation of a sewage system, but awakened the government to the lack of attention given to island's development outside the Port-of-Spain.

The later years of the 19th century saw a multitude of technological changes which included opening a public library, developing a water system and establishing postal service, railway, telephone and electricity systems. Of particular economic significance was the first discovery of oil in the western world in 1867 by Walter Darwent. He struck oil at 200 feet at great cost, but could not figure out how to get the oil out of the ground. Following up on the findings by a forest ranger of oil seepages in the Guayaguayare forest in 1870, Randolph Rust brought in the first commercial well at a depth of 850 feet in 1902.

World War I generated a great deal of interest in oil exploration and Trinidad exported its first oil in 1914. Over a dozen companies were drilling in the 1920's and oil had become the backbone of Trinidad's economy by 1930.

World War II brought the Americans to Trinidad under the Leased Base Agreement designed by President Roosevelt and Winston Churchill. Trinidad had started to make Port-of-Spain a deep water port in 1935 and completed the work in 1941. Its location provided a strategic base for supplies headed for North Africa and it is said that the dependable supply network from here contributed greatly to the defeat of Germany's Rommel. VE-day, celebrating the Allie's victory in the European Theater in 1945, brought a new musical innovation into the streets of Trinidad—the steel band. The number's played in the beginning days were elementary tunes like "Mary Had a Little Lamb" and "Alan Ladd—Gun for Hire." The steel band is now a permanent part of Caribbean culture and the feature of Trinidad's yearly Carnival.

Independence Day arrived in Trinidad on August 31, 1962. This was the end result of a struggle started by Uriah Butler in the 1930's and continued by Eric Willams in the '40's. Eric Williams had been elected Chief Minister, as the leader of the People's National Movement (PNM) in 1956 and automatically became Prime Minister upon independence from England.   Williams continued to win elections and lead Trinidad until his death in 1981. Not only did Eric Williams prove to be a dynamic leader of Trinidad, but he assumed a position of power and influence during the Caribbean's most ambitious political and economic endeavor, the attempt to form the West Indies Federation in 1956. Disagreements between Williams and Jamaica's Manley and concern about the advantages to be gained by Trinidad and Jamaica led to the dissolution of the Federation before it became firmly established.

The Arab oil embargo in 1973 quadrupled oil prices and Trinidad enjoyed 10 years of unprecedented prosperity.   During this time Williams used taxes on oil exports to take over the economy. The PNM purchased key foreign corporations, built roads and other public works projects. They nationalized all oil companies and gas stations and other major industries such as sugar, electricity, water, airlines, banks and insurance companies in 1975.

The Government invested heavily in building factories to produce petrochemicals, fertilizers, cement, iron, steel and automobiles. By 1981 the Government was employing two-thirds of the workers. The drop in oil prices, beginning in 1982, led to an economic depression with high unemployment and the reduction of per capita income from $6800 in 1982 to $3000 in 1989. The PNM lost control in the 1986 election to the National Alliance for Reconstruction Party (NAR) which promised to increase employment and end governmental corruption.

A riot in 1990, supported by Libia's Gaddafi, did not succeed and order was restored. A new emphasis on tourism began in 1994 with the beginnings of the development of a master plan to prevent over development and to protect the environment.

Your island contact:

Mr. Clifford Hamilton, Executive Director
Trinidad & Tobago Tourist Development Authority
134-138 Fredrick Street
Port-of-Spain
Trinidad, West Indies
Phone: (809) 623-1932

Fort Christian, St. Thomas

CHAPTER 28

U. S. VIRGIN ISLANDS

SIZE
St. Croix: 83 sq. miles
St. John: 19 sq. miles
St. Thomas: 31 sq. miles

GEOGRAPHY
All the islands are of volcanic in origin and
have hills that rise to around 1500 feet. St.
Croix has more flat land than the other two.

CLIMATE
Tropical, but trade winds provide some cooling in
the evening hours. They are all in the hurricane
zone.

CAPITAL
St. Thomas: Charlotte Amalie (the administrative
center for all three islands)
St. John: Cruz Bay (main town)
St. Croix: Christensted and Frederiksted (main towns)

AMERINDIANS
Extensive archaeological finds have led to the conclusion that the
Ciboneys, Arawaks and finally the Caribs all inhabited the U.S.
Virgins at various times. The Europeans had their first contact with
Caribs on St. Croix when Columbus sent a well-manned boat
ashore. The Caribs met the sailors with a barrage of arrows in a
short, fierce battle. One sailor died in battle and one captured Carib
died soon after being brought aboard.

When the Europeans began to infiltrate the Virgins, they found
only traces of Amerindian presence. It is assumed that the Spanish
either ran them off or captured them and transported them to other
islands to be used a slaves.

DISCOVERY

Columbus came across St. Croix, which he named Santa Cruz, during his second voyage on November 14, 1493. After his encounter with the Caribs, described above, he sailed forth past a number of island chains which later came to be known as the U.S. and British Virgins. Columbus made no attempt to land on these islands. Apparently, one encounter with the Caribs was enough, for the purpose of his mission was to explore and discover, not to settle.

SPANISH QUEST FOR POWER AND GOLD

The Spanish ignored the U.S. Virgins as they did most of the smaller West Indies islands. They made one attempt to become established on St. Croix in 1650. At this time, the English were in control of the island. The English had driven off the French, who migrated to Guadeloupe, and the Dutch, who migrated to St. Eustatius and St. Martin. The Spanish landed with 1200 men disembarking from five ships and caught the English completely by surprise. They killed around 120 Englishmen and forced the others to leave the island.

Now that the English were gone, the Dutch took the opportunity to attack the ill-equipped 60-man Spanish garrison. The project ended in failure.

The French, now established on nearby St. Kitts, felt the time was opportune to recapture St. Croix. They sent a military force of 160 under de Poincy. After losing 40 men in an ambush, de Poincy convinced the Spanish garrison commander that he was at full strength and convinced him to surrender and sail for San Juan. This ended the short period of Spanish occupation in the U.S. Virgins.

EUROPEAN POWER STRUGGLE AND SETTLEMENTS

The Company

The term "Company" is used frequently in this and following sections of this Chapter. It is now appropriate to introduce this 17th century concept of private enterprise, as applied by the Danish Crown, for the Company had an economic and cultural impact on the U.S. Virgins lasting for 84 significant years.

The Europeans utilized two methods to establish colonies in the West Indies. One was total financing and administration by the Crown. The other was by chartering companies to organize the settlements, with the Crown reserving a percentage of the profits and the right to renew or cancel the charters at will.

In 1670 the Danish Crown established the Danish West India Company, a joint stock company in which King Christian V owned shares. Later, as the slave trade expanded, the name and charter was changed to the Danish West India and Guinea Company. While the Company charter did have the appearance of being a private enterprise venture, the Crown did retain certain powers. When the Company had some financial difficulties in 1675 the Crown stepped in and invoked a 10% assessment per share. Failure to pay would result in forfeiture of a stockholder's entire investment. Also, government employees were then "invited" to invest 10% of their salary in the Company. If they did not voluntarily buy the appropriate number of shares within 6 weeks of notification, the Crown deducted the amount from their salary. Wealthy non-stockholders were taxed an amount for each carriage they owned to support the Company.

The Crown would not see the Company fail in its beginnings for lack of financing. The King issued the Company a charter which authorized it to occupy St. Thomas ". . . and other islands in the vicinity or on the mainland of America. . ." The charter granted the Company all powers of colonial government including a complete monopoly on trade, the right to import all goods from Denmark duty-free and to build forts. They could also establish their own court system and construct buildings for meetings, offices and warehouses.

The Crown recognized the need to populate the island; therefore, the charter empowered the Company to select two enlisted men "from among the strong, industrious men who are married and know some trade . . ." from the Danish military forces. The charter also authorized the Company to select as many as needed for workers "of those who have been condemned to prison or put in irons" and as many women "as may be desired from among those whose unseemly lives have brought them into prison or a house of correction."

Under the direction of appointed Governor George Iverson, 189 of the selected set sail for St. Thomas on February 26, 1672. Eighty-nine died en route and 75 more died soon after landing. In fact, 263 of the 324 persons shipped to St. Thomas died during the first 3 years of immigration. This calculates to a 19% survival rate. To replace the losses the Crown sent more convicts which Governor Iverson described as "lazy, shiftless louts . . of no use." The Company also solicited indentures in Denmark, but the word soon got around that there were few places in the world less desirable to live than the West Indies. As a result, few Danes immigrated to the Caribbean. The Company tried many policies to turn a profit, in spite of internal corruption. They made St. Thomas an open port to encourage trade. It did that to some degree, but also became a recreation center for pirates. While they did refuse an offer by the Brandenburgs (a German-based company) to buy St. Thomas, they did lease some land to them for agricultural purposes and allowed them to use St. Thomas as a distribution center for slaves from 1685 to 1718. The Company was in financial difficulty from the beginning. In 1754 the Crown decided that it could no longer sanction the Company's mismanagement and corruption and canceled the charter.

Settlement of St. Croix

Both the English and Dutch settled on St. Croix, the first of the U.S. Virgins to be settled, about 1625. The English settled in today's Frederiksted area and the Dutch in the location of the future Christiansted. Some French Protestant refugees joined the Dutch about the same time. The English and Dutch bickered continually over land rights and authority. In 1645 the two bodies engaged in a conflict and the Dutch governor killed the English governor. After seeing the bloodshed, they decided to retreat to their homes. The Dutch governor died soon after and the English invited the newly-elected Dutch governor to a dinner to discuss some kind of settlement of grievances. The Dutch governor accepted, but was arrested upon arrival and condemned to death in revenge.

It had become clear that the English would become the dominant colony, so the Dutch and French emigrated, leaving the English in control until the Spanish takeover in 1650. As noted previously, the Spanish occupation was short-lived. When the French re-occupied St. Croix, Monsignor de Poincy, Governor-general in charge of all French settlements in the West Indies, was in charge of St. Croix for three years before deeding the island to the Knights of Malta, a rich and powerful Catholic order. In 1665 French King Charles IV decided the Crown should control St. Croix and placed the island's administration with the French West India Company.

After the company mismanaged the island for nine years, the Crown retook control. This period was marked with almost continual wars with England, illegal trading, piracy and religious conflicts. The Crown decided that defending the island was too expensive and the colonists were tiring of conflict. In January 1695 the Crown moved the entire French population of 1200 to St. Dominique (Haiti) and left St. Croix deserted. The Danish West India Company exercised its option under their charter to acquire islands and in 1733 purchased St. Croix from the French. The island remained uninhabited for 3 years.   The Danish Crown took over St. Croix in 1755 and proclaimed it to be a Crown colony.

The Settlement of St. Thomas

The Danish Company began its settlements of the Virgins with the voyage of the "Pharoh", as mentioned above, in 1672. They established a town in a harbor which they named Charlotte Amalie in honor of the wife of King Christian V.

There were a few Dutch on the island who had emigrated from Tortola in flight from the English, but they offered the Company no resistance. The Danes remained in control of St. Thomas until 1801 when a fleet of English ships appeared and took control of the island until 1802. The island was returned to Denmark until war broke out between England and Denmark in 1807 and England took possession of all the Virgins for 7 years. During this period St. Thomas flourished and friendly relations developed between the English and Danish governmental officers.

At the end of the Napoleonic Wars in 1815, the Treaty of Paris restored St. Thomas and other Virgins to Denmark. St. Thomas and other Virgins remained under the control of Denmark until their purchase by the United States in 1917.

The Settlement of St. John

The Danes claimed control of St. John in 1684, but did not begin to settle it until 1718 because of the closeness of the English stronghold of Tortola. The initial settlement was made by Virgin Island Governor Erik Bredel who arrived with 20 planters, 16 slaves and 5 soldiers on May 8, 1718. His diary reads in part, "I have planted there the flag of our most gracious King, fired the Danish salute and then we feasted and drank to the health of our most gracious King and the welfare of the honorable Company."

By 1720 there were 30 plantations in operation. Because of the small size of its population and the closeness to St. Thomas, St. John has never enjoyed its own administration.

BUCCANEERS, PIRATES AND PRIVATEERS

A glance at a map of the Spanish Main shows a sprinkling of small islands, islets and cays in the Eastern Caribbean. They were strategically located to provide springboards and sanctuaries for those inclined to prey on the gold and silver-laden Spanish galleons or ships carrying valuable cargoes of sugar, cotton, coffee, fine silks, rum and rare woods. When the Crown, implementing their policy of remaining neutral during European conflicts, declared Charlotte

Amalie on St. Thomas to be an open port offering pubs, brothels and a hungry market for   everything, it was natural for the town to become a pirate's lair. It was not unusual for French, English and Dutch crew members to carouse together in a St. Thomas pub one night and find themselves in battle with each other on the following day.

There are romantic stories told about the loyalty pirate crew members had for each other. One tells of a drunken pirate who had been overcharged for his drinks, paid a "lady of the night" for services to be rendered and then thrown out into the street. Hearing of this injustice, crew members of several ships stormed the pub. They first ran the customers to the street. They then boarded up all the doors and windows with the proprietors and "employees" inside and set fire to the building. This was pirate justice.

One of the present-day landmarks on St. Thomas is Blackbeard's Castle. Historians question if Blackbeard (Edward Teach) ever set foot on the property, but some islanders insist the Castle was Blackbeard's headquarters and some of his escapades are certainly documented to have been in the Eastern Caribbean. Yellowed documents show that a Dutchman, Carl Baggaert, built the structure in 1674 over protests that the Governor made to Denmark's King that Baggaert's tower was on higher ground than his Fort.

While the pirates brought some prosperity to St. Thomas, they also brought some problems. In 1696 French privateers lay waiting outside Charlotte Amalie harbor seizing not only Spanish and English ships, but also those belonging to St. Thomas merchants. Captain Kidd was among the notorious visitors to St. Thomas. He appeared at the entrance of Charlotte Amalie harbor with his ship, the four hundred ton Quidah Merchant and 80 men on April 6, 1699 after a voyage from Madagascar. His appearance created a political crisis with England, for while Charlotte Amalie was an open port, England had a price on Kidd's head. Messages were passed between Kidd and Governor Lorentz. Kidd asked sanctuary while he sent documentation to Governor Bellamont in New England to prove that his privateering activities were in England's interests, and that he was not a pirate of English shipping. Lorentz received Kidd's requests and consulted with his peers. He allowed seven persons who proved they were only passengers, and not Kidd's crew, to disembark with their baggage, but denied Kidd landing privileges. Kidd sailed away for Santo Domingo, never to return to the Virgins.

While the merchants, pubs and smugglers of St. Thomas welcomed the business of pirates with pockets bulging with gold and sought after merchandise   the   Europeans   treasured,   pirate appearances presented political problems for the Governors. Lorentz wrote in 1700 that four of nine pirates who arrived "some time ago" had received exemplary punishment. The other five had been placed in the hands of Company directors. Records of pirate activities extend into the 1800's and while a major number of U.S. Virgin historical documents have been destroyed, an earnest reader can come across numerous writings of pirate escapades--but whether they be fact or legend is in question.

THE SUGAR ERA

During the Sugar Era when other islands were reaping the harvest from cane as their major source of wealth, the Virgins were reaping their harvest of wealth from merchandising, smuggling and privateering. But the Virgins did put their "two-cents worth" into the production of sugar cane. Sugar plantations began to emerge in St. Thomas just prior to 1688.

A census was taken, not too scientific in nature, around 1688 that resulted in a count of 11 nationalities: 66 Dutch, 31 English, 17 Danes and Norwegians, 17 French, 4 Irish, 4 Flemish, 3 Germans, 3 Swedes and one each of Scotch, Brazilian and Portuguese. Among the 76 who were adult, 56 were listed as planters, five as carpenters, one as a Lutheran minister, one as a schoolmaster, one as a fisherman and one as a tavern keeper. At this time 90 plantations had been surveyed.

By 1691, one hundred-one plantations were under cultivation with the average being in operation just under five years. Only five of these plantations were devoted to sugar production, while 87 were devoted to the major crop--cotton. After St. Thomas was secured, the Company reached out to establish agriculture on St. John, in spite of the threats of English interference from Tortola.

The Danes found water on St. John in 1718 and provided generous land grants and tax breaks for new planters. The grants required one white man to be on their plantation within 3 months after the grant's issuance, sugar mills to be erected within 5 years and permitted planters to take as much lime and wood as needed. By 1721 thirty-nine planters had received St. John deeds. Governor Moth wrote to the Company Directors on March 16, 1726:

"St. John is now entirely settled, (so) that there is no more land left to give away except at the Fort and the Company's plantation, which is still lying idle, as it is not surveyed. Next year the greater number of St. John inhabitants will begin paying the poll and land tax. There are already about 20 works built and others in the process of building. . "

The Company required the planters to sell their sugar to them at a preset price and when the Company acquired the two major factories for processing the cane, the planters became even more dependent on Company policy-making.

St. Croix entered the Company sugar picture on June 15, 1733 when Denmark purchased the island from France. The Company laid out 300 parcels of land for plantations but had problems finding planters with adequate capital and ability. English settlers did show an interest in St. Croix and plantation prices were lowered and tax advantages made to entice them. By 1742 the Company had succeeded in helping to establish 264 plantations on St. Croix, 120 of which were devoted to growing sugar--the rest to cotton. St. Croix planters exported 11,000 tons of sugar in 1780. Production rose to just over 20,000 tons of sugar in 1815 and the island ranked 4th in the Caribbean behind Jamaica, Cuba and Guadeloupe in that year. A little over 32,000 acres were devoted to sugar production in the Virgins when planting reached a peak in 1796. 86% of the total acreage was on St. Croix, 8% on St. Thomas and 6% on St. John. Clearly, when it came to assessing income from legal negotiations, the purchase of St. Croix was an economic windfall.

As the 19th century came to an end, the Virgins became more of a dependency than a contributor to the Danish treasury and as the 20th Century dawned, the Company showed only a small profit in 5 of the 11 years from 1904-1911. The proposal for the sale of the islands to the U.S. became more and more attractive.

SLAVERY AND SLAVE REVOLTS

When sugar appeared on the scene in the Caribbean and the focus zeroed in on profit-making, the Danes joined other Europeans in the exploitation of African natives. Governor Lorentz observed the profits taken by the German-based Brandenburg African Company when two of their ships brought slaves to sell in St. Thomas in November 1696. A captain of one of the ships confided to Lorentz that the Danish forts along the Guinea coast would be excellent locations to conduct a slave trade. Lorentz then wrote the Company directors, " . . the first experience would give you such joy, that the slave trade would hold its place before all other sorts of commerce and the Company will be impelled to continue it."

The respect the Company and Crown had for Lorentz brought about the issuance of a new charter for the Company on September 28, 1697 which renamed the Company, the "Danish West India and Guinea Company". The first Company experience of transporting slaves from Africa to St. Thomas proved to be a disaster. After a mutiny and an outbreak of scurvy, only 259 of the 506 slaves arrived alive at St. Thomas and 37 of these died shortly after their arrival. The next ship arrived in July, 1699 with two-thirds of the "cargo" of slaves surviving. The men, women and children arrived in assorted sizes and ages. To determine their selling price, an ingenious number of calculations were made. On July 8, 1710 Captain David Diniesen, a private supplier, sold the following slaves to the Company:

Number	Category	Price Pies de Indies
134	Men	134
26	Women	26
11	2/3 Boys	7-1/3
20	½ Boys	10
2	2/3 Girls	1-1/3
5	½ Girls	2-1/2
2	1/3 Boys	2/3

TOTAL   200 Head   =   181 5/6 Pies de Indies at
65 rdl. = 11,819 rdl., 1 mark.

Source: Westergard: The Danish West Indies, 1671-1917 The MacMillan Company. 1917. Page 149.

It is left to the reader to further research and find out why ½ of a Girl was worth more than 2/3 of a Girl, what 2/3 of a Boy was and what a "Pies de Indies" is in terms of current U.S. Dollars. It should be noted that the "cargo" that arrived is described as 200 "Head". This was the mentality of the day in the 18th Century. While the Company did actively participate in the slave trade, it rarely had more than 20 ships in operation at any one time. The majority of slave traffic coming through St. Thomas came from the Dutch, English or a variety of private carriers of other nationalities.

The 1733 St. John Slave Uprising

While St. John was just a speck of a island among the giants involved in the sugar era, a slave uprising that began on Monday morning, November 23, 1733 was to rank as one of the major recorded events in Caribbean history. The numbers involved in the beginning were 208 whites and 1087 slaves.

The spring and summer of 1733 saw a drought, July came with a hurricane followed by a siege of insects which destroyed maize and other foods. The island faced famine conditions. To suppress possible problems with the slaves, Phillip Gardelin, whose faithfulness to the Company had enabled him to rise from bookkeeper to Governor, issued a series of mandates involving severe punishments for slaves who committed or attempted to commit any sort of conspiracy or uprising against their master. The slaves found these new mandates intolerable, especially at a time when they were facing famine conditions. So, on that November Monday morning, 14 slaves carrying wood appeared before the fort overlooking Coral Bay. After satisfying the challenge of a guard, they entered the fort. Once inside, they dropped their wood and drew their hidden machetes. They killed the guard and other six soldiers who manned the fort. The blasts from a cannon which they fired three times, signaled the beginning of a general revolt to slaughter all the whites on the island.

The slaves began their move from plantation to plantation and by the middle of the afternoon their number had risen to around 80, many with flintlock rifles and pistols. There were some slaves faithful to their masters who reported the rebel's advances and some whites were able to flee to plantations with some fortifications. By 3:00 p.m. the news of the uprising reached St. Thomas and later that day reinforcements arrived and retook the fort and dispersed the rebels to the bush. Soon, the entire island was under siege and fear was beginning to mount that the uprisings would spread to St. Thomas and English-held Tortola. After ten weeks of battle, the English sent a man-of-war with 60 men to join the Company to repress the uprising. The English were ambushed and retreated. Repeated attempts by the Danes and English to crush the rebels, which extended into March of 1734 ended in failure.

The apparent success of the St. John rebels was enough to strike fear in the hearts of all planters in the Caribbean who lived from day to day being greatly outnumbered by their slaves. This fear extended to the French in close-by Guadeloupe and Martinique and the urge to help Denmark was also sparked by the possible sale of St. Croix to the Danes and a desire for Denmark to remain neutral during France's impending war with Poland.

The French arrived on St. John on April 29, just after the slave rebels had made a fierce attack on the well-fortified Deurloo plantation. They chased the rebels for 3 weeks, unable to find them and engage them in battle. Apparently, the rebels had resigned themselves to defeat and after breaking up into several small bands, committed suicide.

The French returned triumphantly to St. Thomas on May 27, 1734. In early August a report was received that 14 rebels, without arms, still were at large on St. John. To avoid bloodshed, Danish officer Theodore Ottingen issued an offer of pardon to these remaining rebels if they would surrender. They surrendered, but instead of being pardoned, they were executed in an assortment of ways. This sort of treachery was commonplace for the times. So ended the St. John uprising. Many discouraged planters emigrated St. John to the newly-purchased island of St. Croix and joined others with renewed vigor growing cane and employing the labor of African slaves.

The attitudes toward slavery began to change. The Danish government outlawed the slave trade in 1792 and the British freed their slaves in 1833. In 1847 Danish King Christian VIII enacted a law that would end slavery over a twelve year period. This action displeased the planters and incited the impatient slaves to organize to gain their liberation.

On July 2, 1848 St. Croix slaves blew on conch shells and rang estate bells as a signal to assemble to march to the fort in Frederiksted to demand their freedom. They did this, burning and destroying everything in their path. Governor Von Scholten was so shaken by the extent of the damage and continued threats of vandalism that he immediately issued the following Emancipation Proclamation on his own:

1. All unfree in the Danish West Indies are from today free.

2. The estate Negroes retain for three months from date the use of the house and provision grounds, of which they hitherto have possessed.

3. Labor is in future to be paid for by agreements, but allowance of food to cease.

4. The maintenance of the old and infirm, who are not able to work, is until further determined, to be furnished by the late owners.

St. Croix, July 3, 1848 P. Von Scholten.

The proclamation didn't quell the rebellion. It took Spanish soldiers and a British warship to come to assist the Danes and end the conflict. Von Scholton's proclamation met with governmental disfavor. He was returned to Denmark where he was forced to retire and condemned for "dereliction of duty." General Bordeaux (Buddoe), considered to be the slave's hero in the rebellion, was banished to Trinidad.

POST-SLAVERY ERA

The slaves entered emancipation with no preparation or education as to how to deal with self-survival. The planters had difficulty coming to grips with the fact that their slaves were free. Planters and freed-slaves resorted to a share-cropping arrangement on St. Croix. Freed slaves on St. Thomas despised working the soil and turned to the commercial activities taking place in Charlotte Amalie. In short, the slaves were "dumped" into freedom and having no economic weapons of their own to bargain with were forced to work for their former masters pretty much on their conditions. The white elite retained control of administrative and professional positions and with their military background of officers presiding over their men, a strict social stratification developed. The freed slaves found themselves on the bottom of the social and economic scales.

The U.S.A. Buys the Danish West Indies

It took over 50 years of negotiations and 3 wars to bring Denmark and the U.S.A. to a transfer of ownership. The first attempt was made in 1864, but ended when President Lincoln was assassinated and Seward and his son were injured. The purchase of Alaska from Russia for $5,000,000 and the Danish West Indies came before Congress in 1867. Congress agreed to the Alaska purchase only. Congress refused another proposal in 1868. Denmark made another proposal in 1896 to the Cleveland administration, but it wasn't even considered. Around 1900 Germany began to show interest in the islands and another proposal was placed before Congress, but the U.S. House of Representatives rejected it. Yet another treaty proposal was drafted by the Danes in 1902, but this time German influence on a new Danish government resulted in its withdrawal. The final treaty negotiations began in earnest in 1915 when Germany was posing a threat to become established in the Caribbean. This time the Monroe Doctrine, a policy adopted by the U.S.A. in 1823, came to influence the purchase. Briefly, the Doctrine stated that the U.S.A. would guarantee all nations in the Western Hemisphere protection against European interference that would be "for the purpose of oppressing them, or controlling in any manner their destiny." The purchase of the Danish West Indies would give the U.S.A. complete control of deep water passages into the Caribbean and help secure the Panama Canal and provide essential military sites to enable the U.S.A. to enforce the Monroe Doctrine. When, in August 1916 it appeared that the U.S.A. would likely enter into a war with Germany, President Wilson authorized Secretary of State Lansing to offer Denmark $25 million for the three islands. Denmark agreed and signed the treaty at the Hotel Biltmore in New York on August 4, 1916. Ratification by Congress came four days later. Direct jet air service came to St. Croix from New York City in 1962 and to St. Thomas in 1966. Air service and cruise ship traffic increased tourism 4-fold from the 1960's into the 1970's.

The islands, now identified as the U.S. Virgins, had entered anew era with resounding success in a new industry--tourism. Some problems still remain to be resolved which include the islander's desire to become U.S. voting citizens and to have voting representatives on the floor of Congress.

Your island contact:

Jerry Koenke, Assistant Commissioner
USVI Division of Tourism
Department of Economic Development and Agriculture
P. O. Box 4538
Christiansted, USVI
Phone: (809) 822-4538
Fax: (809) 773-0495

Anneberg Mill, St. John

The Caribbean Today

The Caribbean Today

INDEX

Photographs

M A P S

Further Reading

Rogozinski, Jan. A Brief History of the Caribbean. Facts on File. New York * Oxford. 1992

Williams, Eric. From Columbus to Castro: A History of the Caribbean - 1492 - 1969. 1984

Parry, J.H. Sherlock, Phillip and Maingot, Anthony. A Short History of the West Indies. Macmillan Education, Ltd. 4th Ed. 1991

Knight, Franklin, The Caribbean: The Genesis of a Fragmented Nationalism. New York * Oxford University Press. 2nd Ed. 1990

Southey, Thomas. The Chronological History of the West Indies. Three volumes. Frank Cass & Co., Ltd. First print, 1827. Reprint, 1968.

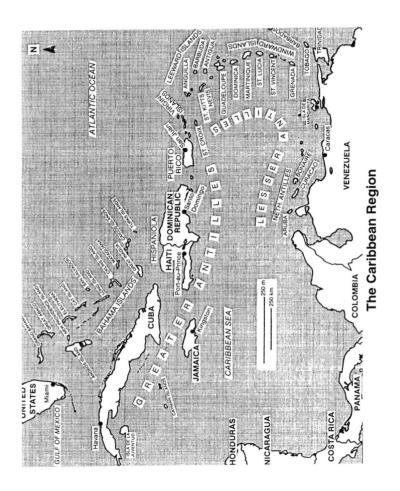

The Caribbean Region

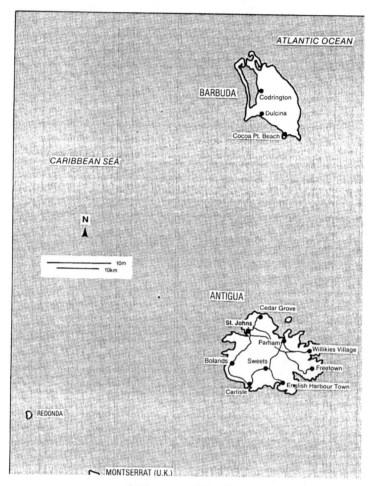

Antigua and Barbuda

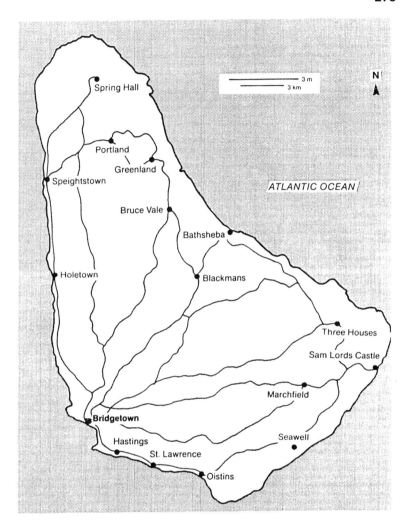

Barbados

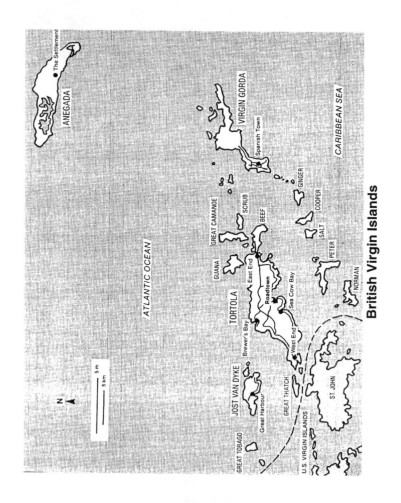

British Virgin Islands

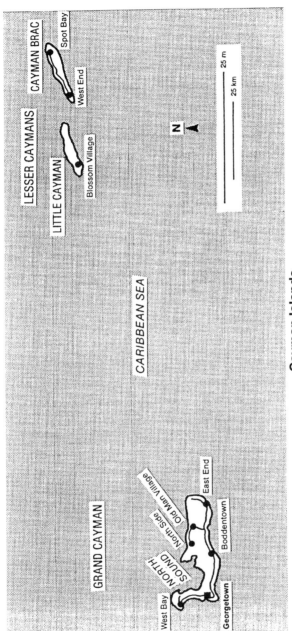

Cayman Islands

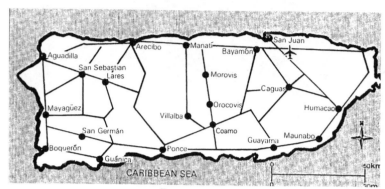

Puerto Rico

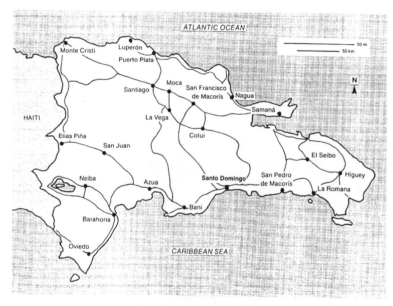

Dominican Republic

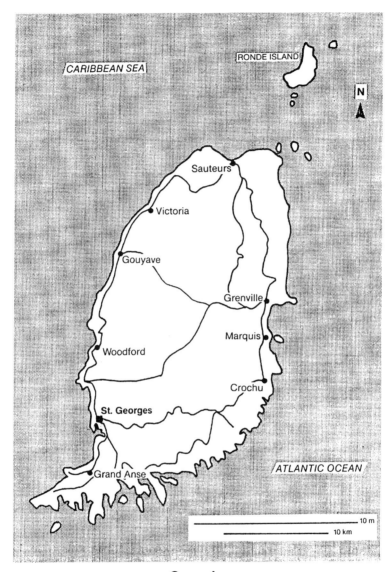

Grenada

Jamaica

N

CARIBBEAN SEA

Port Antonio
Port Morant
Kingston
Ocho Rios
Spanish Town
Old Harbour
St. Anns Bay
Frankfield
May Pen
Falmouth
Mandeville
Montego Bay
Black River
Savanna la Mar
Lucea
Negril

20m
20km

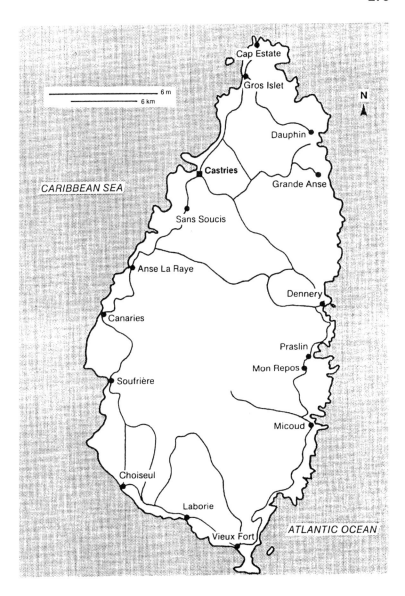

Cap Estate

Gros Islet

N

Dauphin

Castries

CARIBBEAN SEA

Grande Anse

Sans Soucis

Anse La Raye

Dennery

Canaries

Praslin

Mon Repos

Soufrière

Micoud

Choiseul

Laborie

Vieux Fort

ATLANTIC OCEAN

6 m
6 km

St. Lucia

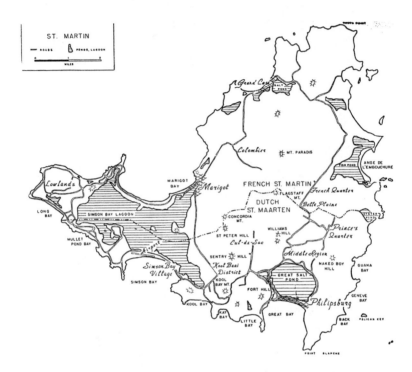

St. Martin/Sint Maarten

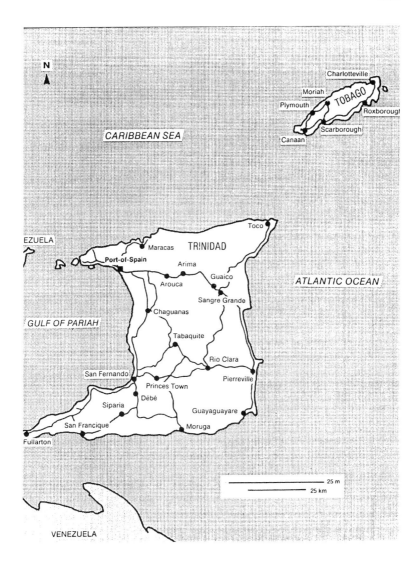

N

CARIBBEAN SEA

Charlotteville

Moriah

TOBAGO

Plymouth

Roxborough

Scarborough

Canaan

EZUELA

Toco

Maracas

TRINIDAD

Port-of-Spain

Arima

Guaico

Arouca

Sangre Grande

ATLANTIC OCEAN

Chaguanas

GULF OF PARIAH

Tabaquite

Rio Clara

San Fernando

Pierreville

Princes Town

Débé

Siparia

Guayaguayare

San Francique

Moruga

Fullarton

25 m

25 km

VENEZUELA

Trinidad & Tobago

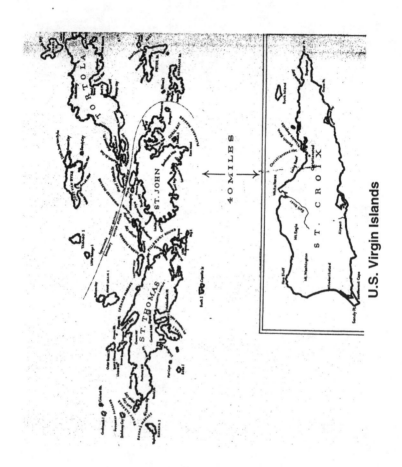

U.S. Virgin Islands